Just Wait 'til Your Dad Gets Home

Just Wait 'til Your Dad Gets Home

KENNETH HAW

iUniverse, Inc.
Bloomington

Just Wait 'til Your Dad Gets Home

iUniverse books may be ordered through booksellers or by contacting:

iUniverse
1663 Liberty Drive
Bloomington, IN 47403
www.iuniverse.com
1-800-Authors (1-800-288-4677)

ISBN: 978-1-4759-7469-0 (sc)
ISBN: 978-1-4759-7471-3 (hc)
ISBN: 978-1-4759-7470-6 (ebk)

Library of Congress Control Number: 2013902502

Printed in the United States of America

iUniverse rev. date: 03/08/2013

Contents

Introduction

The one truism about the beginning of life is that you begin the journey to death. Is this not so?

Lots of times during my life I have lived with a load of guilt over some real or imagined incident. By putting words to paper, I can put it all into the perspective of time. Most people today have no idea how their parents met, where their grandparents or great-grandparents came over here from. Most people I have talked to do not even know what world events were going on when they were born.

My brother, Ron, and I were having lunch one day at the IHOP restaurant in Paradise Valley Mall after just finishing a game of golf at Stone Creek Golf Course. We won't go into how badly I was beaten as that is another story. Eventually, our discussion got around to my writing my life story and Ron commented, "I'm glad you are doing it, but I believe the past should remain just that—the past. It should not be dredged up and the bad memories recalled."

I tried to explain that the book was not about all the bad memories, but life experiences, good and bad. In his viewpoint, he's right, but I feel that if I do not do this book, my life will not be fulfilled.

I believe every human being, of age is a sanctuary of secrets. We all know things about ourselves and others that we will take to the grave and I admit there are many things I know that will remain unwritten and unspoken.

Nostalgia can be addictive. I have found once you start down that path, your life becomes a constant. Remember when and your mind turns to mush. I've been on that path numerous times in the writing of these memoirs. I have made most of the entries in these writings as reflections, ways to vent and to clarify.

I have gathered together fragments of my life and hopefully readers will be able to follow my ramblings and connect the dots that show a full sketch of my life as I remember it.

Was I a good son? If you looked up the definition of good, you would not see my picture by it. Was I a bad son? I would not stray far from this concept. I could have been a lot more to a lot of people, but aren't there a lot of us like that? Hindsight is always 20-20, is it not?

My parents were neither rich nor famous as the world judges. Their lives were neither rich nor full. Their beginnings were humble, but their reach was ever upward as that was the only way they could go from where they were. There were values they either knowingly or unknowing taught their children. The worked hard throughout their lives but had little of life's luxuries.

They are both gone now, and I am not bereft. I would never know the security and unconditional love that every parent should give to their child. To love and be loved, we see it all our lives. Even though I was bitter from the first of my memories, I realize my parents were living in extremely hard times for people without any education to speak of. Dad never went to school or only the second grade, depending on who you speak to, and Mom only finished the eighth grade. They were both alcoholics, smoked and fought with each other incessantly.

I swore to myself that if I ever got old enough to leave their house and start on my own, I would be a totally different person than my parents. I would not make the mistakes I saw them making. I would make something of myself. I would not let alcohol rule my life as I had witnessed it doing to my parents. Who was I to know what lay in my future. I have gathered the material for this book, not only from my memories but from many other sources such as birth and death certificates, report cards, interviews with uncles, aunts, cousins, discharge and other military papers, numerous newspaper articles as well as many other sources.

I think my family members may find it interesting to read about my life as it was lived in another time and in places where, in some cases, very few families were ever privileged to have lived. There are parts of my life that my family is not familiar with and may find interesting. This memoir was written candidly. It describes my life the way it was. I have included the tears as well as the laughter.

This is not a collection of everything, but rather a selection of memories that highlighted my life. I hope you, the reader, will find them to be informative as well as interesting. And, to my children and grandchildren, and others I hope you get as much enjoyment out of reading this as I have out of writing it.

Chapter 1

Mom and Dad's Families

Before I get started with the meat and potatoes of the book, I think I should outline my aunts and uncles on both Mom and Dad's sides of the family. This will be a good reference area if you need to look them up for any reason. I will also list dates of births and deaths for the ones I know.

Starting with Mom's family, oldest first.

Father: Benjamin Franklin Brown
Born: April 11, 1895, Oklahoma
Died: August 12, 1977 in Klamath Falls, OR

Mother: Ellen "Ella" Sarratt
Born: May 17, 1902 in Armore, OK
Died: November 3, 1972 in Selma, CA

Children of Benjamin and Ellen Brown:

1
Mary Katherine Brown
Born: February 29, 1935 in Oklahoma City, OK
Still living

2
Bennie Christine Brown
Born: March 27, 1937 in Oklahoma City, OK
Still living

3
Shirley Brown
Born: May 24, 1942 in Mesa, AZ
Still living

4
Elmer Franklin Brown
Born: September 4, 1920 in Oklahoma
Died: March 26, 1989 in Tulare, CA

5
Ola Mae Brown
Born: June 27, 1922 in Stonewall, OK
Died: February 2006 in Banning, CA

6
Anna Louise Brown
Born: November 3, 1923 in Stonewall, OK
Died: November 1, 2000 in Peoria, AZ

7
Orval Burnett Brown
Born: October 1925
Died: Unknown (from diarrhea)

8
Emma Margaret Brown
Born: November 2, 1927 in Mountain View, OK
Died: February 4, 1991 in Fresno, CA

9
Linnie Evalina Brown
Born: November 2, 1929 in Oklahoma City, OK
Died: July 8, 1937 in Oklahoma

Dad's side of the family was almost as large and would have been larger if all the children had lived.

Father: Robert Lee Haw
Born: December 19, 1873 in Bakersfield, CA
Died: October 23, 1951 in Florence, AZ

Mother: Georgia Virginia Perkins
Born: January 25, 1890 in Longview, TX
Died: October 28, 1951 in Florence, AZ

Children of Robert and Georgia Haw:

1
Albert Haw
Born: 1906
Died: 1909

2
Maggie Catherine Haw
Born: December 20, 1907 in Paris, TX
Died: June, 1953, in Casa Grande, AZ

3
Charlie Earnest Haw
Born: August 23, 1909 in Monkstown, TX
Died: March 31, 1998 in Mesquite, TX

4
Vallie Mae Haw
Born: November 12, 1911 in Milton, TX
Died: April 30, 1996 in Casa Grande, AZ

5
Reba Lee Haw
Born: March 23, 1918 in Howland, TX
Died: July 1, 1982 in Portersville, CA

6
Ivy Haw
Born: 1919
Died: 1919

7
Kenneth R.G. Haw
Born: August 16, 1920 in Grant, OK
Died: February 8, 1991 in Prescott, AZ

8
Aubrey Preston Haw
Born: January 14, 1923 in Wright City, OK
Still living

9 and 10
Twin boys Haw
Born: 1925 in Arthur City, TX
Died: 1925 in Arthur City, TX

As you can see, these families are very large as per today's standards. The number of children who died, either at childbirth or at a very early age would seem alarming today. In the early 1900's, there were very few hospitals, few doctors and they were usually in the major cities. For the most part, children were born at home, sometimes with the help of a neighbor or family member. Those who died at home were sometimes buried on the plot of land the family owned.

This book will deal mostly with my father's family. However, at times, I will refer to my mother's side. This chapter can be a resource for connecting the individuals.

*

Grandpa Haw and Grandma were married November 17, 1904, in New Boston, TX (Bowie County). Grandpa was 31 and Grandma was 14. New Boston is in the far northeast part of the state, just off Interstate-30, just south of the Oklahoma-Arkansas state line. They were destined to become migrant workers as many were in the early 1900's.

They would follow the crops—fruit, cotton, vegetables, wherever there was work, primarily along the coastal line of Texas inland to Arizona and California. In the mid to late 1920's, the entire Haw family lived in the Galveston, TX area, approximately 38 miles along the Nueces River to Mathis, TX. They were living in tents and home-made camp trailers. They were fishing commercially along the Nueces River, utilizing trot lines, hand lines, and nets, anything they could use to catch fish which they would sell to tourists and small cafes. They also ate a lot of fish.

Grandpa apparently was pretty good with his hands and built very sturdy campers. He even built one that looked like the forerunner of an Airstream trailer according to Uncle Aubrey.

*

In 1928, close to where they were living, a bridge and dam were to be built across the Nueces River on the southeast side of what is now Interstate-37. This body of water, when backed up, would become Lake Corpus Christi. Grandpa and Uncle Earnest were hired to work on the construction. This lasted a few years and during this time Grandpa began making moonshine and selling it to construction workers and, eventually, to surrounding bars. Uncle Earnest told me in the early 1990's, he could probably take me back to an area on the Nueces River where Grandpa and my Dad, who was about 10 years old at the time, had to bury a load of moonshine because the "revenuers" were after them. They never returned to dig it up.

The earthen dam they had helped build washed out around 1932 or 1933 and they signed on to help rebuild it. Around this time, Grandma Haw became sick and was pretty much bedridden with what was diagnosed as plural asthma which now would be emphysema. She could only do light chores and not be on her feet for too long at a time.

*

In October 1940, the Haw clan plus a few new additions, as some of my aunts and uncles had gotten married, all were going from Texas to California. They stopped in Casa Grande, AZ, to pick cotton so they could afford to continue the trip to California. They were there for a couple of months and Grandma got to feeling better. Grandpa decided that's where they would put down their roots. Aunt Reba and Uncle Melvin Waller, her husband of six years, decided to continue on to California to settle. Uncle Earnest and his wife, Hazel, stayed in the Casa Grande area for a little over a year then returned to Texas where they would settle, around Dallas, TX. Aunt Maggie and her husband, Tim Lamb, decided to stay in Casa Grande as did Aunt Vallie and her husband, Robert Stanford Jr. All had come over from the Texas area. Talk about "greener pastures."

Uncle Aubrey told me that my Dad was always kind of a loner. In all the moving around, none of the kids received any kind of a formal education to speak of. Uncle Aubrey thought Dad had started the second grade, but never finished. He also said Dad had a big mouth, sometimes said things he never thought through and was always getting into fights. This trait Dad would carry into his adult life. I know what you're thinking, like father like son. Oh, well.

Chapter 2

Mom and Dad, before me

Lee Waller, brother of Uncle Melvin Waller who had married Dad's sister, Reba, decided not to go on to California, but stayed in the Casa Grande area because he liked running around with Dad and his brothers.

Around this time, the Brown family was living in tents, seven miles east of Mesa, AZ, north of the old Apache Trail road, just east of the Arizona canal. Louise Brown and some of her sisters had met Kenneth "RG" Haw, some of his brothers and sisters, and Lee Waller when the Haw clan ventured into the valley area to pick citrus.

Lee Waller began dating Ola Mae Brown in the fall of 1941 and introduced Dad to Louise Brown shortly after this. Knowing the kind of con artist Lee was at the time, I figure he needed the use of a car, which Dad had or could get from one of his brothers. Or at the very least, Lee would have someone to share the expenses and travel with.

On Dec. 7, 1941, Japan bombed Pearl Harbor. The United States then declared war on Japan and Germany on Dec. 8. Shortly after war was declared and because of the number of Japanese we had in the state, Del Webb Corp. was contracted to build interment camps for the Japanese. These camps were built in Sacaton, AZ, which was on the Gila River Indian Reservation between Casa Grande and Phoenix. Dad was hired full-time to work on this project.

In January 1942, RG (Dad) and Louise decided to go to Las Vegas, NV, to get married. In Nevada, you could get married quickly, no questions asked, no blood tests required, just zip in and zip out. It sounded good, but didn't quite work out that way. RG had borrowed a friend's vehicle, a 1937 Ford, for this long drive. They made it as far as Henderson, NV, about 20 miles south of Las Vegas.

They were almost to Las Vegas when RG fell asleep, ran off the road, over corrected and rolled the Ford. Louise, asleep in the passenger seat, was partially ejected. She had her right leg caught when the passenger door closed on it. Her leg was broken in a couple places from the knee to her upper thigh. RG was not injured, but Louise had to be hospitalized in Henderson. The vehicle was totaled.

Louise was in the hospital for a couple of weeks giving RG enough time to hitchhike back to Casa Grande where he would borrow Aubrey's (his brother) 1940 Ford to return to Nevada to get Louise. When he got back to Henderson to pick up Louise, she had a cast on her leg that would not allow her to sit in an upright position. RG had to have the bench seat of his brother's car altered a little bit. He found a place that cut the bench seat in half allowing her to lay down on the back portion of the passenger side so Louise could ride in a laid-back position as they returned to Casa Grande.

*

It should be mentioned that Mom's mother Ella Mae Brown did not care for RG in any way, shape or form and made it very clear that they would not be getting married with her blessing. Because of the outbreak of the war and the situation being as it was, they were hoping to get married as Louise was only 17 at the time. Louise stayed with RG's family in Casa Grande and finally her parents came around to okay the marriage.

On June 3, 1942, Anna Louise Brown and Kenneth RG Haw were married in Mesa. They were sitting in the front seat of an old Ford that belonged to RG. Louise still had her leg in a partial cast and could not stand on her injured leg for very long. Present during the ceremony was Ella Mae and her daughter Christine, Louise's sister. It is not known who, if any from RG's side of the family was present. After marrying, they established residence in a tent erected in the back yard of RG's parents.

On Sept. 24, 1942, RG received his draft notice. He was drafted into the U.S. Army-Air Corps and was to report for active duty status on Oct. 9, 1942, at Smokey Hill Army Air Corp base in Salina, KS. His Army serial number was 39850319. Smokey Hill provided training and advanced training for B-29 pilots. RG was trained as a spotter, working on the firing range, so to speak. He would spot the dropping of bombs during target practice sessions and report back to the pilots.

Early in January 1943, Louise was able to rejoin RG in Salina. She was heavily-laden with a baby. For those of you who don't understand the previous sentence, she was pregnant. In late February or early March of 1943, Louise had a baby boy who died at birth. This information was told to Ms. Jan Moore who was a social worker at Good Shepherd Rest Home during Mom's last months. More on Dad's relationship with Mom in following chapters.

Chapter 3

Me

I am Kenneth Ray Haw. I was born to Kenneth R.G. Haw and Anna Louise Haw (Brown) at 7:45 p.m. Jan. 2, 1944, at St. John's Hospital, Salina, KS. I was six 6 pounds, 2 oz., 18 inches long. Dr. Porter Brown was the attending physician.

In 1944, President Franklin D. Roosevelt, a Democrat, was in his third term of office. The vice president was Henry Wallace. The Dow Jones was at 143.30, an ounce of gold sold for $35, silver for 75 cents an ounce. A loaf of bread went for 10 cents, a gallon of milk for 62 cents and a pound of butter for 50 cents. A new Ford automobile sold for $975 and a gallon of gas for 15 cents. The average new home sold for $3,475 and the annual family income was $2,378.

In the arts, the No. 1 song was "Sentimental Journey" by Homer/Brown/Green. The top movie was "Going My Way," produced by Paramount Studios and starring Bing Crosby who was the No. 1 actor at the time. The No. 1 actress was Ingrid Berman for her role in "Gaslight."

About five years before I was born, on April 30, 1939, the first regular commercial television broadcasts were aired in New York City via a transmitter that had been installed in the Empire State Building. I remember our first television set in the late 1950's. This TV tidbit is just to show that my family was not a family of means.

Well, I think we have Day 1 out of the way. What do you expect? I was born at 7:45 p.m. Most of my first day was already shot so let's head into my pre-school years.

*

Following my birth, we stayed in Salina, KS, for about six months before moving to Ellsworth, KS, just north of Salina. This would have been about June 1944.

Lo and behold Mom was pregnant again. This info was told to me by Mom's sister, Ola Mae, who verified information given to me years ago by Mom that I had a younger brother who died. He was born between me and Ron. However, there was a bit more that Aunt Ola Mae had to add to this saga. According to her, Dad had an affair while in Salina and came down with a venereal disease. She thought it was gonorrhea and that's what is believed to have killed my brother in December, 1944. He was born premature stillborn.

I want to make a note here that the two infant deaths mentioned previously have not been verified or authenticated by any birth or death certificates. I hope to obtain these documents before publishing this book. However, if I am unable to obtain these documents, I do believe these events happened as described.

It must have been something in the water.

*

We had lived in Ellsworth for about seven months when Mom got pregnant again. I was about 12 months old at this time and the events I am relating to this pregnancy were given to me by a friend of Mom's, Mrs. Jan Moore, who had befriended Mom during Mom's last year of life at age 76 in Good Shepherd Rest Home in Peoria, AZ. The events have been substantiated with records I received shortly after Mom passed away on Nov. 1, 2000.

When Mom became pregnant, Dad was furious and did not believe the baby was his. After months of fighting and feuding, my mother's parents, Benny and Ella Brown, came to Ellsworth from California to pack Mom and I up to take us back to California with them. Mom and Dad were going to split up because of this baby.

We were going to California by train and got as far as Grand Island, Neb., when my Mom went into labor. Grandpa Brown and I stayed at the train station house while Grandma and Mom went to the Lutheran

Hospital in Grand Island. My sister, Debra Ann Haw, was born alive at 3:30 p.m. on July 24, 1945. She was six-and-a-half pounds and the father's name was listed on her birth certificate as Kenneth R.G. Haw. This information was given to the attending physician, John Reilly, by my mother. Who really knows besides Mom, whether this was also Dad's daughter. This event on numerous occasions over the next 18 years would cause me a lot of trauma and unnecessary searching of my own soul. More on this in later chapters reference the little bastard that wasn't mine.

My sister, Debra Ann Haw, died at 5:30 p.m., on July 24, the same day she was born. This is substantiated by a death certificate I received from the Vital Records Depository in Lincoln, NE, on Oct. 13, 2000. She lived for two hours and died from cardiac insufficiency, another premature birth.

After a short time, Mom was released from the Lutheran hospital. The exact length of stay in the hospital is unknown, but after being released, her and Grandma met up with Grandpa Brown and me back at the train station. After some discussion as to which direction to go, either continue on to California or go back to Dad in Ellsworth, Mom decided to go back to Dad.

*

We were back in Ellsworth for a short while as Dad was scheduled to go overseas. He packed Mom and I up and sent us to Dallas to live with his older brother Earnest and sister-in-law, Hazel. Meanwhile, the Armistice was signed and Dad did not have to go overseas, but instead he was transferred to Colorado where he spent a short period of time. He was honorably discharged because of a surplus of enlisted personnel in the zone of Interior. He had spent a total of three years, 2 months, 6 days in active-duty status before being sent back to Davis-Monthan Field in Tucson for separation on Nov. 29, 1945.

Mom and I had already moved back to Casa Grande, AZ and was living with my grandparents, Robert and Virginia Haw. Dad joined us there.

After the first year or so, my life pattern had started to develop. Salina and Ellsworth, KS; Grand Island, NE; Dallas, TX; and Casa Grande, AZ. This was to be an unbroken pattern throughout most of my younger years as you will see as this book progresses.

I must have been a beautiful baby, and I have the baby pictures to prove it. I especially like the picture of me at 15 months, the one of me standing alone next to a vase of roses, which was almost as tall as me. Another picture I especially liked was with Mom and Dad. Dad was in his military dress uniform and Mom with her dark hair down past her shoulders with a heavy wool full-length coat on. Mom was a very attractive lady from which I got my looks. These pictures were taken in Nebraska and I would venture to guess around April, 1945.

Mom nor Dad never spoke to me of my sister's birth nor death. I guess from what I have gathered it was understood between them that the subject would never be brought up whether it was from shame, guilt or whatever. One can only guess.

Imagine if Mom would have kept a journal of her life, how it would have read. She only had an eighth-grade education as far as formal schooling. But, if a person were given a degree in life experiences, she would have had a doctorate. Dad told me he had attended the second grade, whether he passed the second grade or even went to school at all is open for discussion. He could neither read nor write, except to sign his name, K.R. Haw. Mom said she had to work with him to get him to write his name.

*

We were living in a tent that we had pitched in Grandma and Grandpa's backyard at 1000 E. 5th Street in Casa Grande. Just east of where we lived, on the southwest corner of 5th Street and Trekell Road lived my uncle Rob and Aunt Vallie, my father's youngest sister. They owned and operated a small service station that was truly a neighborhood-type station.

As per information Uncle Aubrey gave me, he and Dad bought a one-room shack for just a few dollars and moved this into the backyard to replace the tent we were in. This was sometime in 1946. Dad was pretty good at building so he added on to this "house" when he could We still used the bathroom in Grandma and Grandpa's house which had a door directly into it from the backyard. Whether it was built like that or added on for us, I don't know.

We would follow the migrant farmers as we picked cotton in Casa Grande. We picked vegetables and citrus in the Phoenix and Mesa areas, then we would migrate west to Yuma, AZ, with stops along the way in Tacna and Wellton to pick melons, lettuce or whatever the crop of the season was. For the most part we would pitch a tent if the stay over was going to be for a short while or we sometimes would rent a migrant worker's shack if we were going to be there a while. From Arizona, we would follow the workers or, I should say work because I don't think any migrants got close enough to one another to form lasting relationships. We went to various California locations such as Ivanho, Stockton, Eureka, Tulare and Woodlake, just to name a few. We would then go into Oregon, the Portland area to pick strawberries.

Appendix A in the back of this book lists the places I have lived while growing up, including Mesa, AZ, where I graduated from high school. This list is as comprehensive as I can make it, but it is only as good as my memory and research done on various pictures, etc.

*

In December 1946, I was almost three years old when we were involved in an accident in Woodlake, CA. Dad was driving, Mom was in the passenger seat, and yep, yours truly was standing in the middle of the seat between them. What a big kid!. When Mom told me this story, she said Dad and her had been drinking.

He was speeding and another car came at them in their lane. Dad swerved to avoid the head-on collision before running off the road, spinning the car numerous times. When it came to a stop, I was gone and it was pitch dark. I must have gone through an open window because there was no damage to the vehicle we were driving which Mom thought was a 1942 or 1943 Ford or Mercury. The other vehicle had stopped to see if everyone was OK. A search then began for me. It took quite a while but Mom remembers a person from the other vehicle yelling from quite a ways off "I've found him, over here," he yelled over and over.

I had been rescued.

Mom said they took me to the hospital to have me checked because of how far I had been thrown and how dirty I was. I was checked and released. Nothing broken. "Everything was A-OK." This was the same hospital my brother Ronnie Lee Haw was born in on Dec. 19th 1946, a few days after the accident.

*

This is probably a good time to mention some of the clothing I wore. In my early pictures, 15 months to about four years old, I assume I had some pretty flashy duds. At least my long and short sleeve T-shirts looked nice. I wore a lot of overalls, so I really don't remember what I had for pants if I wore any.

When I started school, I remember Mom working for many hours making my shirts. I think the fabric was cotton and the pattern was always the latest fashion for whatever the large containers of flour came in. This is what my shirts were made from, flour sacks. Mom was a very good seamstress and they always seemed to fit nicely. The bags must have been washed before I wore the finished product because I never remember having an unusually white appearance. We must have eaten lots of stuff that required flour because there never seemed to be an end to the fabric Mom used.

I might add that I was not malnourished. I was always a little porky, and had good clothes to wear. The two go hand in hand. I mean me being porky and the flour from the sacks. I can't remember my shoes all that well, but I know I had some because one of my favorite games was "Kick the Can" and I can remember Mom telling me to quit because I'd ruin my shoes. Well, Hell, I didn't have any flour sacks to kick.

Two of the main ingredients for life were never denied me that I can remember. I am talking about food and clothing. I can't even say that the most important one of all was denied me when I was younger, I don't really remember at what age they started denying me their *love*.

I do not remember going to pre-school or kindergarten with my sense and sensibilities. I rushed right on into the first grade. The first three reporting quarters of this exciting step in my life took place in the Elbow Creek School, Tulare County, CA. My teacher's name was Gwendolyn Glover and after only three quarters of the four gone, we moved back to Arizona, but she knew I belonged in second grade.

I have the report cards to prove it guys, what can I say. This is the same year that we bought our first brand new car, a 1949 Mercury in Tulare, CA. I finished the first grade in Casa Grande. After beginning the second grade in Casa Grande, we moved to Coolidge, AZ, after a third of the school year. We rented a trailer in a trailer park and I finished second grade in Coolidge.

*

Sometime before the beginning of the third grade, we moved to Superior, AZ, where Dad worked on the Queen Creek tunnel. He was a high scaler, hanging from ropes and drilling holes for the dynamite charges to blast out the rock for the concrete tunnel to be installed. We lived in a rental house that has since been demolished and was located where the road to Ray, AZ, passes over U.S. 60.

I started and finished the school year in Superior and it had some good memories for me. Sometimes after school Mom would take Ron and me to watch Dad work and then we would go to Oak Flat Pond, just east of where they were building the tunnel, and we would fish for crawdads. I don't remember ever catching a fish, but tons of crawdads.

Almost every Saturday, I remember Ron and I each getting a quarter. This would get us a cherry milkshake at the Rexall Drug Store in downtown Superior, right next to the movie theater, which was our next stop to spend the rest of our quarters.

One day, while walking home from school, I got in a rock fight with one of the boys from my school. I remember he ran into his yard, picked up something and threw it at me. It was piece of chain link wire about six inches long. It caught me in the right temple and I went home bleeding. Mom took me to the hospital to have it removed. It wasn't lodged in very far and it didn't take any stitches. When Dad got home and heard the story he and I both went to the boy's house where an argument ensued between Dad and the other boy's dad about who would pay the hospital bill. A fight followed and Dad ended up being arrested and also had to pay the hospital bill.

The Queen Creek tunnel is located on U.S. 60, about two miles east of Superior and is 1,149 feet long. This is a beautiful site for me to see in my travels as I know the work that went into it and the memories of the area.

*

The latter part of 1951 was not very happy for the Haw family as Grandpa and Grandma both passed away. At the time, we were living in Coolidge in a trailer park.

As mentioned previously, Grandma Haw was not in the best of health and had not been for many years. However, it was Grandpa who came down sick first and had to go to the Casa Grande general hospital. He was quickly denied care because they had no income and did not have the money needed for admittance. Grandpa was taken to the Pinal County hospital in Florence, about 35 miles away, but a long 35. He was transported by Aunt Vallie who also signed him into the hospital.

Grandpa was in the hospital about seven weeks and was diagnosed with carcinoma of the stomach, stomach cancer. I remember he either seemed to be drugged and asleep or in quite a bit of pain when we could see him. I was told this by Mom and Dad as in those years you had to be at least 12 years old to go into a patient's room.

Grandma was at such a loss for Grandpa that after a couple weeks, they set a fold up bed in his room for her. Grandpa passed away on Oct. 23, 1951. Five days later, on Oct. 28, 1951, having never left the hospital room where she had stayed by Grandpa's side, Grandma died. It is listed on her death certificate that she either died from: A. Heart failure; B. Nephritis; C. Arteriole sclerosis. It was a multiple choice-type thing going on here, but from what doctors told Mom and Dad, she died from a broken heart, pure and simple. She just lost any will to live when Grandpa died.

They are both buried in the Mountain View Cemetery in Casa Grande.

Chapter 4

Travelin' Man

After Grandpa and Grandma were buried, we moved from the rental trailer in Coolidge into their house in Casa Grande. This was the first place I can remember that we lived in with inside plumbing and indoor bathroom. Even with the house we had rented in Superior, we had to use an outhouse and pump water.

I was walking in tall cotton this school year, fourth grade, living in a house with an actual address on it, new flour-sack shirts. Both Ron and I had identical printed shirts. There must have been a push on those flour sacks. I walked back and forth to school, accompanied by my little brother who was in the first grade.

I am thinking there's absolutely no way I'm going to blow this situation. I'm going to be the best student in my fourth-grade class. It's going to be yes sir and yes ma'am to my teachers and I will always have a smile on my face. But, I haven't quite made it to school yet.

I was never real quick to make friends and the first reporting period of the fourth grade, I believe it was after six weeks, my teacher, Mrs. Curtis, sent a note home with me to my parents. It simply stated that I had not learned to get along with my classmates, either on the playground or in the classroom. She even had the audacity to put in there that I was very dependent and was in need of help. Where the hell this was coming from, I don't know, but let me explain what I think the real problem was.

My first experience and memory with what I thought would be a fight occurred during my fourth school year in Casa Grande, I can remember a classmate who was at least twice my size. Well, he was a lot larger than I was and had called me a sissy, threatening to knock me down and sit on top of me.

Let me explain this "sissy" part first. I always had good hands, quick hands. I was the marble champion in the third and fourth grades and also came in second in "Jacks." Now Jacks is a funny game where a lot of physical dexterity is required and that was me. You toss this little rubber ball into the air and pick up from one to a dozen little metal objects in a variation of fast, swift, sweeping motions.

Tubby thought this to be a sissy game. I only called him "Tubby" that one time and I guess I rightly forgot his real name. I don't know if Tubby is what irritated him or that he didn't like Jacks. I do know that if he ever carried through on his threat to knock me down and sit on me, he would probably kill me, so I found out that my feet were also quite swift, never allowing him to catch up to me. I am not saying I was scared of him, but my clothes were pretty much hand made in those days and I had to protect them at any cost.

I remember numerous days I had to run from him before school, at recess, my favorite class, and after school. The making of the me to follow was that one day, my fleet feet betrayed me and Tubby pushed me to the ground and dirtied my shirt pretty good. To my good fortune, I managed to scramble, get up and shag out of there like a rocket. I can still remember the kids laughing at me to this day.

That afternoon, Mom, after seeing my dirty shirt and skinned-up elbows, made me tell her what happened. I thought she had sympathy for me until dad got home and she told him. They called me into the kitchen where they had been having their little confab over a couple of beers. Dad told me in no uncertain terms that I was going to school the next morning and have it out with this kid and if I did not, he would have a belt for me when I returned home. Now having felt the power of the belt a few times before, I didn't reckon a few bruises to be nearly as bad.

The next morning, I knew what I had to do, but upon arriving at school, I didn't see a 2x4 or a baseball bat anywhere, but I did see Tubby, hanging around with a bunch of kids that used to hang with me.

I guess I caught him off guard because I walked straight towards him. The sneer was just leaving his face as I replaced it with a round-house right hand which I was right proud of. I guess, because I had momentarily closed my eyes as I threw the punch, it landed solidly, but he didn't go anywhere. It seemed like an eternity before he opened his mouth and started crying, turned around and ran off. Sissy.

We ended up becoming pretty good friends after that.

*

I believe the year was 1952, but I'm not sure. I do know Mom, Dad, Ron and myself went to visit Mom's family who were living in tents, south of Washington Street in Phoenix—somewhere in the neighborhood of 42nd Street, a few blocks east of the Phoenix Greyhound Park.

The Arizona Canal was just a few feet from where we were camped. It was a canal with dirt embankments, not concrete lined as most are today. We had to dig out an area at this canal where the women could get to the water to wash our clothes. I do not remember how long we were there, but this morning in particular was the day after Christmas.

As usual on Christmas morning or sometimes Christmas night, Ron and I got our presents which mostly consisted of one item each that we had pleaded with Santa for months prior to the big day.

I was ecstatic when I opened my Daisy Red Ryder BB gun. This was a lever-action, spring-piston air gun with adjustable iron sights, similar to the one Ralphie got in the movie "A Christmas Story." It had a gravity-fed magazine with a 650 BB shot capacity. I even got a tube of BB's that came with it. I was in heaven.

I couldn't wait to get the OK to start hunting or just shooting. When it was light enough out to see what I was shooting at, I was out of our tent like my pants were on fire.

I shot at every bird I saw. These birds were relatively safe as I was just learning to shoot. I was getting somewhat discouraged by not being able to hit anything when I noticed a target next to the canal bank. It was wide enough target even I couldn't miss.

Mom's sister, Kathleen, was doing the wash. Her bulbous butt was in the air as she bent over alongside the canal washing clothes. Stealthily, I snuck in as close as I dared to get my prey without giving myself away. I sighted down the barrel of the rifle and fired right into center mass. A direct hit.

Now, I am not a rocket scientist, but when she shot up from her crouch and started yelling some cusswords I hadn't heard before, I

20

thought I had better change locations, which I did, quite promptly I might add.

I started running straight down the canal bank. I probably had only run about 20 or 30 yards when I was yanked backwards by my aunt and into the canal I went. I was airborne before I could utter a word. The next thing I remembered was climbing out of the canal sans my prized Daisy Red Ryder BB gun.

By this time everyone from the camp was waiting for me. What could I say? Maybe, I could make amends by agreeing to take a gun-safety class or who knows?

I did get to cut off my own switch from some trees in the area. Aunt Kathleen was first to administer a few swats of justice with a switch, or should I say switches. Then Dad added a few more and promised there was more punishment to come if I didn't retrieve the BB gun from the canal.

After a few hours, I came back to the tent carrying another switch as I was unable to find the rifle. I did learn that the thicker the switch, the less it hurt. That said, corporal punishment still was quite painful.

*

The kids who lived around us, Ron and myself, would play games in the evenings such as "Hide-and-Go-Seek," "Cowboys and Indians," "Cops and Robbers," "Quick Draw," and "Kick the Can."

Kick the Can could be played anywhere, anytime. I remember walking home from school one day and the route we took home was usually littered with cans and other debris. After kicking this one particular can, a bunch of paper flew out of it. This paper was money and what appeared to be receipts from a drugstore that was in the downtown area. I took everything, can included, to Mom. Mom drove me to the drug store and made me go inside and return the can and money. I don't know if Mom ever believed I had actually stolen the money or not. But, just for the record, I did not, have not nor ever would steal money from another individual.

I know how hard money is to come by. I picked cotton on weekends and when school was out. I made $3 per 100 pounds of cotton and gave this to my parents. Let me tell you what I remember about picking cotton.

We picked two different kinds of cotton:

1 Regular cotton. It would get about 3 ½ to 4-foot tall. We earned about $3 per pound.
2 Pima cotton with stalks 5- to 6-feet high. It was a better grade of cotton, harder to pick because of closer, tighter balls. We earned about $3.50 per pound.

I remember going to the fields, sitting there all day babysitting Ron. Not that I could do a hell of a lot except run to get Mom when he needed changing or got hungry. Mom and Dad worked from sunup to sundown in the fields—long, hard, sweaty, dirty, filthy work.

I think I was about eight or nine when I got to strap on my first cotton sack. I was walking in high cotton so to speak, no pun intended. These sacks were made from heavy canvas and I remember some having black bottoms covered in tar so they would drag easier in the dirt. My bag was probably seven to eight feet in length. The object was to pick the cotton, put it inside the bag and when you got to the point your couldn't put anymore in, you had to take and shake the bag to work the cotton to the bottom. When you got enough cotton in the bag, you now would lie down, place your legs in the bag and push real hard to pack the cotton good and hard, then start picking again. I remember on a good day, I picked over 150 pounds and made about $4.50.

The balls had sharp, needle-like points on them. If they weren't opened up all the way, they would jab into your fingers. Your fingers would get sore and bled, but you kept picking. Eventually, you would build up a tolerance and calluses.

I had to drag my bag to the weight area that consisted of a wooden tripod with a scale and a large "J" hook that you draped your bag over. After weighing, the weight was recorded into a log book with your name in it. After the bag was weighed, you had to take the bag, strap it over your shoulders and climb a ladder onto a large wagon, walk out onto a 12- to 14-inch plank that ran from one side of the wagon to the other. You then took your cotton bag and shook it empty into the wagon before climbing back down and start all over. At the end of the day, it was fun for us kids as we could actually play in the wagons full of cotton. We would go out on the plank and jump off into all the cotton that was in the wagon. We'd do flips. This was the most fun of the day.

We, numerous families, would follow the cotton crop from one farm to the next to the next. This was sure exciting, especially at the end of each day and you got paid in cash. I would see my Dad getting wads of money and I couldn't wait to get older. Dad and Mom were both hard-working, dedicated people. I saw my Dad in more fights than I can remember. Some he won, some he lost, but boy could he fight and boy could he drink. The more he drank, the more he would fight. Boy, I thought and wished I could be just like him.

To all of you impressionable young people reading this, I should insert a warning: Be careful of what you wish for. It just may come true.

*

I passed fourth grade and was going into the fifth. I had become quite an entrepreneur. I spent almost all the money I came by for comic books. I loved to read at an early age and after school and on weekends, I would walk the neighborhood, knocking on doors and trading comic books. I would have a box full of mine and if they had any I hadn't read, we would trade for one. Sometimes, people would just give me the ones they had. Times were a little simpler in the 1950s, even adults with no children read comic books.

*

I remember the first business venture I went into came straight from the pages of some of those comic books. It was a seed business. I would order all these seeds—flower seeds, vegetable seeds, any kind of seed imaginable, I could get. I frequently doubled my money by selling these seeds to friends, relatives and some people I was trading comic books with.

With my parent's blessing, I went into the seed business. Back then, they put a lot of seeds in those little packets, which I believe, was the downfall of my first business venture. Not a lot of repeat business as the seeds lasted for years.

*

I was nine years old and still in the fifth grade when a friend, a Mexican boy who lived around the corner from us, was visiting. Dad had left his pack of Camel cigarettes, non-filter, a real man's smoke, on the kitchen table. The temptation was too great. I got the pack and some matches and we beat feet to the bathroom. Now, I had never attempted to smoke before, but my friend said he had and he'd show me how to light up. He got it going and I couldn't believe how much smoke he was making. I was getting ready to light mine when the door burst open and there's Dad with a beer in his hand.

Remember, as I had said earlier, the bathroom had a door going into the backyard. Well, when I looked from Dad to my friend, all I saw was the open door. Here I was standing, matches in one hand, package of cigarettes in the other and one in my mouth, unlit. I don't remember how many cigs were left in the pack, but Dad made me eat all of them. I wasn't doing too bad until I swallowed. That probably wasn't the sickest I have ever been in my lifetime, but it ranks right up there. To this day, I have never smoked a cigarette and have no craving for one.

*

Back to school. My fifth-grade teacher, Mrs. McKean, says I am growing up, doing better in school and becoming an average student. Average? What the hell is average? From a 70 to an 86.5 overall grade? Was Einstein average?

School was pretty much a repeat of 1952, still picking cotton and helping Uncle Rob at his service station.

Chapter 5

'What Mother Means to Me'

Grandpa Brown got a job in the Jamestown, CA, area, laying pipe. It apparently was a job with some stability and would last a few years. He told Mom and Dad about it and thought he could get Dad on if he wanted to come out to California.

I started the school year at Jamestown school, Tuolumne County. Jamestown was really not a town, but an area that had a lot of farms and ranches. It also had a one-room school house with one teacher, Anna Belle Mann, for grades one through eight.

This was a beautiful area, green, near a lake and lots of trees. I remember shortly after the school year started, we heard about a western movie being made nearby. The stars were Randolph Scott and Forrest Tucker. Ron and I were both western addicts, having our own cap guns, holsters, etc. I pleaded with Mom to take us to see the movie being made. She didn't need much prodding as Randolph Scott was a Hollywood heart throb and all women loved him.

We spent a good full day watching a western movie being made. At the time, it was not titled and they had just started production. I felt sure with my two holsters, cap guns and my rolled up cuffs on my blue jeans that I would have a part in the movie. I wasn't quite sure about Ron, who was dressed identically to me including rolled up cuffs. These cuffs just weren't rolled up, but really rolled up at least eight inches. These jeans were bought to last at least as long as we grew and probably would last at least a year or two past that.

This was probably one of the prettiest areas I had ever lived in and I knew we were going to be here for a long time. However, within the first month, Dad had all the good drinking places located and he was in one of these when he got into a fight with a foreman (boss) off the construction site he was working on. Dad got his jaw broken and he was beaten pretty badly. I was there. He had to be taken to a hospital in Stockton, CA, about 30 miles away via ambulance. I could not go with him, but had to wait at the bar for Mom to come and get me.

When we arrived at the hospital, they were wanting to operate on Dad's jaw, but Mom had to give the OK, probably because Dad could not talk because of the broken jaw nor could he read or write.

They did surgery and had to wire Dad's jaw shut and he remained in the hospital for a couple weeks. He lost his job because he couldn't make it to work and possibly because of the fight with his boss. You think?

When Dad was released from the hospital and had to recover for a few weeks, it was enough time for me to finish eight weeks of school. We moved to Visalia, CA, where I attended school for a short while and then we moved to Stockton, CA, where Dad had been offered another job as a pipe layer. I think it was around this time when Dad joined the AFL-CIO laborers union. We probably spent about two months in this area before Dad decided we were going back to Arizona where he was going to work construction. We moved back to Mesa, AZ, and bought a mobile home.

*

Dad joined the local chapter of the AFL-CIO and landed a job doing road construction midway between Mesa and Payson at a little place on the side of the road called Sunflower. The construction Dad was involved with was from Sunflower towards Payson. The thought was we would move to Sunflower where we would join a laborers commune, a group of other people with trailers located just east of the little general store which was all there was to Sunflower.

We established our home site under some giant sycamore and cottonwood trees right on Sycamore Creek. The construction company, which I believe was Fisher Construction, set up generators in the area where we could run lights and have electricity.

There were no school buses going in either direction and Sunflower was in Maricopa County which would necessitate our going to school in Mesa. Mom wanted us to go to school in Payson because Dad was working that way. Payson is in Gila County and Mom had to apply for and get a variance to take us to school in Payson which was about 35 miles one way. This 35 miles was on narrow, sometimes steep mountain roads. Oh, did I mention the roads were dirt and not maintained well? The drive, one way, took close to 1½ hours.

Mom had to go before W.W. "Skipper" Dick who was the state school superintendent at the time. Mom told me later that the superintendent was very reluctant to grant the variance.

Mom drove us every day for the last six weeks of the school year. She would wait at a local park until school was out, then drive back to Sunflower, only to get up early the next day and do it all again. Ron and I were the only two kids who went to school from our little commune.

*

We spent most of the summer at Sunflower. There really wasn't a lot to do to get in trouble, or so I thought. But, if there's a way, I could find it. One grand summer day, I was hiking along Sycamore Creek eastward and strayed away from the creek going south when I noticed a few mounds piled a couple feet high from ground level with rocks.

I am thinking whoever put the rocks on top of one another really didn't have any more rights to that land and I had to remove them. There was a bunch of neat stuff with some really old-looking bones. The neat stuff was some pretty neat pieces of pottery and old pots still in one piece, a leather pouch with pieces of blue rocks in it. There was more than I was going to be able to carry back to the trailer. I came back later that day with a small cardboard box I had retrieved from our local dump which we shared with the Sunflower general store and café.

When I returned to the trailer, I stashed my treasure under the wooden steps leading into the trailer. I didn't think I had better tell Mom or Dad about this for a while. The next day, we were sitting down for supper when someone knocked on the door. I jumped up and looked out the window to see who it was. I didn't recognize the man standing on the steps in a dark green uniform with patches on the sleeves, but I did recognize the box he was holding. I'm thinking this can't be good.

As things worked out, I was only given probation by this U.S. Forest Service ranger. He said I had defaced an old Indian burial site and had stolen artifacts. The facts of the matter was I could not hide or lie my way out of this. The next morning, this ranger and Mom supervised me as I put the rocks back into a mounded area. I never saw the artifacts again and I am sure I never covered them back up.

*

I believe this time in my life is where I really developed my love for hiking and being by myself. I still love both of these things to this day.

We got to know the owners of the Sunflower General Store quite well along with their hired help. I especially remember a very likeable man by the name of "Stubby." I don't know and never asked about his name, but I think he had all his fingers. He was kind of an overall caretaker, gas station attendant, cook, etc. He also was not opposed to tipping a few beers with Mom and Dad when the occasion arose which was usually nightly and weekends.

This is also the time that I realized the loud conversations Mom and Dad had on a regular basis were what some would think of fighting. They were bounced out of the General Store on a few occasions. This really wasn't a problem as Stubby would just bring the booze to our trailer.

A couple incidents that stick in my memory occurred on our drives to or from school in Payson. I had never heard of the word vapor lock and probably still wouldn't if I had not asked Mom how come we were always broke down on the side of the road. It was explained to me that a vapor lock was when something in the fuel system of the vehicle would overheat and the vehicle would cease to get gas, thus stopping until it cooled off enough to restart.

The other thing which we never got an answer to and may not want one.

We were driving back to Sunflower along a very steep section of the Mazatzal Mountains when we heard a very loud roaring noise from our vehicle, a 1950 grey Ford (the color becomes significant later) and the vehicle began to shake. Mom was so nervous she had to stop the car, get out and walk around a bit. Then, she had me drive into Sunflower. Yes, this was the first time I had ever driven and we made it without any further incidents. However, I don't think she was as nervous about the UFO as I was driving for the first time.

When we told dad what happened, we checked the car over for damage. We still have no idea to this day as to what could have burnt the paint off the top of the car, leaving it black. It is not possible it was an airplane as we were on a narrow road on a pretty steep cliff. Possibly a UFO, do you think? Your guess is as good as mine, but I would lean in that direction.

*

Towards the end of that school year, we had to complete a writing assignment, "What Mother Means to Me." This is what I wrote.

"What Mother Means to Me"

My mother mean a lot to me. When I want to go to the show she lets me. She brings us to school each morning and sits out in that old hot car every day except when we are sick or on the weekends.

When we go to town she asks my father to give us some money so we can have some fun. She fixes our lunch and gets us ready for school each morning.

Sometimes we argue back to her when she tells us to do something for her. Sometimes we say no we aren't going to do it she tells us we shouldn't say it, that means a lot to us. And she does many more things to help us and to make us happy.

All good things must come to an end. Time to move again.

*

We had been living in an 8-foot by 35-foot mobile home and what was neat was we could just hitch it up and pull it anywhere we went, which we did and often.

I started the seventh grade at East Mesa Junior High School. Dad was in between jobs, but he knew he wanted to make his home in Mesa. This lasted for about two report periods before Dad got a job helping build a portion of Interstate-8 which ran through Gila Bend where we moved to, actually a few miles east of Gila Bend where the construction company had its equipment parked within a chain-link enclosure. That is where we parked our trailer. Dad got paid a little extra for being the watchman at the construction site.

My first tryout for any kind of sport was the basketball team which I made. But looking back, Gila Bend didn't have a lot to choose from, which could have worked in my favor. We eventually moved into the town of Gila Bend, a trailer park just east of the town, behind a Texaco service station.

I remember a friendship I developed with a school mate named Roger Clement. A few weeks before the end of the school year, Dad had taken a job in Superior at the mines and we were going to move back to Mesa where he would commute and come home on the weekends. Roger's parents, with our prodding, talked my folks into letting me live with them until school was out. We won out and I moved in with them, finishing my year out there. They were also going to be moving to Yuma, AZ, once the school year ended or I would have tried to stay the summer with them also.

Robert's parents took me home to Mesa a couple weeks after school ended. My parents and Ron were living in a trailer park on South Country Club Drive. It was nice to see my little brother again.

Dad's job was not going well in Superior. He had been injured slightly when he was hit in the head by a rock while working in a pit. I think he decided there were other jobs out there he hadn't yet tried. Not many, but possibly a few. After all, we did have a trailer and a pick-up to pull it with.

*

I don't think I've properly described the trailer we were raised in, but I think it is appropriate to do so. The one I can remember most vividly was approximately 8x35-foot. The living room was in front and consisted of a small couch. The dining room table folded out from the wall next to the living room. We had two metal folding chairs that were also used for more seating in the living room. We just turned them around. The kitchen was next with a small 3-burner butane stove. If you turned around from the stove, there was the refrigerator which was also small, real small. Continuing on down the hallway about three paces were twin bunk beds on one side and a built in dresser on the other. I slept on the bottom bunk.

Next came a small bathroom with a shower, no bathtub. The entire back part of the trailer was Mom and Dad's bed with built-in dressers and a tiny closet. We had two doors leading outside. The front door divided the living room from the kitchen area. The other door was at the rear of the trailer, out of Mom and Dad's room.

*

Dad decided he had had enough of the heat and we were moving to Flagstaff where he would gain employment, again. Flagstaff had a union hall where the unemployed would meet, usually on a daily basis and various sundry jobs would come in. The next in line could either take the job or pass. If he passed, he went back to the end of the line.

Dad didn't know how to say pass and surely couldn't spell or write it. This probably accounted for some of our movements. One of the neat things is with all the men (I do not remember ever seeing a woman in the union hall), there would always be drinking and gambling. I remember getting to sit up on the pool tables during some of the gambling sessions and raking in the money when Dad won.

One of the first jobs Dad got was outside Flagstaff by a few miles. It was a road construction job and he had to place the stakes outlining the proposed roadway.

It was still during the summer months and I was a budding entrepreneur. Remember the seed business? This time I decided I would shine shoes. It was only a mile or so into town from our trailer park and what would I need for supplies? Black and brown polish, a couple rags, a shoe brush and something to carry it all in which also would allow the person something to rest their foot on while I polished the shoe. I would supply the spit for the spit shine. It took me a couple days to put everything together, but I was well on my way to total independence for a 13 year old.

*

I walked into town everyday for about six or seven weeks. I built a steady cliental, mostly in the bars on the main drag of Flagstaff (Santa Fe Avenue, Route 66), wherever the job took me. I started out charging 25 cents per pair of shoes and usually I got tips. I didn't have one particular corner, but I walked around a lot. I remember some of the business people would bring me shoes from home to shine.

I had a good thing going until one day I let a stranger talk me into going across the street past the railroad tracks where he had some friends who needed their shoes shined. We walked across the street, across the railroad tracks, past the train depot and down into a wash (possibly the Rio de Flag Wash). The stranger stopped and started undoing his pants and told me to take care of him or I would be sorry. I pretty much had this figured out and I was already sorry. But I still had a hold of my shoeshine kit and it was put together pretty sturdy. Besides, I didn't think this guy could run all that fast with his pants down around his ankles. I ran into him with my shoeshine kit which contained about four to six cans of polish, two brushes (one for black shoes and one for brown), numerous rags cut in strips for really singing a tune on the shoes. And, oh yeah, all my money in a can that I kept in the box.

When I ran over the guy, he started falling backwards. I didn't know he would be able to grab hold of my shoeshine kit. He was on his way down when I let go of the box and beat feet to the other side of the tracks, never stopping until I got home.

My shoeshine days were done. Most of the money I had made was in a can in the box in the hands of God only knows who. I remember when I got home I would tell Mom and Dad and maybe we could go back to see if we could recoup some of my losses. It wasn't to be as I learned we were going to Holbrook where Dad had taken a road construction job close to the New Mexico state line.

*

The good thing, or bad, depending on your view point, is when you are the owners of a trailer house, you can pick up and move at a moment's notice or less.

We had just passed Winslow, east-bound, when the sky turned black. We had to pull off the side of the road next to a fence because we couldn't see. This was the biggest locust/grasshopper migration anyone could remember ever seeing, literally millions upon millions of them. They stripped all the vegetation off the ground which wasn't much and then started on the wooden fence posts. All we could do was sit and watch. It didn't last long and when the swarm passed, there was nothing but devastation left in its path.

This should have been an omen, but we continued on to Holbrook where we were met with more bad news. The job Dad had taken was being put on hold, but they could use him for a couple weeks doing manual labor on a site just outside Holbrook. Dad took this job. I really can't remember ever getting out of the trailer because the wind was blowing so hard and it always seemed to be dusty and hot.

The next thing I remember is just a short while after arriving in Holbrook, I was told we were going to go home.

*

Home? Casa Grande here we come, again?

I thought we would arrive after school had already started. It didn't matter because we hadn't been in Holbrook for more than a month.

But, it wasn't Casa Grande. It was back to Flagstaff where Dad took a road construction job with Tanner Construction. This could be a great place to live and make friends if we could live in one of the larger trailer parks where there would be other kids. Ron and I didn't seem to ever have anyone our own ages to play or associate with. The only things my parents seemed to do or even want to do was drink, primarily at local bars. They would take Ron and me and we would have to wait in the vehicle which was now a 1954 Mercury four-door with a hitch to pull the trailer.

This one night, Mom and Dad, after one of their drinking binges, were on the way home with Ron and myself in the back seat. Dad could curse pretty good when the occasion warranted it which is what happened when the cop behind hit his siren and red lights. Dad was arrested for DWI (driving while intoxicated). Mom was allowed to follow the patrol car to the police station in downtown Flagstaff, corner of Beaver and Birch streets, where Dad would be processed, and then Mom could take him and us home.

This should have and possibly could have worked out okay because Mom was pretty good at acting sober or at least more sober than Dad. What I remember most is Mom and Dad did not come to actual blows before they got back to the vehicle. Then they did. Dad was blaming

Mom, Mom blaming Dad. Mom pulled out in the middle of the intersection right in front of the police station, stopped the car and the fight was on. By this time, it was getting light outside because I could see a few police officers running from the police station our way. The next thing I know is Mom, Ron and me are being driven home by a police officer. They kept Dad and, if not for Ron and me, the probably would have kept Mom also. They did keep our car somewhere.

When Dad got home from jail, he had been transferred to a road and bridge construction job north of Flagstaff. We moved to a little place called Cameron about 52 miles north of Flagstaff on U.S. 89.

*

When school started, we were bused to school in Tuba City. Yep, this is the Tuba City, right in the middle of the Navajo Indian Reservation.

My idol was Randolph Scott, a cowboy and great Indian fighter in many movies. This was not a good combination for white boys going to an almost all-Indian school. I got into a fight a day, usually with the same kid, not always. He probably had to take a couple days off to heal his hands injured when hitting my head. My thick skull had to hurt his knuckles.

The coach of the PE class finally had enough of the fighting and to settle things once and for all, we were to battle in front of the entire PE class, inside, with boxing gloves. It went well "for both of us" as neither of us would admit defeat. We fought hard for a few minutes. Then when we couldn't stand any longer to throw punches, exhausted we both went to our knees, but kept throwing leather. The coach finally called it a draw and let both of us know, the fighting would stop then and there.

To my surprise, I was accepted or at least tolerated the rest of the time we went to school in Tuba City. We had moved a couple of times due to Dad's job locations, but we remained in the general area. We moved from Cameron to a little place we called "Shadow Mountain." We got to call it what we wanted to because no one had ever lived here before. It was just an area set up for the construction workers a little ways off the road. This mountain, just west of us, when the sun set, would cast a long shadow, thus "Shadow Mountain." There were probably a half dozen trailers in our little community, but none of the others had kids.

I made friends with a few kids although my entire class consisted of 13 kids, four were girls. The class consisted of six white kids, five of which had lived with the Indians for years. One had not and would not for much longer as we were moving again.

*

The last six weeks of the school year found us back in Casa Grande. I did not find out until later years that Dad, Mom and my Uncle Aubrey and his wife, Virginia, had conspired to buy a not-so-flourishing truck stop restaurant. They renamed it the "Haw's Truck Stop."

I went to register for the eighth grade at the Casa Grande middle school. They had to have transcripts from my other schools in order to register me. This took a week or so and they would not let me go to school until their received the necessary paperwork. When I had collected all the paperwork, I again went to get registered. I was told the courses I had been taking were not the same as was required by this school district. It was recommended I sit out the remainder of the school year and begin the eighth grade again at the beginning of the next school year. My grades were not the best so they did not think I could catch up to graduate with the current class.

This was fine with me and Mom didn't put up much of an argument so I got to "quit" school.

We were living at the La Pasada Trailer Park on the north side of Casa Grande, directly across the street from the only bowling alley in town. Directly adjacent to the trailer park was a small store ran by a Chinese couple where I got a job bagging groceries and stocking shelves. This was during the day and Ron usually went with Mom and Dad to the truck stop. I also got a night job for a few hours each night setting pin at the bowling alley. This was before automatic pin setters.

Setting pins went like this: The first ball was rolled and however many pins were knocked down I would jump down from my perch, pick up the ball and roll it back on the return ramp. I would then pick up the pins and place them in the appropriate positions in the pinsetter. The area I worked in was not well lit. Sometimes the bowlers might not see me and roll the second ball while I was still in the back area placing pins.

Did I mention they also sold liquor at the bowling alley? This caused some frantic moments as some bowlers were less than sober. I always had at least two lanes, sometimes three or four. I got paid so much per game and I really had to hustle.

One night, after bowling was over, I had cleaned up my stations and was getting them ready for the next day. This girl, her mother and other people were still there when I was leaving. They said "Hi" to me as I walked by and apologized for having nearly hit me with a bowling ball as I was picking up pins to reset. I really did not remember this particular incident, but I took time to talk to her because I was in no rush to get home.

*

Her name was JoAnn Chandler. She told me she lived in the housing area just west of the bowling alley. She and her mom bowled there quite often and claimed her dad worked in Hollywood and was never home. His name was Jeff Chandler and he was a movie star in a number of movies, including many westerns. This took me by surprise as I was a western movie fanatic and I didn't remember hearing his name although he received an Academy Award nomination in 1950 for best supporting actor for his role as Cochise in "Broken Arrow."

We talked for a few minutes before she introduced me to her mother prior to their leaving. She said she was going into the eighth grade. JoAnn also had a genetic disorder where she could not tolerate the sunlight. She had to stay inside during the days and when she was in school, she had to stay in the classrooms until she was picked up by her mother.

I started the eighth grade in Casa Grande and whenever I had some spare time, I would walk to Jo Ann's house and visit with her. We talked about school and her condition, whatever kids 13 or 14 talk about. I was very hesitant to make any lasting friendships, boy or girl, because of my transient lifestyle. I didn't think it would change and it didn't as not too far down the road, Dad would take another job, thus ending forever this friendship.

*

I could sense the truck stop was not going that well as my parents were drinking more than ever and arguing incessantly. One night I agreed to go with them to work and watch after Ron. I soon learned why this restaurant venture was not working.

Mom was working her butt off behind the counter, waiting on customers. Dad was supposed to be cleaning tables and instead was sitting at the counter drinking beer after beer. Aunt Virginia, who was supposed to be helping Mom wait on customers, had not shown up yet. Mom started drinking beer also and I'm thinking this is a job I want when I get older—Be your own boss, drink while you're working and keep all the money you make.

I learned a valuable lesson for later on in life. "Be careful what you wish for, it may come true."

Aunt Virginia and uncle Aubrey came in a couple hours later. Uncle Aubrey was very seldom around as he was working elsewhere and was out of town a lot. Very shortly after they arrived, the shit hit the fan. Remember Mom was also drinking and had probably put a few away by this time. She started yelling at Aunt Virginia. I had heard most of the cuss words, so I thought, but some things Mom called Virginia were over my head.

The cursing progressed to pushing and shoving. Yes, there were customers in the truck stop. This instantly evolved into a hair-pulling slugfest that went out the front door of the restaurant onto the sidewalk with the customers following as well as Dad, Uncle Aubrey, Ron and me.

I can't say there was clearly a winner or loser, but Mom had her fair share of cuts, bruises and thinning hair. Uncle Aubrey nor Dad tried to intervene, at least I never saw it and so I thought this was a long time coming. The truckers surely got their money's worth that night.

Shortly after the above incident, the partnership was dissolved and Dad was at the union hall looking for work. I hadn't finished half the school year yet, but I knew we were moving again, but to where?

*

Fredonia, AZ. Where the hell is this?

If anyone is really interested, it's as far in northern Arizona as you can go and still be in Arizona, right on the Utah state line. Wow, a new place for the Haws to visit. An all-Mormon town, another who, what is a "Mormon?"

Dad had taken a job as a high scaler at Glen Canyon Dam. I remember packing up all our worldly possessions, in two boxes, hooking up to our 8-foot by 35-foot trailer and heading out. We had upgraded or downgraded depending on your viewpoint to a pickup truck. This came in handy because we kept a small freezer we got from the truck stop. This came in handy because while we were traveling, I had a place to sit or sleep on while we moved.

It seemed like weeks as we traveled north to Fredonia, but in reality, it was only a few days. I remember we had to stop quite often because the pickup was either overheating or vapor locking.

I was in a rage because I just knew I would have to quit school again because I couldn't take the same classes as I was taking in Casa Grande. I could visualize a 21-year-old graduating from high school. Not graduating was never an option I entertained.

Fredonia city limits I think. At least there was a trailer park across from a dilapidated looking hotel. I hadn't seen any thing else at that point, but the town was a ways up the road.

I returned to school in Fredonia, but God, it was cold up there. Our trailer didn't quite do enough to fight off the bitter cold. The other kids were very cliquish and Ron nor I felt at home. Ron's was becoming more of a little rebel, taking after his big bro, huh?

We were in the same school and I saw him often which was good. Occasionally, we had lunch together when our schedules overlapped. This school went through the 12th grade.

It's not long before trouble comes, but not for me. Ron's was starting to get a mouth on him and it seems a 10th grader had enough and messed him up a bit. This must have been on a Friday because Dad only came home on Friday nights, thus we only saw him on weekends.

Dad was working about 100 miles away or probably 75 as the crow flies, at a new construction site called Glen Canyon Dam. When this dam was completed, there was to be a new town developed around it to be called Page, AZ. He lived in a Quonset hut set up for the workers in an area close to the dam construction site. I know he had a very dangerous job and one which he got paid good money as far as the union scale went. He was a high scaler which meant he hung over the sides of cliffs drilling holes for dynamite charges. This was in the very first stages of the building process.

He came home Friday night late and left early Sunday afternoon to return to work. At home all he wanted to do was drink and relax. It seemed like more drinking than relaxing. Mom was more than happy to relish his homecoming by having a supply of beer and hard liquor available.

Back to the 10th-grade bully that was picking on my little bro. Like I had mentioned before, the reason I thought this was a Friday at school is because when we got home and Ron told Mom why he was scraped up, his clothes so dirty, she mentioned words that were to become scary to me and so hurtful that I would never say them to anyone I loved. She said, "Wait 'till your Dad gets home."

Well, I really thought Ron was in a world of hurt, but I was soon to realize it wasn't Ron, but me that was in a world of hurt.

When Dad returned home, Ron and I were in bed, but in a small trailer, such as ours, you heard every creak and noise. We knew when he came in as you could hear Mom and Dad talking. Within a short while, Ron and I heard Dad say, "Ken, Ron get your asses in here." This part I probably cleaned up because of the PG rating on readership.

I knew he was mad. I think he was mad when he stepped in the door when he got home. He asked Ron what had happened at school that day. Ron told him about the 10th grader pushing him around, a real sob story. Hell, I even had tears in my eyes. Then Dad looked at me and asked, "What did you do about this?"

I was stunned, but told him I didn't even know who the kid was, talking about the 10th grader. I was told in no uncertain terms that I would take care of the situation Monday morning before school started because he was more my age than Ron's. If I didn't take care of it, he would make me wish I had.

Monday morning, Mom drove Ron and me to school and we sat in the car at the entrance until Ron spotted the guy and pointed him out. I got out of the vehicle and approached the kid. I told him I was going to have to fight him because of what he did to my brother. He was with a couple of friends and they kind of backed away, just looking at me. There wasn't much difference in size. Remember, I should have been in the ninth grade.

He asked, "Do you want to box or wrestle?"

I immediately said box and he laughed as we got into a boxing stance. I hit him, not once but three or four times and now I guess he wanted to wrestle as he dove into me. We went to the ground. Somehow, I came up on top and hit him a couple more times before he said he had enough.

He was bleeding from the nose and a cut on the side of his face. When he stood up, he backed away and just stared at me. It wasn't a hate stare, but I think one of admiration. No teachers or anyone else had attempted to break us up, and to my surprise, nothing further was ever mentioned to me about this incident. We never became friends, but they left Ron and me both alone after that. I ended up graduating from eighth grade in Fredonia.

*

There actually was a lot to do in the Fredonia area and I had a lot of time to myself because Mom had taken a job working late afternoons and evenings at a motel in Kanab, Utah, which was only seven miles due north of Fredonia. She would pick Ron up from school and take him with her to work.

I had met a couple boys who lived in the same trailer park, Billy and Alvin Bishop, who were about my age. We did a lot of hiking, looking for arrowheads which were plentiful around a mountain called "Steamboat." I didn't know it at the time, but this area was on the Kaibab Indian Reservation. There were a lot of Indian ruins on the sides and on top of the mountain which was not difficult to climb. We collected nothing more than old arrowheads as I had previously learned my lesson about artifacts. The arrowheads would fit in my pockets.

The Bishop boys had heard about my fight at school and had told their father, Al. Now all this time we had lived in this trailer park, the Bishops were there and secret boxing training lessons were going on behind their trailer which could not be seen from ours.

I was invited to attend the next weekend and it was exciting. It didn't take me long to get to liking Mr. Bishop who told me to call him "Al." I finally got to put on the boxing gloves and spar a couple rounds with one of his sons, Alvin. Al told me I reminded him of himself when he was the Arizona state middleweight champion in the early 1950's. I didn't have much boxing skills, but I had fast hands and I hit hard. When I left, I was feeling pretty good about myself and Al said when they had another session he would send one of the boys to get me.

When I got home, I told Dad about Al and the boxing sessions. He already knew all about him. They worked close together at the dam project where Al was the tugger operator who lowered Dad and one other person over the side of the cliff to do the drilling. Their seating platforms were operated by a large gas-powered wench with Al at the controls.

Dad said Mom and him had known Al and his family for quite a few years. Al was from Payson and that's where he lived while he trained and boxed.

*

There was a motel across the street from where our trailer park was and families of Glen Canyon workers stayed there. The adults became more of my parent's drinking buddies, as if they needed more. They were doing OK on their own.

*

The workers would car pool, three to four per vehicle, for the drive to the construction site. This one couple, new to the area, his wife was alone at the motel and frightened to stay alone. She had approached Mom and asked if I could spent some nights with her. I would sleep on the couch and she could help me with my homework. I think Mom probably agreed because I was usually by myself until sometimes late at night. (Remember she would pick Ron up at school and take him to work with her at the motel in Kanab).

This was a good arrangement for me as I usually got supper, something besides the sandwiches Mom had left for me or I'd fixed myself. Even the sleeping arrangement was OK. The couch was a sleeper couch that made into a bed. The first time we made it, we couldn't return it back into a couch. I didn't spend every night there, just three to four nights a week. This arrangement must have been OK with her husband because he thanked me for watching after his wife.

It was about the third week I was staying there when she invited me to share her bed because every time I moved on the fold out, the springs would creak, waking her. This made sense to me and she would only have one bed to make the next morning.

I soon found out that she had roving hands and she woke me up stroking and playing with me in areas that were quite arousing to say the least. She also had me using my hands on her and she sometimes would get quite loud which scared me because I thought I was hurting her. This wasn't the case. I was 14 or 15 years old.

On Friday night, shortly after these new sleeping arrangements, her husband was driving back to Fredonia with two passengers. He was driving some sort of convertible when the car hit a cattle guard across the road that someone had removed. The two passengers were both killed and her husband had the top part of his head scalped back. I remember when I saw him at the Flagstaff hospital sometime later, he had stitches all around his head where they tried to reattach the scalp.

The only reason Dad was not in the vehicle is the group in the collision had gotten off a couple hours early. The next group down the road found the vehicle and bodies. They transported the woman's husband to the Kanab hospital. Because of the head injuries and after he was stabilized, he was transported to the hospital in Flagstaff.

I graduated from the eighth grade with a proper graduation ceremony at the Fredonia school. The next day, the whole family went to Kanab to look at a new trailer house. Mom was going to quit her job at the Kanab motel and café. Our first stop was the motel. There was a lot of activity in the parking lot which was not big. Mom told us that they must be taking a break from making a movie west of Fredonia.

I got to see, albeit from a couple hundred feet, Alan Ladd and Clint Walker who were the stars in the movie. I remember how short Alan Ladd seemed to be in comparison to Clint Walker who was probably the largest man I had ever seen. Mom had been cleaning their rooms for weeks and had not said anything about this to me. She thought the name was "Fort Utah" but she wasn't sure.

According to various websites, Alan Ladd was about 5-foot-6 at the most while Clint Walker by most accounts was 6-foot-6, a whole foot taller.

*

Buying a brand new 10x50-foot Champion trailer paled in comparison to seeing the movie stars. The dealership would deliver our new home to the trailer park that Monday which allowed us to take that week to transfer all contents of our old 8x35-foot into it. Dad was at work at the dam so he missed all the fun. Ha, ha!!

The plan was to sleep in the new trailer Friday night and hitch up the pickup to it Saturday morning and head to a place called Wahweap General Store and Trailer Park. This was within walking distance of where Dad was working at Glen Canyon Dam. We would leave the old trailer to be picked up by the dealership that sold us the new trailer.

This was a nice trailer, but we never really got a chance to set anything up before we were on the road. Ron and Dad were in front with Mom driving the pickup. I was riding in back atop the freezer. This was good way to travel for me as I could move around a bit and sleep on the freezer which is what I was doing as we rounded a curve. I slid off the freezer, hit the dirt road and the trailer tire ran over my left hand. I remember lying there stunned, seeing the whole family running back to me.

My left hand was bleeding pretty good, affirming Ron's diagnosis as he began yelling about the blood and that I was going to die. I hadn't even looked at my hand prior to this, but when I noticed it I thought I just might die. It was bleeding profusely, but Mom had the foresight to get a couple towels from the trailer and place them around my hand. She had me sit up and put my hand between my legs and press my legs together in an effort to stop the bleeding.

We were probably half way or a little more to Wahweap and no way could we turn around with the trailer. If we went back to Kanab, which had the closest hospital, we would have to uncouple the trailer, someone would have to stay with it and the other drive me to the Kanab hospital. After 30 minutes or so, Mom looked at my hand and the bleeding had pretty much stopped. So, it was decided we would continue on to our destination.

Mom had given me a couple pills and a couple shots of what tasted very much like alcohol—vodka or gin, not the good stuff. I don't remember having any really bad pain with the hand, but when I looked at it, I thought I saw a small rock lodged in the open wound. I sat in the bed of the pickup the rest of the way to Wahweap.

*

Wahweap was probably the most desolate, God-forsaken place I have ever seen or would ever see again in my lifetime. It was still daylight when we arrived and I could feel the numbness wearing off as my hand was starting to throb. I needed a couple more shots of whatever!!

The lady running the general store and gas station came out to look at my hand after Dad and Mom got us registered. She proclaimed I would live, but she needed to pick out some gravel and wash the wound good. What a way to make our appearance in Wahweap.

We parked our trailer at the end of one of the rows of trailer houses. Not many trailers as grand looking as our new one, but there were some as long or longer. There were two rows of trailers that were spaced far enough from each other that you could park your vehicle between them and still set out a couple chairs between the vehicles and trailer. There were probably between 30-40 trailers set up in two rows. At the end of the rows of trailers, nearest the store, were coin-operated washing machines. There were not many machines in the buildings and I remember Mom had to wait quite a while sometimes to get a machine.

The Bishops were also there and only a few spaces down from us. The boxing lessons were fewer and farther between and this was OK because there were quite a few kids, both boys and girls, who liked to hike and explore as I did. This was going to be one of the best summers I could remember.

*

There was a foot bridge that stretched across the canyon from east to west. A small flag pole was set up and when the flag was raised on windy days, you were not to cross the bridge because of the swaying. Oh, yeah, it was 700 feet to the bottom. This just added to the thrill of having to sway the bridge with just your body weight. "Just don't look down," is what we said to the "scaredy" cats who didn't want to go out on the bridge.

At first, I was one but soon realized this was a natural high. I don't know who ratted us out, but soon there was a spotter, usually a worker who would not allow us on the bridge when the flag was stiff because of the wind. We still went out at night when we could, but the novelty wore off.

I was given a bicycle by the Greens who operated the general store. It was OK to ride on the flats, but it had no brakes. Where we had to dump our trash was a dirt road that went down a pretty steep hill to a small wash. The road then made a sharp left and ended a short way from the dump site. We had to back our pickup down this road and toss our garbage over the edge of the cliff.

Some of the kids had nicer bikes, with brakes. I would watch them speed down this hill and go around the curve. Then, they had to push their bikes back up the hill. I didn't want to attempt this because I was a little scared and having no brakes on my bike was a pretty good excuse or so I thought.

This one day, one of the boys, whom I considered a professional at this thing, explained to me how to use a stick (he even supplied the stick) as a brake. When braking, he explained, the stick should be placed between the tire and frame. To slow down, all one had to do was apply pressure while lodging the stick against the frame and onto the tire. So, all I had to do was lean over and place the stick between the frame and tire when I was approaching the curve and apply pressure. This sounded reasonable to me and when he explained it for the umpteenth time, I decided to go for it.

I took off down the hill with the stick clutched in my right hand. I was going pretty fast and the curve was coming up even faster. As my speed increased, I leaned over and tried to shove the stick between the wheel and frame, but at the same time I looked up and put the stick into the spokes. The stick was ripped out of my hands and the bike started making very weird movements. I knew right then I was road kill.

This was assured a few seconds later when I became airborne sailing into the garbage heap and beyond. I knew I was dead when I woke up from some stinging on my right hand. I looked and there were a couple scorpions on my hand. I was lying half in the sandy wash, on top of broken bottles and all kinds of trash. I don't remember where the bike was and I never did find out. I knew it was ruined and so was I.

A couple of the kids ran down the hill, yelling at me. They got me back up the hill, but nobody wanted to go back to my trailer with me. Maybe, it was the way I smelled. Then again, maybe they were afraid of my Mom.

When I got inside the house, I told Mom I had been stung by a couple scorpions and I was "gonna die." The only thing she did was to put some ice in a washcloth and tell me to keep it on my hand. Surprisingly, I lived through the night. She never questioned me about my bike. Truth be known, the dump is where my bike would have been from day one if my parents had their way.

*

Within a few days many of us kids were planning a hike into the canyons. We had hiked around the rim, especially along the west side because most of the girls were afraid to cross the foot bridge. I wonder why?

During some of our hikes, we noticed slits or spaces where if you squeezed through sideways, you could drop down into a wider opening and possibly get all the way to the bottom where the Colorado river was flowing. None of us kids had ever been down to the river. That became the challenge.

The first time we went down, we were not prepared at all. Some of us had munchies, but no drinks except for a couple canteens with water. The first couple hundred feet down was a real hoot and holler. We had to manage a couple jumps of maybe five or six feet, usually onto sand. Duh, I don't think anyone thought we might have to return the same way. Our goal was the river, then find an easier route out.

The decline got a little steeper in places where the jump down was 10 or more feet, if we elected to do that, but the sand was also thinning out exposing more rock. Some of us guys had to take our levis off and tie the legs together to lower the girls. The last guy or two would then jump as the others would try to break his fall. This was not so much a hoot and holler anymore as it was getting to become work. We kept our descent into the unknown for what seemed like hours and probably was.

I had brought a flashlight that ran off two what appeared to be 9-volt batteries. They weighed at least five pounds, maybe 10. By the time we finally heard the river running, it was the only illumination we had left.

After a few more minutes, we were at the base of the cliffs, probably at least a 700-foot descent we had made. The Colorado River is right there. It's running well over 100 mph. There's absolutely no way any of us were going into the water that looked like chocolate milk. Well, maybe not quite 100 mph, but the milk part is right.

At the bottom of a narrow canyon, we didn't have full sunlight for very long and we needed to find a way out. We knew there wasn't anything we could see from the top that was closer to the trailer park, so we proceeded to go further away looking for a better route up. None to be found.

Now we can't even find the route we took down. Shit, what to do? We ran the way we thought we had come, but we weren't sure. Finally, someone yelled they thought they had found a way up and all of us congregated to the escape route. It looked familiar. This could be the way. It was, but it was much more difficult going up than coming down.

We had to place the smallest kid on top of the bigger ones to reach the inclines and even then it was a momentous task to get from one level to the next. Our flashlight batteries were dim at best and it seemed like hours had passed before we reached the top. When we exited, it was dark. But, lo and behold, when we exited this canyon crevice we saw lights from who knows what, a search party.

We had dilly-dallied longer than we thought, but we did answer the voices calling in the night. The searchers, consisting of concerned parents and any others they could round up at the trailer park, were looking for us.

My parents were not among the searchers and I was elated. Maybe, they would not miss me and I could sneak home. I watched as the parents engulfed their kids in their arms, weeping. Then they transferred from Jekyll to Hyde, spanking their children while asking them what they thought they were doing taking part in such a crazy stunt like exploring canyons.

As an observer to these "family reunions," I was a little amazed at the emotions displayed by some parents. When I returned to my trailer, I was able to sneak in unnoticed as we never locked the doors, thank God. I quickly undressed and snuck into bed. Ron was sound asleep and there were no lights or sounds coming from Mom and Dad's bedroom.

I laid awake for a few minutes and thought, "Hell, maybe they are still out looking for me." I ventured to their bedroom door and quietly opened it. They were both lying nude on the bed. I closed the door and thought, "OK, they don't know about the search party."

They didn't. I guess I was a little relieved, but having years to reflect on it, I'm not so sure. Not caring was in their minds. I don't know when, but I learned later that every mobile home or trailer resident was asked to assist in the search. My parents did not join the search party.

*

Shortly after this episode while talking to the proprietor of the trailer park, Bill Greene, he invited Ron and me to fly with him to Flagstaff. Wow! I had never flown in a plane and when I mentioned it to my parents, who Mr. Greene had already received permission from them. They were fine with it.

While flying in a plane, up above the ground in a place where I had never been, I began feeling ungodly sick. I looked at Ron and he looked great. I then thought, "Oh, shit, I am older and should be setting an example which is hard to do with your stomach is in your throat. Then Mr. Greene asked, "Ken, do you want to pilot for awhile?"

"Oh, shit," I said to myself again before agreeing to. To this day, I have no idea where that sound came from. Mr. Greene told me to climb to the front, as I was sitting in the seat directly behind him, and take over.

Bill slid over to the passenger side and I grabbed the wheel. When I moved up, I grabbed the "wheel" and pulled back. This was the wrong thing to do as this put us in an upward move.

Bill said, "Don't touch anything until you get in the seat and I will instruct you. I said OK, but my mind said "You're an idiot." I slid into the pilot's seat and it was absolutely amazing to be at the controls for quite a few miles that is until Bill took over the controls and landed the plane in Flagstaff.

There are many memories that stand out referring to my few months at Glen Canyon, but I remember this flight with Bill Greene as being one of the best.

*

While in the Wahweap area, I had developed a friendship with this one girl "Jane Unknown." Her dad was also a high scaler who worked in tandem with my father.

One day, we were playing near a gorge, the canyon walls, we heard a loud siren blaring. We ran back to the trailer park/gas station to find out what happened. There was a man, I believe, there who was fueling up at the gas pumps. We ran up, as curious kids will do and looked in the window. There was a dead body inside the vehicle. Jane started screaming. It was her dad.

Her dad and my dad had been working side-by-side on seats, high scaling, drilling holes for explosives when her dad's seat broke. My dad was sitting right next to him when it occurred. Al Bishop was the hoist operator, the "tugger."

Dad, who was employed as most were by Kiewitt-Judson-Pacific-Murphy Co., had "froze up" and it was a long while before he could be pulled to safety.

Oh, what a summer this was. If only every kid could experience these life moments. Who was I to know at 14 years of age that death would be at my doorstep for many years to come and I would applaud it.

*

We stayed at the Wahweap park for a short while longer. There were at least four or five families that would be leaving at the same time and we were one of them. Safety in numbers so to speak. This was the time of the year where rain storms were known to fall frequently and oftentimes wash out the road. I later learned this was called monsoons. Rain didn't have to be falling on or near where you were to cause problems because the washes ran fast and didn't soak up a lot of water.

We were about two to three hours on the road to Fredonia, a dirt road not well maintained, when the lead vehicle and trailer stopped. The driver walked back letting everyone know what the problem was. The wash which usually just trickled across the road was roaring about eight- to 10-feet wide and just as deep. As we were stopped, the rain began to fall. Right where we had stopped was right where we stayed as no one would be going in either direction for a while.

The fun thing about being a kid is not having certain cravings like adults do about malt beverages such as beer or spirits such as whiskey. The good and bad about this was no one had stocked up on these life essentials. But, the darker it got this first night out we could see a faint flickering of a neon sign only a mile or so up the road, naturally on the other side of the wash which was roaring pretty good as evidenced by the 50- to 500-gallon barrels, supposedly stock water barrels, rushing down the wash. Parts of the banks were falling in, thus the wash was getting wider.

This was not a good sign as no one wanted to disconnect the vehicle from the trailer and return to Wahweap to stock up on staples such as beer and whiskey. The thinking of all the great men and minds gathered around the fire pit, was what if the road to Wahweap is washed out and "What if I can't get back." Everyone was gathered around the big fire pit that served as our cooking stove that night and for a few nights as well.

Slightly after midnight, someone suggested strapping a couple of step ladders together, laying them over the wash which now was more like a large river cutting a canyon. The thought was to crawl over the ladder to the other side and hike to the bar. If it's closed, we could wake the owner or break-in. This was now a matter of life or death even though it is our first night. They agree, this is better than camping out. A couple hours and many beers later, the trailblazers were carrying flashlights and the makeshift ladder, going down the wash in an attempt to find a narrowing to dock their bridge.

They did and they did. We hadn't walked long before we found a narrow enough area where the ladders were dropped across and were stable enough to crawl over. The only loss was a lantern that was dropped and was last seen bobbing up and down before disappearing altogether in its rush to the Colorado River.

Well, if this isn't the shits. All the men were able to cross, leaving Ron, me and another boy on the other side without a light to await the return of Daniel Boone and group so we could help guide them back to the ladder. We could hear them talking and walking for what seemed like a long time, then nothing but running water.

When they returned, they were in the bed of a pickup that let them out on the road across from their vehicles and the raging wash. There were people on that side of the wash who were trying to get to Wahweap for work and couldn't. They knew it would be a few days because of the repair crews would have to come from Fredonia and Kanab to complete the repairs.

They finally got the cases of beer and whatever down to the ladder and everyone crossed over carrying their wares without incident. It was decided to leave the ladder for a future return trip. I don't remember how long we were stranded, but I think only a couple days because the men made only one additional trip to the cantina for "supplies."

*

We did not have a destination firmly in mind, but Dad, Mom and Ed Bishop had been talking about Payson on numerous occasions because of the nice weather, the availability of work and the relatively cheap land. It was decided by Mom and Dad, never taking the subject up with Ron and me. Really, Payson was a place we had lived already and I liked it. They wanted to buy a business and spend the rest of our lives there.

Well, OK, cooler than many other places I have lived, but dreams come and go. Dad wanted to get out of union work, especially after his experience with his partner falling 700 feet. This, I could understand.

In the Payson area, if you exited off 87 North and took Bonito Street and went about 100 yards you would come to Ash Street. Take a left or go south to the first right would take you to Pecan Street which is about 200 yards long and has six houses on each side of the street. We bought a lot somewhere in the middle of this block.

As you come into Payson on State Route 87 before you get to main street, the Bee Line Café sits on the west side, still open and doing a booming business as of this writing. Mom and Dad bought this business minus the apartments that sit in the rear of the restaurant. Do I know how they got the money? No, I am not a psychic. But they must have had the money. I learned later, the owners sold it with various contingencies which I will mention later.

Mom ran and operated the café and for a while Dad assisted by handling cleaning and maintenance chores.

Ron and I started school in Payson. I was in the ninth grade and Ron was in the fifth. This was a dream come true, a nice small town, beautiful weather and we had our own place. This was a first for me. A home, a place where I could get to know some kids, make lifetime friendships, etc.

This lasted a couple months. Dad got restless and got a union job in the Florence area, drilling and dynamiting. We sold the café back to the owners we had purchased it from. They had first right to repurchase. Remember the contingencies? We got a little money and a 1949 Mercury four-door that didn't run as our going-away present. Remember the car though as it would become a big part of my life.

*

We moved to Mesa, AZ, locating in a trailer park on South Country Club Drive. I enrolled at East Mesa Junior High School. This was a big city compared to others I had lived in. It was huge. Have I mentioned that I didn't get along well in crowded places and large crowds? East Mesa Junior High was huge. My first couple days there were memorable. The first day me and a couple guys were walking from one class to our music class. One of the guys says, "Did you see that dog?"

"No," I said.

He then says, "If you just yell 'Here, Bull Dog, here Bull Dog.'"

Well, I did not see a four-footed creature come back around the corner, but what I did see was a rather large man, about 5-foot-6, stocky, and a face that definitely resembled that of a bulldog.

Now, I might not be the most brilliant person on this planet and it didn't really take a rocket scientist to tell me I was in a world of shit. I looked around for my new-found friends, but guess what, I was standing by myself when this teacher came up to me, grabbed me by the shoulder and said to come with him. I knew I was supposed to be going to music as my next class, but to have the teacher personally escort me. Neat, until he walked me to the back room and took out a paddle with holes in it. I asked him, "Can you really afford that paddle?

A paddle with holes is less resistant to air and after 10 swats, I know he had invested well. If he expected me to cry, he was swatting the wrong kid. It's not my being all that macho or resistant to pain, it' that I had received a lot worse at home on a lot more consistent basis.

I vowed to myself that the next day I would get even with my "buddies."

The next day, I was waiting outside my primary class when Buddy No. 1 showed up all smiles. I hit him so fast and hard in the stomach, he threw up all over my shoes. Well, these shoes would be handed down to Ron in a couple of years and I'd clean them as best as I could.

But when I looked up Buddy No. 2, he had seen what had happened and took off running. The chase was on. We ran and ran and when I rounded one of the corners, Buddy No. 2 was sprawled on the ground and I tripped over him. I hit his head with my head and apparently was knocked out for a couple seconds. I was abruptly pulled up by two teachers who declared, "He needs medical attention, take him to the nurse."

I remember thinking I hit Buddy No. 2 pretty hard when I fell on him, but was surprised when they started walking me to the nurse's office. I couldn't see real well from my left eye which had seemed to close on me. I kept wanting to push on it to open it up, I had a real problem when I lifted the big bag of puffed skin over my left eye. When I released this bag of skin filled with blood, it would fall back down over my left eye, obscuring my vision.

When I got to the nurse's office, she did not even try to help me. She called my mom who said she would be right down. Mom took me to a doctor who ended up having to lance my eyebrow to drain the bleeding. The area on my left eye brow had not been broken when I hit Buddy No. 2's head, but blood vessels had burst and created a large swelling, full of blood.

When we got back home, we had a phone message on the trailer door to take me back to school. I don't think I had mentioned we did not have a phone and all calls came through the trailer park office.

We went back to the school administration office where Mom and I were both told that I would be suspended for the rest of the week for fighting. This was not a first-time occurrence for me, nor the second, nor maybe even the third, but when I explained to Mom the circumstances, her reply was, "Just wait 'till your Dad gets home."

This wasn't the first time I had heard this, but I knew Mom didn't want to deal with me. I knew Dad wouldn't listen because when he came home on the weekends, he was usually drunk or had been drinking. I got the usual dose of the leather belt with buckle, but I would not cry. I was determined that I would not.

Now Mom and Dad were great believers in "spare the rod, spoil the child." Even though I tried to be the best kid I could, I was always labeled the screw up, not worthy of their love. I really don't know if Ron was receiving the same or similar treatment, but I learned to tune out my surroundings at home as much as I could.

I do know Dad felt an obligation to punish me as soon as he got home for something I had done or if I had done nothing obvious, he would whip me for something I may have gotten away with. I remember numerous times I would cry to myself before Dad was to get home because I knew I would be punished for something. Sometimes, he would even let me cut my own switches off the willows or cottonwoods that were numerous in the park. Well, what the hell, wasn't every other kid getting the same treatment from their parents? Not so.

*

Dad was apparently making pretty good money because after a few months, we purchased an acre of land at 230 W. Southern Ave., in Mesa. This was one of the most exciting moments in my life. A real home without wheels, and with a lot that provided ample space to run around.

I had joined the track team at my junior high school and I was really good at running three-quarter mile, 1320 yards. I met new friends and was enjoying my school year much more than earlier. Also, something else happened around this time. Dad had been given a 1949 Mercury as part of the payment when they sold the café in Payson, as mentioned earlier. He told me I could have this vehicle if I could get it running and showed I could be responsible. Well, hell yeah. I could bullshit anyone for a short while. Like father, like son. Right, or not.

I met a new friend while running track who would eventually be a friend for life, Terry O'Conner. He also ran the same event as I did and we were highly competitive. I remember running quite a few events, never losing one, but I also can see Terry's smiling face beside me at the finish line. Somehow, I knew this guy was going to be a lasting friend. I hadn't had any true friends prior to this and it scared me.

*

Even though we had an acre of land and what passed as a house, I was leery at having friends over. Our house was about 40 feet by 40 feet with floors covered by a wood-grained linoleum. It had two bedrooms, kitchen, living area and a bathroom, but it was ours. We had room for chickens and a cow that provided ample milk and related dairy products like cheese and butter. We also planted a garden.

I was glad when track season was over because Mom had taken a job to help pay house payments. She was a nurse's assistant at the Mesa hospital on Main Street and Mesa Drive where she worked the evening shift, 4 p.m. to midnight. She would take Ron and me to work with her, but kids under the age of 15 were not allowed in the hospital.

For months, Monday through Friday, Ron and I would stay by the vehicle or in it while Mom worked. On the southwest corner of Main and Mesa Drive was a Pete's Fish and Chips stand and every night we would get food and drinks there. I still do not know if the owner took pity on us or Mom paid, but I'll go with the pity part.

This wasn't as bad as it might sound because we would spread a blanket out onto the grass and sleep most of the time.

We had a number of chores to do around the house. Feed the Cow, a jersey that came with the purchase agreement, was milked at least once a day. We also fed the chickens which we let run loose. Later we got a lamb and this creature wanted to follow us everywhere we went, a real pain in the butt. Where was Mary when you needed her?

The first year we lived there, the oranges and grapefruit trees were carrying quite a load and the neighborhood kids would steal quite a few of them, not like we didn't have plenty to go around. This really pissed Dad off. I remember one Friday night we were sitting in the family room which overlooked Southern Avenue and our front yard when Dad saw some teenagers come up our drive and pick some oranges before walking off.

He jumped up, ran out the door and started chasing these kids for felonious theft of oranges. He ran towards the street and disappeared, hands in the air, yelling obscenities at the top of his lungs.

I forgot to mention that in front of our property paralleling Southern Avenue was a small irrigation canal with running water. After a few tense seconds, Dad re-appeared, crawling out of the canal. Not a good time to laugh, probably a good time to go milk the cow or do something else.

*

I applied for a paper route delivery with the Mesa Tribune in our area. I had an old bicycle I could attach racks to the front and be good to go. I got the job. It started at 4 a.m. when they would drop my papers off at Main and Southern, the far eastern end of my route. Prior to starting my delivery, I would get there, roll the papers and put rubber bands around them.

Now this might seem like a piece of cake, but this area was pretty remote. Although I only had 40 to 50 houses on my delivery route, most of the houses, however, were on numerous acres (10 to 40 acres) with long driveways to the houses. But, what the hey, I needed this job to help get my car running, providing I'm wouldn't be too tired to drive it.

After delivering the newspaper, I had to really hustle in order to get home, get cleaned up and catch the bus to school. The bus stop was about a quarter mile east of our house and down a dirt road along a canal bank. I liked the job pretty well and decided to get a new bike, one that would be a little easier to pump and a little faster/reliable than the one I had.

Mom, Ron and me went to the Western Auto store where they sold bicycles. I picked out a really nice, sleek-looking Western Flier. This was a pump, not a 3-speed or whatever, but it was new and would get the job done. I had saved a little money, but not enough for the full amount. I talked to the manager and arranged for weekly payments to be made by me at the store every Saturday morning.

I was a true entrepreneur and a responsible kid, per this guy who didn't even know me, but was willing to take a chance on me. This felt good and no way was I going to let him down. I was a 15-year-old kid with a job, ambition and a means of making my weekly payments. Also, when I went in to make my payments, I would assemble other bicycles that had been sold and were awaiting pick up, thus lowering my balance owed.

By this time, the school year was about half over and I made my last payment on my bike. (Side note: I saw a similar bicycle on E-bay recently selling for $475. These bikes are collectors' items today)

One Saturday morning, I went in and paid the remaining balance for my bike. What a thrill!! I was flying high on my Western Flier. I polished the spokes, tires, seat, the entire bike was sparkling. I was ecstatic. This was mine, the only thing I had ever really owned.

I decided to treat myself to the movies that Saturday night at the downtown Mesa theater, taking my bike. They had a bike stand in front of the theater where you could lock up your bike and I did. I did and I didn't. I locked up my bike and watched the movie. But when I came out, I didn't have a bike. I was devastated, probably crying and cussing. I had the manager call the cops and I filled out a report. I still had the papers from earlier in the day with all the numbers for the bike so they knew what to look for.

I had the Sunday edition of the paper to deliver the next morning and no bike. My older bike had been "shit canned" but for one wheel and tire that was salvageable. My parents were pissed at me for not locking the bike up, even though I swore to them that I had, but to no avail.

Sunday morning, I left the house at about 3 to meet my delivery person at 4. I had a cloth sack over my shoulder to carry the papers. I told the delivery person that this would be my last day. I gave him my sob story about the theft and told him I would get the papers delivered, but some may be late because of the transportation I didn't have and the amount of walking I had to do.

I didn't get home until late morning and my feet were killing me. My eyes were wrung out, but I got the job done. Some of the customers had met me at the entryway to the drive and said they knew something was wrong because their paper was never late. A couple even offered to help me get another bike, but my pride and my prejudices at the system kept me from taking their offers.

It seemed only the bad people make it in this society so maybe I could learn to be bad in this huge environment. Who knows?

*

To add insult to injury or vice versa, the next day, Monday, when I got off the bus to come home from school, two high school boys got off at the same stop. I thought this was a little weird because I hadn't seen them get off here before and they were heckling me from the time we got off the bus until I heard them say they needed to throw me into the canal, books and all.

Well, it wasn't many days that I even brought books home with me and I hardly ever opened them when I did. I knew they were talking about me as it was only the three of us at this time because the other boys had turned off in their driveways a while back. Again, I might not be a rocket scientist, but propulsion of my feet is what I elected to do. I probably made it about 50 yards or so when I was jerked back hard, landing on my back with my books flying every which way. My shirt was ripped almost all the way off me.

I stood up and faced the guy. The other one was standing back a ways and I knew who the trouble was. I didn't say a word as he pushed me at least twice as I staggered backwards into the canal. The water wasn't running deep, but there was a lot of mud. Apparently, on Mondays most people don't get irrigation. Thank God. When I stood up in the canal, the guy, I never knew his name, started kicking my books in the canal. I just stared at him and after a while both of them left, walking back the way we had come.

Mom still made most of Ron and my clothes from whatever the flour or sugar sack design was for the month. The one I was wearing was pretty well shredded and the buttons were ripped off. It was also muddy and wet.

I couldn't find all my books or hardly any of my papers. However, with some work, I did manage to extricate myself from the canal and continue home, perplexed and confused as to "What in the hell had just happened?"

I still didn't have a reason or an excuse when I walked in the front door of my house. Any other day Mom would have been outside feeding the cow or chickens or something, but not today. She was sitting on the couch and when she looked up at me, I thought she was looking at an extra-terrestrial. She was shocked. So was I when she lit into a litany of profanities that simply boiled down to "What the hell happened to you?"

After I told her the story, she said I was not going to school the next day, but we were going to be at the bus stop after school and confront the boys who had done this. The next day, we went to the bus stop and waited until the bus showed up. I was right proud of my Mom because she was going to stand up for me and maybe she even believed me. I only hoped these boys had taken the bus today or maybe she wouldn't believe me.

When the bus pulled up to the stop, Mom went to the driver with me in tow and explained what had happened. Mom had me point out the one who had thrown me in the canal. I did and she told him to get off the bus as he was going to fight her son man-on-man. Wow, so much for standing up for me. Only one boy stood up, the right one. He was bragging about how I ran from him and how he had caught me. He also said he would make short work of me and be back on the bus in no time. Mom asked the driver if he would wait and he said "Yes."

When he stepped off the bus, I remember I took a solid hit to the head and thought "This is all you have." My first punch hit him straight in the mouth and my left hand hurt as I had one of his teeth sticking in my knuckles and was still throwing blows. The next thing I remember he was down and I was on top of him, still flaying away when the bus driver pulled me off of him and said "I think that's enough."

The bus driver had a couple of the kids help him load the guy back onto the bus. He told me they were up to no good when they followed me the day before. He thanked me for the show and indicated he may not have a job the next day, but said it was worth it.

I never saw the boy again, on or off the bus, but the driver was there and always had a smile when I got on the bus.

*

The rest of my school year was uneventful other than going home, milking the cow, a jersey we had named Daisy, feeding the chickens and working around the farm, so to speak. Mom would make butter, Ron and I would take turns working the hand churn. Mom would skim the butter from the top of the churn, wrap it in cheesecloth and hang it on the clothesline to dry. We never wanted for milk, buttermilk cheese or eggs. This was a staple to go with our pinto beans and fried chicken. We also had a good-sized garden with tomatoes, string beans, radishes, carrots and okra among other seasonal veggies.

The couple next door, the Howeth's had hundreds of chickens and sold the eggs to local markets. I would help them at times and they would keep us supplied with more eggs and little chicklets that I got to watch hatch in an incubator.

*

On Feb. 7, 2004, my wife, Beth, and I went to Mesa to verify some addresses and look up some of the areas I used to live and work. The house on West Southern Avenue was no longer there, but would be 232 W. Southern. There was a large tin shed with construction equipment parked beneath it. I parked in a vacant lot to the west of this area and walked back to get an address. Southern Avenue is now a well-traveled paved road with two lanes going east and two lanes going west. Not at all like I remembered it, but this was 48 years later.

I approached the house at 230 W. Southern Ave. which appeared to be within the fence line of what enclosed the acre we used to own. I introduced myself to Mr. Marvin Gatz who was standing in the doorway at this house. I explained I was writing a book and had previously lived here. He asked my name again and was somewhat surprised. He stated

59

he bought the acre next door from my parents and had also inherited a jersey cow with the purchase.

We talked about 20 minutes and I asked him about the house. He said he sold the house to a gentleman who tore it down for the lumber, but he had kept the land as a place to park his construction equipment.

The city had widened Southern Avenue and had covered up the irrigation canal. I asked him about the two fig trees at the northern end of the property. He said he still has them, but since his wife passed away, no one eats them any more. When I mentioned the older couple next door to the east of us, he said he knew them well. Mrs. Howeth passed away in the late 1960's. Mr. Howeth, he said remarried a couple times before passing away a few years ago in his nineties.

I asked him what he remembered about my parents. He said Mom was a looker and Dad was always looking for trouble, noting that Dad seemed to be ready to fight at the drop of a hat. Mr. Gatz said he got a pretty good price on the property as it seemed my parents were ready to relocate as soon as possible.

*

Back to my story.

I was still living on Southern Avenue as I entered the 10th grade at Mesa High School. I had been spending almost every penny I earned from mowing lawns, picking citrus, and a variety of other jobs trying to fix up my car as I would soon be getting my driver's license.

The only thing I really enjoyed was running track. When I ran the 1320 or three-quarter mile in the ninth grade, I was undefeated, so now in the 10th grade, the track coach thought I should run the quarter mile, 440 yards. Terry O'Connor, my old nemesis from junior high, also was on the track team.

I also met a guy who would become not only a life-long friend, but a confidant, a compadre, a bosom buddy so to speak, John Allen. John and I would become very close as his home life was not much different than my own, meaning we didn't have much of one. John lived close to Apache Junction with his stepfather, Buster, and his mother, Rose. He had to take a bus to get to Mesa High School.

John was also on our track team, but was kind of a recluse as I was. We stayed together as much as possible, either me at his house or he at mine, but really at neither.

I had a car, but couldn't afford gas until I learned the secret of the "Oklahoma credit card," a 6-foot long length of garden hose and a five-gallon can. Any vehicle was our gas station, especially late at night or early morning when no one was awake. We would sneak into their carports, open the gas cap, put in the hose and suck on said hose until gas came out. We would fill up the can and run like hell.

We also became quite proficient at keeping up on the top 10 tunes which were on 45-rpm vinyl records, small enough to put down the front of your pants and walk out the store with it. Payment? No such thing. You needed money for this? I was getting into the mode where if I couldn't steal it, I didn't need it.

*

My home life hadn't changed much. If I wasn't there, I wasn't missed. If I was there, they wanted to know what I was doing. I mostly was staying at John's or if it were John's parents asking, he was staying at Ken's.

In the 10th grade, I went out for the junior varsity football team and made the team and then quit as this was going to interfere with my running around. Too much work. I missed 15 days of my sophomore year as I became very adept at signing Mom's name to absentee excuses.

We still did not have a phone so I wasn't particularly worried about getting caught. I kept this up pretty much the whole school year, not caring, not being cared about until I got into a fight towards the end of school. This in and of itself would not have been a problem except for the fact that before I could be re-admitted to school, after a five-day suspension, my parents had to appear with me at the principal's house. This was for a consultation as to my fighting and the 11 days I had missed from school.

Elias Brimhall, my principal, was a prince of a man. He always said hello to me and had good words to say to me. I was flunking almost every class except PE and social studies, when my parents and I met with him. As part of the consultation, my parents became aware of my misdeeds in the classroom.

Did they expect I was getting straight "A's" and hadn't missed any days of school except for the five days for fighting? Oh, well, we all have our imaginary worlds.

They were aghast. My parents actually seemed to be awestruck at the revealing of my improprieties. Well, when I heard this coming from Mr. Brimhall, I admit I was kind of in awe myself.

I knew I was going to be kicked out of the 10th grade to only repeat my inconsistencies for another year. I was as surprised as my parents when they were told by Mr. Brimhall to have me back in school on Monday. Mom and Dad didn't know what to do or say. So with a collaborative effort, they decided to take my car way for one week. That's OK. I was almost out of gas again anyway.

I somehow survived the 10th grade as I got my grades up to passing. I got a 3 in English, a 1 in PE, a 2 in social studies, a 4 in business math, and fours in biology and Spanish. Not commendable, but passable.

*

The summer was pretty much a repeat of my school year, but no notes to forge for missing school. There was no principal's house to go to when I got into a fight, which was often.

However, there was a bombshell towards the end of the summer vacation. My good friend John Allen was moving to Albuquerque, NM. When track began during the 10th grade, I was also interested in boxing and was traveling to and from Phoenix whenever I could and working out with Ed Bishop, Glen Canyon era. I had amateur boxing bouts around the valley and I was still running the 440, watching the back of Terry O'Connor.

I also made some new friends on the track team who would become my sidekicks—Leslie Miller, Jim Heimer and Marvin Whittier. They were all better at running than I was, but I had a car. Keeping gas in it was a problem, solved by my Oklahoma credit card which needed two people. So Marvin and I would get gas whenever and wherever we could. Marvin lived the closest to me and had the least homework or so it seemed. Jim lived way out east and could only get together on weekends. Leslie was always doing homework.

The weekends were ours. The Carnation ice Crème Shop on North Central knew us well. We ate ice cream and picked fights with kids from Phoenix schools, Tempe schools and anyone else who didn't like Mesa High.

By this time, either Marvin or me could buy beer at some place along our route. We couldn't afford much, but a couple six packs amongst the "car pool" was sufficient. We would party hardy and just be high school kids.

I continued to keep up with the latest top 10 records via pants concealment and other things that could have gotten me in trouble. I was a restless soul, looking for something, but I didn't know what. I was becoming more of a delinquent. I would like to place blame somewhere besides myself, but I was living it. Consequences be damned.

There was a hot dog and hamburger stand called "The Stix" that was near where we lived on North Country Club Drive in the trailer park when we first moved to Mesa. I knew they never locked their windows at night. This place had a seating area around the service area. When you arrived and sat down, the waitress would come out, take your order and deliver it to you. I think she or he was also the cook as service was slow, but the food was OK. They had a little sliding window next to the cash register that I would always see open just a crack. Right inside this window were the treats—candy and gum.

One night, I visited The Stix, after hours, when I knew it would be closed. I parked in the trailer park in front of a trailer—I don't know whose—and walked to The Stix. It was good and dark as I hopped over the seating area and slid the sliding door open. I cleaned out as much candy and gum as I could load in my pockets when I saw headlights turning into the area. The place set a little ways off the road and they had to be coming to The Stix.

I hid under the counter area opposite where the seating was. I then remembered I hadn't closed the window. Someone got out of a car and shined a flashlight through the windows and all around. It was a Mesa police officer. I freaked. What should I do? Stand up and turn myself in or what? I waited. It seemed like hours, but was only a few minutes. The flashlight scanned the entire area, except for where I was hidden.

Even when I heard the door of the police car shut and the car drive off, I waited a few more minutes for the cop to return and say, "Ken, you can come out now."

He didn't, but I did. I got out of there like my tail was on fire. I made it over to where I had parked and made my getaway. I did close the window before departing. I still can't tell you to this day how much candy and gum I stole, but that was just the start.

*

I thought I was doing pretty well in school during the 11th grade. At least I thought I was trying harder. Dad had taken a job for Mastercraft homes as a laborer. This would keep him in the Mesa area and got him a discount on one of their new homes.

About midway through my junior year, 11th grade, we moved into a new home at 1362 West 6th Ave., built by Mastercraft Homes.

My grades at the end of the first semester had not improved. I had a 1 in PE and a 2 in Audio Visual. This was something I elected to do, carting the audio equipment to the appropriate classrooms, set up the equipment and operate it. This is not as easy as it sounds. You had to thread the film through the machine and leave just enough loops to run it. Not like today when you can put in a VHS tape, CD or DVD and push a button and be good to go.

Typing, I got a 3. I thought I had done better although this belief may have been enhanced with my lust for my teacher, the best looking teacher at Mesa High. English, American History and Bookkeeping were all 4's. I thought I was trying. I even took books home with me. But, then again, I never opened them.

*

Dad got a good discount on our home at 1362 West 6th Ave. because he was an employee of the builder. I think it was a little under or over $7,000. A block house with three bedrooms, two bathrooms, family room, kitchen with an eating area and a large backyard. Another stop on the Haw's westward movement.

We moved into the huge home towards the end of my junior year. This was high-scale living. It was the first time we had ever had carpet except for throw rugs. My own bedroom with room to turn around in. This was a good-sized community with houses right next to each other and paved streets. Our house was just east of the house on the corner of 14th Avenue

64

which ran north into Broadway. There was a service station on the corner of Broadway and 14th Avenue that I applied for and got a job.

I also hooked up again with Al Bishop and he thought I had potential for Golden Gloves boxing. He lived in Phoenix and told me that if I could get to Central Avenue, just north of the river bottom at the Riverside Ballroom a couple times a week, he would be willing to meet and train me. This is something I wanted to do, but it was 18 to 20 miles each way and I was having a hard time stealing enough gas just to get back and forth to school. I'd have to hitchhike to my boxing session. Hey, I'd give it a try.

Today, if you even drive this stretch of road, you will cross numerous gang-infested areas. I'm talking violent gangs and they were probably there in the 60's, but I didn't know about them. I did know the population once you crossed out of Tempe into Phoenix was primarily black. I never had any bias, wasn't raised that way. To me Black, Mexicans or Anglos were all folks trying to make a living as were my parents. We had worked side by side with all nationalities during our travels.

I know I am getting ahead of myself but I want to continue on this subject because I think it's important. Not having said prejudices, I treated everyone as I wanted to be treated. When I couldn't get a ride, I walked for many, many miles, and sometimes would run not from fear, but to get my roadwork in. Hitchhiking was a hit-and-miss proposition. Sometimes the same people would pick me up, but never to take me all the way to my destination.

So I would walk through areas where people would yell at me, "Hey, white boy. What you doin' in our neighborhood?" I'd stop and talk to them, tell them what I was doing, training for the 1962 Golden Gloves tournament. I garnered their respect and sometimes when I was coming home, someone would be barbecuing in their front yard. They would yell at me as I walked by to come eat with them. They made me promise to let them know where and when I'd be fighting so they could try to be there.

Numerous folks who became friends seemed to care about me. I ate good, sometimes not knowing exactly what it was I was eating. Sometimes the people would give me a ride a few miles up the road to where I may have a better chance of more traffic. Broadway Road in the Phoenix area was paved, but it was a narrow two-lane road with not much traffic.

When you reached the Tempe city limits, Broadway Road widened somewhat with much more traffic, eastbound in my direction on the return trip which was usually after dark. Whenever, and it was not often, I had enough gas to drive to the workout facility I would stop by on my way home, if someone was cooking outside and eat with them. They treated me like family and genuinely seemed to care for me.

*

John Allen and I kept doing our things. Mostly, this consisted of skipping school at least one day every two weeks or more if we thought we could get away with it. I forged a pretty good signature of my Mom's and apparently, it was believable. As for making up homework, you can tell by my grades that I made a concerted effort. Yeh, right.

John and I were getting more brazen and were really working the Phoenix downtown area between First Avenue and First Street on Washington where there was Newberry's, S.S. Kreske's and a couple other five-and-dime stores. Nearly all these stores carried 45 RPM records and many small items that were to be targets of our random thefts. We very seldom worked any stores in the Mesa area in case we got caught and recognized.

One particular weekend we had a pocketful of firecrackers and cherry bombs—round fireworks a little larger than a quarter and very destructive. They had fuses and were waterproof. We were in Newberry's. In Newberry's, the bathrooms were close to the stairs leading to the bottom floor. The restrooms were perfect to light a cherry bomb, put it in the toilet and flush it. We had a good plan with John keeping an eye out the door and on the stairs as we planned on running down the stairs, leaving plenty of time before the blast. Well, we thought it was a good plan.

This toilet was slow to flush as I hadn't counted on the water swirling and swirling. Just as I thought the bomb would go down the drain, it detonated. Water and parts of the toilet went everywhere. Water was running all over the floor and there was no stopping it. We skedaddled down the stairs and became innocent, curious customers. It wasn't long before water began flowing down the stairs.

We decided we had spent enough time in this store and as we topped the steps to the first floor, there was a large gathering around the men's room.

*

Later that day, we were back in downtown Mesa. We had time to spare before John had to catch his school bus back to Apache Junction. We also had a few explosives left and felt destructive. We were standing on a downtown corner in front of the theater.

Across the street on the east side was a recruiting officer for the U.S. Air Force. On the northeast side was the downtown VFW. The recruiting office had a huge plate glass window and a ledge in front, perfect for a cherry bomb.

It was early afternoon and there was very little traffic when we placed the bombs, lit the fuses and ran across to hide in the front entrance of the VFW, which nobody ever used as everyone parked in the rear to enter through the back door.

We had almost made it across the street to the VFW the cherry bombs exploded and we heard glass shattering. We were laughing like hyenas when we looked at the stop light directly back of us. You guessed it, a City of Mesa police car was sitting there with the lone police officer looking at us. The driver's window came down and he yelled, "Ken, stay right where you are, I'll be right over."

Now, I didn't rightly think I was that popular and I only knew one policeman on the force. He had taken Ron and myself home a couple times on Friday/Saturday nights when Mom and Dad had forgotten us at the theater. Well, guess who this was. What a small world.

We were ordered to get in the back seat and wait while the police officer went to the scene of the crime. The entire glass window had been blown out with most of the glass lying on the sidewalk. An awful lot of glass was occupying the desk just inside the recruiting office. If someone had been sitting at the desk at the time, they could have been seriously injured which wasn't at all our intention.

Off to the police station.

By the time we got there, we had surreptitiously stuffed the firecrackers and cherry bombs down the crack in the back seat as we sat uncuffed. We had made up a story that we had cut school and were walking around when we found these two firecrackers. We explained we had no idea they would cause any damage such as was done to the window of the recruiting office.

Hell, we told the officer, both John and myself were considering joining the Air Force when we graduated—in my case, if I graduated.

The police officer left the room to confer with people from the recruiting office and another police officer. After a while, they returned and asked if we had been in school all day and where we found the fireworks. At this point in time I couldn't have told the truth if I was reading from a script.

A few minutes later, this second police officer knocked on the door and was standing there with his hat in his hand. I didn't think he was paying homage to our interrogator and I was right. When he came over, he dumped the contents of his hat all over the desk exposing dozens of fire crackers and cherry bombs, quite a few more than the two we had admitted finding, but about the right number we stuffed under the rear seat in the police car.

Right then, I knew I was going to prison. This was a big time screw up. No judge, no jury. Don't collect $200 when you pass go. Just go. The wheels of justice, however, sometimes does not work as it does on television.

The things that probably saved us from dire consequences were: The police officer knew me and my family. He thought if I could finish high school, join the Air Force or military service, in his words, I would probably could avoid prison time by the time I was 18. The recruiting officer was already getting the window repaired and there was nothing further needed from us. They knew how to reach us if further information was needed.

*

John had missed his bus and we were on the way to Apache Junction in my '49 Merc. We were cruising down University Avenue when we passed an LDS church with no vehicles in the parking lot. John told me to pull over. After I did, he told me he was moving to Albuquerque. His step dad, Buster Cox, was being transferred and he probably would not finish the school year before leaving. We were both angry, hungry and broke. I would have to steal gas to put into my vehicle before I could even get home.

It was decided to burglarize this church. Wow, what a high. Even though I didn't get to wear the "camo" clothing with black paint on my skin, this was a clandestine operation. The doors we tried were locked, but the windows we tried were allowing us to gain entrance about 20 feet from where I parked. After crawling through the window, we headed directly for the kitchen area. Refrigerators, food and collection plates of money. I'm talking money. This was like a bank with no tellers. Just put the "dinero" on the counter and whoola "first come, first served." No!!!

We argued a little about the money, very little. We were hungry and broke. We had food and had access to probably a few hundred dollars. We did not count. We came to an amicable decision, we would eat, steal some food for later, but we would not take any money.

Looking back at this day in my life, I should have known that I was not a bad person. I might be a thief, a sneak, a liar, but I wasn't a bad person and neither was John. He was probably the worst thing to happen to me and probably the best.

*

During my junior year, I really began to pay attention to what I was doing and why. The what being a lot easier to figure out than the why.

While on the track team, I had met some teammates who would become very important in my life and would take the place of John. Leslie Miller and Terry O'Connor both ran the half mile in his junior and senior year. However, I remember our junior high years when Terry and I ran like Siamese twins. When we turned around, the other was there, always.

Jim Heimer was a true anomaly. He was crazy. This guy had a death wish more than mine and I'm not even sure I had one. Sometimes after practice, I would drive him home. He lived in a mobile home, something I could identify with. He ran the quarter mile and was unbeatable as he was at everything else. The mile relay team with him on it, set various school records.

These were the tame things!

When we had a few brewskis, beers, we would challenge people, usually those with hot rods to a race across Grand Avenue. This was a 5-way stop where Grand Avenue would intersect with either 51st or 59th avenues. The bet would be that Heimer, on foot, could beat the vehicle across the paved intersection—vehicle vs. runner. Heimer always won. It was like money in the bank.

When he was really "skunked," drunk, or whatever, he would leap over oncoming cars, usually mine. This was absolutely crazy. Jim would stand in the road and run at my car. When he thought he could leap over it, he would. If he couldn't, he wouldn't. A lot depended on the speed. He knew this and would abort if the situation wasn't right.

Marvin Whittier was also a quarter-miler and I don't remember him being in my rear-view mirror. It seemed he was always ahead of me. I don't know and don't really care to remember because if you look at the senior yearbook, all of these guys are listed, but not me. I ran unattached because of the AAU statutes. Marvin and I lived pretty close together and did a lot of raids on vehicles for gas. We had some close calls, but escaped.

*

Girls! This is a subject I wanted to avoid, but doing an autobiography, how can I?

I wasn't a virgin when I met Jody. I might have pretended to be, but I wasn't. I was buying books for the second half of the school year and I was at the cash register. I had the money to pay, I wasn't going to steal them, but the girl at the register made me forget where I was. Jody Greer was a sophomore. I was a junior. This couldn't work. Why? I had become tongue tied, tied tongue or whatever. I couldn't focus. She played tennis and I could come watch. Wow, can I? I did. She was beautiful.

Shortly after meeting Jody, a female friend of mine had gone to a party at Apache Junction where she had been beaten by Billy Coker. This girl was only a friend, not a girl friend. The only reason I even knew about this was I was in the Administration Office to show my absentee excuses when she came in with black and blue marks all over her. I asked her what happened and she told me. I put out the word I was looking for Billy Coker, not knowing or really caring who he was.

Coming back across the field from the east side classes to the lunch area, Billy Coker was waiting for me. He heard I was looking for him and he was ready for anything I had. Let's get it on. He threw the first punch and hit me pretty good alongside the head. From what I was told later, I looked at him and smiled. The beating began and I was pulled off him and hauled to the principal's office.

Would I be kicked out of school for at least a week? Would my parents have to go to Principal Brimhall's house and talk to him to get me back into school? Nothing much changed. I got back in school. My mother was quite a looker and I believe Mr. Brimhall might have been smitten with her.

I had fallen head over heels with Jody and we were able to spend a lot of time together alone during the lunch hour as her Mom and Dad both worked and she lived close to school.

*

I was still stealing gas to keep my Merc running and I was thinking about switching out my V8 flathead for a 1953 Ford overhead cam V8 with 3-2 barrel carbs.

My dad helped me. There was a garage, on 6th Avenue and Alma School Road, just a short ways from where we lived, that would lease bays by the day, week or month. You brought your own tools or could rent them, but your vehicle was secure at night. This project was not easy, but I do believe Dad knew what he was doing as we got it done. This was a real hot rod. The fastest car at Mesa High. The closest to me was Billy Coker and his 1953 Ford.

*

Back to Jody.

I was in love with her. I had met her parents. The family was from Kansas and her dad, Leland, had to come out here for health reasons. A lot of people who had heart attacks, breathing problems, etc., were told to move to Arizona because of the dry heat which would allow them to live longer.

Leland and Becky Greer were to me what I wish my own parents were—role models. They were non-drinking, non-smoking, God-fearing parents. In a way, they scared me as I thought they knew about Jody and I spending so much time alone together, especially during the lunch hour. I just knew they were waiting to drop the hammer on me. If they ever knew, they never let on. The even invited me to go out to visit their family in eastern Kansas for a couple of weeks in the summer. This was something to look forward to and my parents seemed to approve it.

*

Towards the end of my junior year, Dad informed me he was going to get me into the union, AFL-CIO, and there was a job opening in east Mesa that I could probably get, helping build a new school. I would be working as a laborer. Dad had to lie about my age to get me in the union, but I was OK with it as the pay was a lot better than non-union work. This would probably interfere with the trip to Kansas.

I knew why Dad was so anxious to get me on as a union worker. Three reasons. One was so I could start paying rent at home. Two was so I would quit school and be able to make a better living than a non-union worker. The third reason was the one I chose to think was more likely and that was he didn't want me to make anything of myself. Like father, like son.

I hadn't been working on the school for very long when I was assisting a group of workers in lifting a steel beam that was to span the walkway through the school. We almost had it in place. I was to the far left side, when the worker next to me let the beam slip from his hands. I knew right away that I had screwed up something in my lower back because of the intense pain.

A few weeks of working with a chiropractor on a daily basis, my back was pretty good so I was able to go on the Kansas trip and I had a great time. Jody's relatives accepted me as a member of the family and we had a great visit which culminated with a giant family reunion at Pike's Peak, CO, where we spent the last few days.

I didn't work any other union jobs that summer. I had barely made enough before I had gotten hurt to pay my union dues.

*

My junior year almost replicated my sophomore year. The only A's or 1's I got were in PE. I had six D's or 4's, but the teachers really didn't know me. I deserved better even though I missed nearly 15 days of school. I know I deserved better, at least B's or 2's. I probably had the best returned books of anyone I remember. If they had been wrapped in plastic when I got them, they still would be for the most part.

As my senior year started, we were still living on 6ᵗʰ Avenue and I was still stealing gas to keep my car running, still stealing the latest 45 RPM records. In other words life is going on for me as I'm still seeing Jody, at least seven days a week.

Dad was now working as a hod carrier or cement mixer and hod carrier for block layers. He can get me on the Saturdays they work at good pay, but back-breaking work. I enjoyed the physical labor and it kept me in good shape for boxing, track and cross country.

At the beginning of my senior year, my best friend, John Allen, was moving to New Mexico as his step dad was being re-stationed from Williams AFB to Kirkland AFB just outside Albuquerque. This was a devastating blow for me, for both of us as we had done an awful lot together. Not many good things, but the bad things we did together, we usually never thought twice about.

Well, thinking about it, maybe I could straighten out my act. Do better in school, get in fewer fights, etc.

The very next week, I was dressing after PE class and felt my back pocket for my wallet. It was gone. I asked the kid to my left if he had found it. He said no, but I remembered he and I were the last two out for PE and, if I had lost it while dressing out, it would have fallen in front of his or my locker.

I knew the kid, but had never really had an occasion to talk to him. I did remember his locker and reported the loss to Coach Mutt Ford, a legendary high school football coach, who was also my PE teacher. He indicated that he would report the loss and my suspicion of the kid whom I thought might have found it.

The next day, I was called out of my Audio Visual class to go to the principal's office. I had no idea why at that time, but I knew I hadn't screwed up in this class because it was probably my favorite class and I was getting good grades in it.

When I reported to Mr. Brimhall, Mr. Kilbourne, the assistant principal, was also there. I knew this could not be good, but I was on my best behavior. They advised me the other student next to me in PE was already being looked at for other thefts and that they would handle him.

I was not to take things into my own hands as they would handle things and return my wallet, if possible. I should let things fall into place and keep my nose clean and graduate. I told them, "Yes, sir, I will."

I spent the lunch hour watching this kid and learned where his book locker was. I didn't see anyone else, or at least any authority-type person on the same mission. However, they would already know which locker was his. I was unable to see inside his locker during lunch, but made it a point to be in the area a couple times that afternoon when he opened his locker. Maybe, I would see something. Only a fool would not have tossed the stolen wallet by now.

But, this kid was a fool.

He opened his locker and I was only a few feet from him. My wallet was lying there among his books. I reached in as I shoved him aside and retrieved my wallet. I don't remember what he said, but he should have kept his mouth shut and I wouldn't have hit him. But he did and I did.

I knew the way he went down, he was hurt. I walked away and went straight to the principal's office. I wasn't feeling good about what I had just done, but I felt I owed Mr. Brimhall an explanation. I sat outside his office for what seemed an eternity. As other teachers were going in and out of his office, I saw Mr. Kilbourne walk past me into the principal's office. At that point, I knew they already knew what had happened.

When they called me in, the first thing they asked me is if I had gotten my wallet. I patted my back pocket. They asked me to have a seat back outside the office. I was there for a long time. School had long since let out and not many people were left in the Administration Office area when they called me in again.

The kid had to be taken to the hospital where he was treated for a possible fractured jaw. The police wanted to talk with me and I would probably be there for a while longer. The school administrators told me they would either have to suspend me or expel me. No charges were brought against me, but I was suspended from school for five days and my parents were to both meet with Mr. Brimhall at the end of the suspension. They did and I was readmitted.

*

The week off allowed me more time for Jody. During this week, Jody and I had planned a trip to Mexico to be married. We left on a Friday, after she got out of school and was spending the weekend with a friend from school.

We stopped just outside of Tucson and purchased a six-pack of beer. I had never had a problem buying beer because I looked older than I was. We had decided to drive across the Mexican border to find a preacher. We were both very nervous as we passed the point of entry, and perhaps, a little tipsy also.

We parked my Mercury and got a cab to find a priest. We did and we did—I think. The cab driver, upon hearing we were to be married, offered toasts, which was a bottle of tequila passed around amongst us. He told us we would need witnesses so we stopped and got his brother and sister before proceeding to the preacher.

To this day, I do not remember anything until waking the next morning on the American side of the border in the backseat of my vehicle with Jody. Her recollection was slightly better than mine except she remembered the ceremony. She paid for the ceremony, but would not tell me how much. I did not offer to repay her.

*

I got back into school, again. Did I mention my mom was a very good-looking woman and persuasive when she wanted to be. I missed more than 20 days of school my senior year, but with everything else going on, I graduated on May 29, 1962.

On graduation night, my parents were there, Jody and her family, and Principal Brimhall (who had been reassigned to Westwood High School, a new high school that had opened that year in Mesa).

Mr. Kilbourne was the new principal at Mesa High school and presented the diplomas. As I received my diploma and was heading off stage, Mr. Brimhall approached me, shook my hand, congratulated me and told me he never thought he would see this day. But for him, I wouldn't be here and I told him that and I actually think I meant it.

I was still in the AFL-CIO and Dad had gotten me a job as a drill operator on a microwave tower construction job which started Monday following graduation. The job site was at Usury Pass between Apache Junction and Mesa. I also had received an invitation to John Allen's graduation in Albuquerque, NM. Then there was Jody.

John and I were corresponding quite frequently, maybe to see if each other had ratted on the other one or maybe because of a pure friendship. We had plotted to go into the military together on the "buddy" plan which was a new concept to keep friends together during their first enlistment of four years. This was also kind of a promise I had made to the Air Force recruiter following the cherry bomb incident as mentioned earlier. I had made him a promise that if he did not press charges that I would join the Air Force after I graduated. Be careful what you promise!!

*

I had never used a jackhammer-type drill in my life. Dad had been a driller for years, many of which he had put his life in danger as a high scaler/driller. My job began at "00 daylight hours' and by the first break, I had broken two drill bits. The foreman was a little less than impressed.

I had lunch with the rest of the guys on the crew, some of whom knew Dad. I told them goodbye, walked down the hill, got in my car and drove home. Nobody was there when I got home and it wasn't until after I had packed my car, Ron and Mom arrived in Mom's car.

I was sitting in the living room drinking a beer, an A-1 pilsner, as best as I can remember from Dad's stash. This in itself was a no-no. I think he counted his beers or carried abacus beads to keep count. Mom was wild-eyed and Ron just smiled and went to his room.

After all the years and years of Mom and Dad fighting, arguing and the knock down drag outs between the two of them, I knew I was leaving. I had had enough.

But, there was Ron. I went into his room and explained the situation as best as I could to him. We cried and held each other, but I knew where I was going and he could not go. I would probably be living out of my vehicle and he still had three more years of school left. So, it was better for him to stay.

I got as far as the living room and Dad was there. I hadn't heard him drive up and he must have seen my vehicle loaded. He was waiting for me, holding the empty beer can in his hand, smiling. He asked me if that beer was his. I smiled and said not anymore. He called me a few names, one of which was "You bastard!"

Now on any other occasion, it might not have sparked much reaction from me, but this day it did. I don't really remember my exact words, but to the effect of "But not your bastard."

This lit some incendiary device within him and he said, "You aren't going nowhere. Do you think you are better than me?"

I said yes I was and I was. He blanked at that and I am sure he did not get the full drift of my answers.

I said goodbye to Ron and told him I didn't have a good feeling about leaving him. I thought I would even have a hard time leaving the house. He started to follow me out of his room and I told him to stay here, I would be OK.

I could have left the house by just going down the hall and leaving through the front door. Instead, I went to the refrigerator, got me another A-1 and walked out the back where Mom and Dad were standing, arguing.

I offered Dad a sip of the beer, he slapped it out of my hand and then told me the only way I was leaving was over him. I smiled, reached to open the screen door and he kicked it shut. I knew then only one of us would be going through that door standing up.

He asked me about the drilling job. I told him it sucked. When I realized I was being him, I had to quit. I also realized he had a few beers before getting home and talking was going nowhere. As I reached for the door, he swung at me and hit my shoulder. I turned at looked at him and turned again to open the screen. He hit me in the side of the head.

From that point on, I only remember Mom telling me to stop. As she was yelling, I realized I was holding Dad up so he wouldn't fall as I was hitting and hitting him. I let him fall. I walked through the house, out the front door and was on my way to Albuquerque.

Chapter 6

The Military

John Allen and I entered the U.S. Air Force on June 29, 1962 in Phoenix. We enlisted on the "Buddy" plan which meant we would go through basic training together and on to our permanent duty stations together.

Upon enlisting, we underwent various tests—physical, mental, blood and everything else known to man or so it seemed. After completing the tests, there were at least a dozen recruits and we were taken to a downtown Phoenix hotel and given separate rooms, all on the same floor. We were not allowed to leave and had to eat in the hotel restaurant. The recruiters monitored the hallways and we were not allowed visitors. I was fortunate to have a room with a fire escape and telephone.

I snuck Jody into my room via the fire escape the second and third nights we were there. She had been very supportive of my decision to go into the Air Force and we both hoped I would get a decent assignment after I completed basic training.

The fourth day we were called together and it seemed there were fewer recruits than what we started with (possibly some may not have passed their physicals). We met in the lobby with our baggage and were loaded onto a bus bound for Sky Harbor International Airport.

*

In just a few hours, we landed at the airport in San Antonio, TX, where we were met by an instructor who verified our names before escorting us to an Air Force bus for the drive to Lackland Air Force Base. My life was about to become more structured than I had ever dreamed it could be. Before the first day was done, I had lost all my hair, literally it was shaved. I also was introduced to my DI (drill instructor), Sgt. Altamirano.

There were numerous buses and at least 40 of us standing around when our names were called to form up and be marched to our barracks, which would be our homes for the next eight weeks.

The barracks were metal Quonset huts with bunk beds on each side. Behind the beds were metal trunks (foot lockers) for storage and racks with hangers. At one end of the hut were the showers and toilet facilities. At the other end, a set of offices.

Next we were marched to the supply section where we were issued boots, socks, "fatigues" or pants, shirts, etc. Everything we would need for a while, including black shoe polish and brushes.

Adjustments were not easy and discipline was top priority. The military has a set way of doing things, especially in basic training and some recruits would not make it for one reason or another.

Every day began at the same time, before daylight! We were awakened by the same tune, revelry, I think is what it is called. Usually, we marched in formation to the physical training field where we did calisthenics and various marching formations.

Then we went to breakfast which was a hurried affair, a buffet line where you would rush through the line before sitting down to eat at long tables. You ate fast, but properly while sitting ramrod stiff. The 40 or so people who made up the flight did everything as one. You may have eight to 10 minutes from the time you entered the chow hall until you were back in formation. All through this, our DI never took his eyes off us.

It took about two days before I got stuck with the nickname "Shitbird." How that came about I really don't know, but I tried my best to live up to it.

Classroom training was almost on a daily basis as we learned the history of the Air Force, the various ranks. Every day, however, started with physical training.

Cleaning the barracks was done every evening. Everything—floors, toilets, sinks, showers. Showers? You had at the most one minute to shower with 20 or more other airmen because the showers had to be completely dry and cleaned before we could all sit around shining boots and brass buckles.

Barrack inspections were done on a daily basis at the very least. The DI would conduct an inspection every morning prior to formation.

Then there was the "brass," normally a lieutenant or captain, who would conduct surprise periodic inspections and, if it didn't meet muster, the DI would be "written up" if any thing was out of order.

For the infractions, we would receive GIGs. If you received so many GIGs, you could be rotated back to a beginning flight and start over. I don't remember this happening, but my flight lost a few because of the physical fitness challenges.

Towards the middle of training, it became much more fun for me. The obstacle course, firing range and combat training, were ahead but I was enjoying it. After the fourth or fifth week, we got our first weekend pass.

I went into San Antonio, I had to see the Alamo. This was a shock as there were curio shops set up in every room and all around the structure. This was supposed to be an historic landmark/shrine. I remember thinking what a historic mess. I spent most of the day just walking around the area.

I considered myself to be in excellent physical condition at 165 pounds and I had no trouble with basic training. The extreme heat and humidity took its toll on a lot of the guys in my flight. At least two more were ushered out of the service during the last few weeks. I heard two airmen had died from the heat during the first part of August, from other flights not mine.

I was told just before graduation that my orders for permanent assignment had not been cut and no one knew where I was going to be stationed. However, in just a few days, my orders as well as John Allen's were delivered. We were finally relieved from basic military training and were assigned to the 12th Strategic Aerospace Division, Strategic Air Command, Davis Monthan Air Force Base, Tucson, AZ. We were to report "no later than 12 Sep 62."

We were assigned ranks of A3C, airman third class, and would both be assigned to the base supply section. I had about two weeks before I had to report so I returned home to Mesa and stayed with Mom, Dad and Ron.

*

I spent considerable time with Jody. We talked frequently about where we would be officially married (remember our ceremony in

Nogales, Sonora, Mexico) and when. We set a tentative date for January 1963.

Upon arriving at Davis-Monthan AFB in Tucson on Sept. 12, I had a lot of paperwork to do, not to mention various shots and medical and dental physicals to go through. I was staying on base in the Airmen's Quarters. Two men to a room and rather small quarters, but much better than basic.

I was assigned as a material handler to Base Supply 803rd Combat Support Group (CSB). Even though the regimentation was much more lax than in basic training, there were similarities such as pressed and creased fatigues, spit-shined shoes and brass and an absolute gig line, meaning your belt buckle had to be centered with the line of the zipper on your fatigues.

One supervisor I remember distinctly and will mention again later was Tech Sgt. Harold Radcliffe Jr. He was not my immediate supervisor, but he was my most memorable.

Almost as soon as I was settling into a routine, the Cuban Missile Crisis broke and had us on "Red Alert," restricted to base. For those of us who lived on base, it really didn't matter as we were already living on base.

American and Soviet Russia battleships were about to square off in the south Atlantic near Cuba. Missiles had been placed all over Cuba, aimed at the United States, 90 miles from Miami, FL. There were no rules now, only who would fire the first salvo.

Russian Premier Nikita Khrushchev had declared "We will bury the U.S." Between the U.S. and Russia, there were more than 15,000 nuclear warheads aimed at each other's throats.

The U.S. Army, Navy and Strategic Air Command bomb squadrons had gone to DEFCON 2 (defense readiness condition). DEFCON 2 means the next step is nuclear war while DEFCON 1 means nuclear war is imminent.

This was the first time in U.S. history that we were at DEFCON 2, meaning we were just a heart beat away from all-out nuclear war. And, here I was at Davis-Monthan AFB, one of the largest SAC bases in the country. We were on Red Alert and confined to the base. But we did have the Airmen's Club.

The only outlet we had as young airmen under the age of 21 was the Airmen's Club. At the time you could join military service at age 17 with parental consent (which John Allen had) and you were allowed to drink beer at the Airmen's Club at age 17. I saw a lot of young men wasting their lives with alcohol at a very young age.

The crisis lasted a few weeks, but everyone was on pins and needles, knowing DEFCON1 was imminent and we were going to war with Russia.

*

I started traveling to Mesa on the weekends, driving my 1949 Mercury back and forth. One weekend, I had someone offer me a fair price for my Merc, which wasn't really reliable for my weekend excursions to Mesa so I sold it and relied on hitchhiking in uniform to and from Mesa.

Jody was in her senior year at Mesa High School when we made plans to get married on Jan. 26, 1963. We vowed to her parents that she would finish her senior year before moving to Tucson.

I didn't know it at the time, but I had to get my squadron commander's permission to get married. So, I submitted the paperwork to Major Nielsen and received his approval with the stipulation I visit the base chaplain, which I did.

Some evenings when I could borrow my roommate's vehicle, I would cruise the area around South Tucson, searching for an affordable place to live after marrying Jody. I located a nice one-bedroom apartment which was situated behind the owner's house. This duplex had a stairway to the top apartment which I liked.

I was making $100 per month and would get an additional $105 for dependant allowance. This was OK. Plus, I would have to allow for some sort of transportation. Mom and Dad had talked me out of buying a car immediately after I had sold my Merc. I couldn't figure out why at the time, but a couple weeks before Jody and I were due to get married, my parents gave me a 1956 Chevy 4-door Bel Air, free and clear.

Having years to reflect on this, I believe they were trying to make amends for the previous 18 years. Did I appreciate the gesture? Yes. Would I forgive them? No.

Jody had talked with her guidance counselors about the marriage and move to Tucson. They told her she would be allowed to finish the semester via correspondence and graduate with her class.

We were married on Jan. 26, 1963, at the First Christian Church in Mesa. It was a big wedding. My brother, Ron, was the best man. Ushers were Leslie Miller, Jody's brother, Johnny Greer, and John Allen.

Jody had not seen the apartment until we moved in a couple days later. She was happy with it. It was nice and clean. I already had all my belongings in it although the rent wouldn't start until we actually moved in. The owners were pleased to meet Jody.

The apartment was furnished with everything we needed and what we didn't have—such as pots, pans, dishes and silverware—the owners furnished these items to us newlyweds.

*

Trying to get by on just a little more than $200 per month was difficult. We were really scrimping and were not able to travel to Mesa to visit our parents as often as we wanted. Jody had walked to the corner drug store, which was only a short block away, and purchased a few necessities a few times. The drug store owners talked to her about a part-time job as a counter waitress. She decided to do this mostly to get out of the house while I was working. We would have the weekends together and also enough money to go to Mesa a couple times a month.

Jody made good on her promise to her parents and graduated with her class of 1963. She did not attend the formal graduation as she was about seven months pregnant. Neither of us had any idea she was pregnant when we got married.

The owners we were renting from had friends about two blocks away who had a two-bedroom apartment that was coming available and we looked at it. We rented it, as Jody was having trouble climbing the steps to our current apartment. The owners and myself were worried about her.

On Aug. 16, 1963, our first child was born at Tucson Medical Center, We named our daughter Debra Dee. Both sets of grandparents were elated.

*

Everyone old enough to remember President John F. Kennedy probably remembers where they were and what they were doing when he as assassinated on Friday morning, Nov. 22, 1963, in Dallas by Lee Harvey Oswald. I'm no exception. I had just returned to base supply from making daily deliveries. When I approached the delivery desk, everyone on duty was clustered around a radio. Some appeared to be crying.

I asked what was happening and was told the president had just been killed. I became one of the mourners. I had nothing but respect for the president and what he had done for the nation such as keeping us out of a war with Russia when times were extremely tense.

Now, what would happen was anyone's guess, but it couldn't be good the way I saw things. I am not going into a volume of details here because numerous books have been written on the subject. I do not think the true story will ever come to light. There has been so much speculation, conjectures and out right cover ups relating to the event.

There's an old saying, "If more than one person knows a secret, it's not a secret." The only way to keep a secret is to eliminate the others who know. This is what happened immediately upon the arrest of the supposed shooter Lee Harvey Oswald. Two days after Oswald murdered our president, Jack Ruby murdered Oswald.

*

In the early part of March 1964, Jody seemed to be getting sick a lot, losing her appetite. I took her to the base doctor and had her checked out. We were told that probably sometime in October we would be having another child. On Oct. 23, we had another girl, Karen Denise. However Karen got her nickname DD, I don't know. The obvious choice for a Dee Dee would have been Debbie Dee. But, no, Karen became our Dee Dee and Debbie was Debbie.

An airman I worked with lived in a real nice two-bedroom apartment in a single-level complex with a swimming pool. He was getting ready to transfer to Vietnam and his wife and kids were going back to his home to stay with his family. He was getting a great deal cut off his rent by taking care of the pool and if I wanted, he would put in the good word with the owner to get me the same deal.

I talked it over with Jody. We had been over to the apartment a couple times and we both loved it. It was our third move in less than two years, but the owner had agreed to the same deal he was giving my friend. You see a trend developing here.

I had started drinking a little more and running around with my buddy, John Allen, who was still single. This did not bode well on the home front. But the way I figured it was if I wasn't home much there would not be a third surprise. Not really, I loved what I had but I also liked a little freedom at times and was probably scared to death of going to Vietnam although I knew I was going, I just didn't know when.

Jody was getting pretty upset with me and with good cause. I was never home and when I was, I was working the pool area or sleeping. She threatened to take the girls, go to her parents if I didn't change my ways. I helped pack some things for her and the girls and drove them to Mesa. I couldn't bear facing her parents so I helped unload the stuff to the front porch, kissed Jody and the girls and left.

*

The following week, the AF Special forces were at Davis-Monthan to recruit for their unit. This was a one-week assignment then. The ones selected would go elsewhere for more specialized training. The training at the base consisted of different facets of physical fitness—sit ups, push ups, rope climbing and many other activities, including pistol and rifle marksmanship.

As the week progressed, I knew I was at the top of the class and was really hyped. I had quit drinking and was feeling great about my possibilities. Jody and the girls were still away, but I was calling every night. Jody was not as warm to the idea of what I was doing as I was but we both agreed if I had to go to Vietnam, it would be better to go with the best.

At the end of our fourth day of training, I was called into an office in the gym being used by the overseers of the program. The officer in charge wanted to talk to me about my family life. They had conducted a quick background check and I was told that everything was fine, but they had real concerns about the ages of my two daughters. They were cutting me from the program and I could not re-apply.

I felt like a failure. How was I going to tell Jody? I could tell her I flunked out, but she wouldn't believe that for a moment. I had been telling her how great I was doing and how I thought I was at the top of my peers and now, I flunked out. I guess the truth would win out. I needed a drink or a whole six-pack. I stopped and bought a six-pack of beer on my way home. I called Jody and told her the truth. She said she wanted to come home. I dumped the six-pack down the drain. I had to work my regular job the next day and then left for Mesa.

Jody and the girls were kind of camped out in the living room at her parent's home, but they were comfortable. I spent the night at my parents as Dad was at work, someplace out of town, allowing me to visit with Mom and Ron for a few hours. Ron said he couldn't wait until he graduated from high school and after graduating, he would leave home. The situation with Mom and Dad had not gotten better, but with Dad gone out of town working, most of the time at home it was tolerable.

*

The situation with the war in Vietnam was escalating and it had gotten John Allen. He was over there working in a supply depot and had been for a while. The tour of duty in Vietnam was for one year and then you rotated back to the states or were discharged. When John returned, he and I talked at length about his tour. He was never in the line of fire. He ran a supply depot and had made a few thousand dollars on the side by dealing in what he called black market items.

He would sell or trade cigarettes, beer and booze, but never any narcotics which was rampant over there, according to John. He told me how he would requisition the items and exactly how his scheme went. It sounded simple enough. I figured with a few thousand dollars in my pocket when I got discharged would really give me time to go back to school under the GI bill, a system used to assure young military veterans would have the opportunity to get a college degree or go to a training institute.

On July 1, 1965, I extended my tour of duty for one year and put in a transfer request for Vietnam. I got my extension of enlistment on Aug. 11, 1965 with Senior Master Sergeant Robert Morris who gave me my oath of enlistment for my extension.

We talked about Vietnam and he said that in my career field, supply, I would undoubtedly be sent to an area where they were still building supply depot runways and air fields. I left feeling really pumped, ready to go. I had to wait for orders to be cut, but that shouldn't take but a few weeks. Little did I know.

Earlier, I mentioned Tech Sgt. Radcliffe who was my highest NCO supervisor. Jody, the girls and I were invited to his home near the power plant southeast of Tucson. A beautiful house in a nice neighborhood. The sergeant had purchased it new just a few years earlier. He had put in a transfer request to Italy and it had just come through. His wife, being Italian, was elated.

He was taking his whole family and was in a situation with his house I could help him with. They did not want to rent the house, just to have it trashed when they came back. So, he said, he would love to have me and my family move in until they returned in about two years.

I was stymied as was Jody. The sergeant told us that all the neighbors were very nice and looked out for one another. They were dependable if help was needed. Most, like him, were original owners and had considerable pride in their neighborhood. He said he knew I couldn't afford to make their payments, but they would let us make the same payment as we were paying at the apartment and he would make up the difference, feeling confident that the house would be well taken care of.

I pretty much knew what Jody would decide because she did not particularly want to continue living at our apartment. Once I left for Vietnam, she felt the rent would go up. She also did not feel real safe when I was gone, even during the day. We'd take the deal and never looked back. Well, at least not for a while.

Special Order A1285, dated Oct. 1, 1965, promoted me to Airman First Class (A1C). The promotion came with a pretty good pay increase and with the dependant allowance, we would do OK.

*

Special Order A1419 dated Oct. 25, 1965, finally came. I was being released from my duties at the 803 Supply Squadron to the 4082 Strategic Wing APO New York, N.Y. My original orders, which I never saw, were rescinded and I was going to Goose Air Base in Canada for 18 months.

What?

Goose Air Force Base? Where the hell is Canada? What happened to Vietnam?

These were questions I would demand and get answers. Well, you don't demand and you don't get answers that are satisfying in the USAF. I was one hot SOB, but soon to be a cold American in Canada. I was to report to McGuire Air Force Base, Trenton, NJ, no later than 0600 hours Nov. 15, 1965.

Jody's brother, Johnny, was in the Navy, stationed in Virginia, within driving distance of McGuire AFB. Johnny wanted me to come by so he would show me around New York, New Jersey and the Virginia areas.

I spent a week with Johnny who was assigned to a Navy aircraft carrier. The one he was assigned to was currently dry docked. He was a cable operator for jets landing aboard the carrier. I spent some time aboard the carrier and was awed by the sheer size and magnitude of the operations aboard this carrier. It's like a city in itself. Johnny was dating a girl from the Bronx in New York. The best part is yet to come.

Are you ready? Her extended family all owned a bunch of bars. The beer in New York was better than beer in Arizona. It came in big mugs and didn't cost a penny. This was to be a great week.

Johnny took a few days off and he really went overboard, sailor's talk, to show me the sites such as the Statue of Liberty on Liberty Island. The tour of the statute would only allow us to get as high as her crown as the torch arm was under construction. Ellis Island, just to the south of Liberty Island in New York harbor, was the port of entry for all immigrants coming by boat to the United States. I'm sure they have a library listing of all immigrants who passed through, but I didn't think to look at the time.

In Washington, D.C., we saw the Lincoln Memorial, the Washington Monument and numerous other sites. The week went by much too fast.

*

I caught a military aircraft from McGuire AFB to Goose AFB which is located in the very far northeast portion of Canada. When I reported to duty, I was advised that the sergeant I was replacing as the Supply TOC (technical order compliance) Section had already rotated back to the states and I would be responsible for aircraft at Thule, Greenland (which is in the Artic Circle) as well as those on base at Goose.

I was given reams of paper work and documentation, but very little help from my superiors as they thought I would be there in time for OJT (on the job training) before the sergeant departed. This was a one-man operation with one secretary, a civilian and native Indian who lived in the town of Goose Bay, just outside the base. The job was relatively simple and consumed very little time.

The entire base was pretty much accessible by underground tunnels which were lighted, but always cold and damp. There were numerous barracks for NCO's (non-commissioned officers), officers and airmen. There were two civilian barracks, one for women and one for men. I was assigned a double room with another A1C, a military policeman who had been there a few months.

He showed me around and gave me advice of what to do when the weather got bad and where everything was. At the time, some snowdrifts were well past first-floor windows. We were on the second floor and could see out the windows. Every thing was white, broken up by barracks and buildings here and there.

My mentor, if that's what you want to call him was a Staff Sergeant (S-Sgt.) one step above me. He led me through what he thought my job curtailed and let me know in no uncertain terms that if I got my job done and wanted to go to the gym or whatever, it was fine with him as long as I let my secretary know how to contact me.

The gym was one of the biggest single-story buildings on the base. Basketball court, boxing ring, two handball courts, weights and a shower.

This is where I spent most of my working day, as well as evenings and weekends. I did a lot of shadow boxing. I also spent a considerable amount of time playing handball which is just like racquetball, but without a racquet.

*

With my weight fluctuating between 175 and 180 pounds, it didn't take long for the sergeant in charge of the gym to notice me. At the time, I didn't know the base had a boxing team that traveled a few times a year to various Air Force bases in Canada for matches. At the time, Goose AFB didn't have a light-heavyweight (168-175 pounds) and he thought I could make the weight and complement the team.

The matches were not structured. The way they worked was whenever we had a cargo plane (usually a C135 or KC135 refueling plane going to Quebec, Ontario or wherever in Canada), the sergeant would make arrangements with that Air Force base, setting up matches for the time we would be there.

This was a good arrangement and I was assured I could go. I traveled on three different trips during my nine months. I fought two light-heavyweight bouts and one heavy weight bout. I won all three by "stop contest" which was the same as a TKO (technical knock out).

*

My real passion, however, was handball which required good hand-eye coordination as well as playing angles. I spent literally hundreds of hours playing by myself, hours at a time. My right hand was so calloused by striking the ball so frequently, I seldom wore a glove.

My first match was with a captain and he was good. Good footwork, reflexes and although he beat me, I learned a lot. In 4-wall handball, you sometimes have to use the rear wall. Putting yourself in position is key for staying in the game. This is something you have to work on in order to develop this shot. The captain was good at this and I asked him to explain his thoughts when playing the back wall.

He gave me some tips I could practice and praised my game. He asked how long I had been playing. I told him this was my first game ever. He didn't believe me, but said this was one of the better games he had played in months on this base.

My roommate was really into crafts and movies, never entering the gym. He was good company. He and I saw almost every movie to come to the base while we were there. He neither smoked nor consumed alcohol. On occasion, he would meet me at the Airman's Club for a meal while I had a beer or two.

Bob Hull (not related to the National Hockey League star) was next door in my barracks with a room of his own. He was a large man, easily 6-foot-6, 250 pounds. He was in charge of food services which probably explains his weight. He also was a waiter at the Officer's Club, which on weekends was very busy. Bob would occasionally call and ask me to be his clean-up boy or bus boy as some call it. He would split his tips with me and sometimes they were quite good.

*

I hadn't forgotten about Jody and the girls, but telephone conversations were few because of one phone per barrack and, usually there was a line waiting in the evenings. I did try to improvise by writing every other day.

Around the end of April or the first of May, Jody was writing about someone in the neighborhood stalking her. The person would leave stuff on her vehicle or in front of the doors so she might trip over them. She had no idea who it might be. The only thing I could advise was to call the police and report these acts as vandalism. Even though nothing was damaged, I felt the police might be able to do something.

The problem escalated to the point where clothes were being taken from the clothes line in back of the house, usually underwear, hers and the girls. I could only offer suggestions from long distance. The neighbors were all aware of the situation and were supposedly keeping an eye out.

In June, I received an emergency phone call from Jody's dad informing me she was in the hospital from what they thought was a nervous breakdown. She was asking for me to come home and told everybody she wasn't going back to that house.

I put in for an emergency leave which was granted. I got all the way to Davis-Monthan on Air Force shuttles. I hitchhiked to Mesa where Jody and the girls were staying with her parents.

Jody was extremely thin and frail. The girls were well, probably oblivious to the adult things that were happening, I hope.

The culprit was caught. He was a teenager living two doors down who had a fixation on either Jody or the girls or all three. Jody was very adamant about not going back to that house and I didn't blame her.

However, this was problematic in a few ways. I or we had given our words that we would remain in the house until Sgt. Radcliffe and his family returned. I couldn't afford to keep paying him and relocate the family to an apartment in Mesa, which Jody insisted on in order to be close to her parents.

Another problem was how quickly could I get this done. When you got leave in the Air Force, it's usually non-negotiable—you returned on the date listed on the papers you signed. I requested an extension and after the brass learned about my circumstances, it was granted. I now had 30 days instead of the two weeks I had requested.

Needless to say, Sgt. Radcliffe was not a happy camper, nor was I after learning the teenager was not going to be punished for stalking my wife and girls. Why? Because he was a teen and teens sometimes behave that way was what I was told.

Eventually, we found a nice apartment just east of her parents house, 559 S. Belleview Apt. E. It was a two-bedroom located in a nice area of Mesa.

I got a temporary trailer hitch for my 1956 Chevy and a small utility trailer to make the move. We did not have much of our own at the house except for personal items, baby bed and a few odds and ends. Jody refused to go with me and I thought I got everything, but who knows as I had other problems to think about.

We were paying the utilities. Do I have them turned off? How do I secure the house for the next year or so? What do I do with the keys?

These answers were all supplied when I returned to the house. A neighbor from across the street came over and said Harold and he had been talking and after I loaded up to drop the keys off at his house and he would have the utilities read in a couple days. The bill would be sent to me and Harold would pay them forward.

The move went smooth and before you know it, I'm on may way back to Canada. My emergency travel orders allowed me to utilize military transportation when available. This is how I got back to Goose.

*

My phone calls became more frequent because when I could get patched through a base switchboard operator, my calls would go out free of charge.

I began spending a lot of time alone. I was described as unsociable. If possible, I even spent more time in the gym. This was noticed and not in a nice way, or so I thought at the time.

I was called into the base commander's office and I was to be in dress blues. My sergeant had no idea why I was going before the commander, nor did I. The commander, a full-bird colonel, immediately put me at ease by calling me by name. He asked about my family. How did he know? Well, he would have to approve my leave extension request. I thanked him for that. He seemed very concerned about the situation my wife and kids had been put in.

We talked a length and before he dismissed me, he asked how my handball game was coming along. One of his captains had told him I played a mean game. I emphasized without bragging that my game had gotten better because of Capt. Fasano who was looking forward to playing me again sometime soon.

Col. Herberg then laid a bombshell on me. The sergeant in charge of the gym, which was a special services position and directly under the base commander, was transferring out within the week. His position had not yet been filled and I had the job if I wanted it. I would keep my current AFSC of 64750 and be assigned temporary duty to the Special Services Division.

He wanted to know if I wanted to think about it and get back to him. I said yes, I would like to think about it. I thought about two seconds and said, "Thank you, sir, I will take it."

The colonel said he would make it happen. That's how I met Col. John A. Herberg.

This proved to be an excellent move on my part. Although it was boring as hell at times having to be at the gym instead of sneaking time at the gym. I got to know everybody who came into the gym. Capt. Fasano and I did play another handball game and he beat me again, although the score was in the high 30s. He beat me by two points.

*

At the end of September 1966, the captain and I got to go to the Air Force Handball Championships at McGuire Air Force Base in New Jersey. He was playing in the open division and me in the novice. We both took back first-place trophies. The captain started calling me Ken, but I kept calling him "Captain."

We were both invited to dinner with the colonel and his family in celebration of our victories. We had moose steak and a very memorable evening as we got around to talking about our families. The colonel asked about Jody and the girls. I told him the truth, the way I saw it at the time. I unloaded on the request for Vietnam and then getting Goose AFB only after I had extended.

I was not going to make the Air Force a career. I also told them Jody wasn't doing good at all and the entire time I was home on leave, even though I hadn't really expected it, we were not intimate. They asked what they could do to help. I had no idea as I was scheduled for discharge in June 1967.

The captain asked what my plans were and I told him I really didn't know. I said maybe go back to school until I could figure where I wanted to go, but right now my focus was on my family and trying to put it back together.

*

A few days later, the captain showed up at the gym and asked me where I planned on going to college and when enrollment started. I didn't quite know what to make of this and asked the all-universal question any person with intelligence could utter, "Why?"

He said the colonel and he had talked a little longer that night after dinner and he was advised by the colonel to see how they could help me and my home situation. So the captain asked again, "What college would I like to go to?"

I replied Mesa Community College and then maybe Arizona State University in Tempe. He told me to write Mesa Community College and see when its next semester started and if they would accept me at that time.

He added that if the credits were transferable from the community college to an accredited four-year university, then maybe they could help.

I wrote Mesa Community College and explained my situation to them, seeking acceptance to their next semester. On Oct. 18, 1966, I received a reply from the college informing me I had been admitted in good standing for the spring semester 1966-67, beginning with enrollment on Jan. 23, 1967.

I wrote my letter to the captain on Nov. 8, 1966, requesting an early release from my military obligations to attend a recognized institution of higher learning. I hand carried it to the captain. The captain immediately wrote his recommendation to the colonel recommending my early release. I don't think he wanted another handball match.

On Nov. 17, 1966, the colonel approved the request effective Jan. 13, 1967. I received special order No. A-1334 on Dec. 22, 1966, stating I was relieved from duty at Goose Air Force Base, Canada, and assigned to McGuire Air Force Base in New Jersey for separation from service effective 0800 hours Jan. 10, 1967.

*

Jody and the whole family were elated. Jody wanted to know how I had done this and I told her I would talk to her about that when I got home.

It's nice to know you have people who are concerned about what they can do for you more so than what can I do for them. It's also appropriate to point out I could have written much more on the friends I had at Goose, my roommates, my secretary, the people of the area, but I leave that up to the Internet.

Chapter 7

Life prior to the Dallas Police Department

Jody and the girls were still living in a two-bedroom apartment at 559 S. Bellview #E, close to her parents' home in Mesa, AZ, where I had helped them move into a few months earlier. I joined them on Jan. 13 and immediately enrolled at Mesa Community College where I had been pre-approved for the semester.

I did not have a job for the first few weeks after my discharge and I had no idea what I wanted to do. I was leaning towards something in the criminal justice system, but I didn't know what or why.

Again, I met up with my friend John Allen who was living with his step-father in Apache Junction. John was working as a packaging supervisor for Frito Lay and wanted to get me on there, but I didn't see the fit.

I had gotten back into social graces so to speak with my parents and Dad was starting to get a lawn service business going and needed some help. My schedule would be as I needed because of my night-school schedule. This seemed like something I could get into for the short term.

We were building up the lawn service business pretty well. But, again I started my wayward ways as I was not happy in my marriage and I don't know why. It was nothing Jody was doing or not doing, it was just me.

*

I started running around on Jody after just a couple months of being home. John Allen had introduced me to an ASU nursing student who was in some classes with his girl friend. I started making time for this clandestine relationship, time I really didn't have. I was lying to Jody about where I was going and what I was doing. I was lying to my parents to get time off now and again.

Eventually, I forgot what lies I was telling and to whom. It got to a point that I really didn't care. Jody knew I was running around with John Allen again and we had more than a few words on that subject. I know she knew I was now seeing someone else, but never asked me about it.

I guess you might say I was a lost soul who could not foresee anything good in my future. I think it was sometime in July 1967 when my aunt, uncle and cousin (Christine) from Dallas came to visit my folks and I spent some time with them.

At about this time, I had come clean with Jody about my running around and I thought if we both worked at it, we could patch our failing marriage back together. I thought it was about 99.999 percent my fault and that I could, if I worked at it, rectify the problem and all would be well. How little I knew, but when one only looks at the problem as being his own, sometimes you will not see the big picture. But, I'm getting ahead of myself.

*

My cousin, Christine Haw, was the personal secretary to the chief of the Dallas Police Department. We visited for hours on the subject of the JFK assassination and the overall turmoil this had created within the Dallas Police Department.

She told me that Dallas PD was hiring at a rapid pace and that my chances to become a Dallas police officer might be pretty good if I wanted to move to Dallas. I also was told I would have a place to stay until I got a job and, after settling in, I could send for my family. I told Christine I would think about this and get back with her after I talked to Jody and reached a decision.

During the next few days, I talked to Jody, my parents and hers about the move to Dallas and if I could get on with the Dallas Police Department, things would be much better. Warning bells should have been ringing in my ears because Jody was all for it, agreeing that once I got on with the police department and completed the academy, she and the girls would join me.

At this time, we had two vehicles. Jody was going to keep the 1964 Chevrolet Impala station wagon and I would take my 1963 Volkswagen Carmen Ghia to Dallas. I would be staying with my aunt, uncle and Christine in Mesquite, TX, an eastern suburb of Dallas. Maybe this would be the turning point in my life where I could feel good about myself and save my family, living happily ever after. Yeah, right.

The only money we had set aside was a nice silver coin collection I had been developing for a few years. I took what I thought I would need to get to Dallas, all the clothes and personal items I could fit into the Carmen Ghia, which really wasn't much. Remember, this was Volkswagen's answer for a sports car so it had even less room than the normal "Bug."

Did I mention that my Carmen Ghia used about a quart of oil every 200 miles. Yes, a quart every 200 miles. My adrenaline was pumping and I was finally going somewhere in life. I knew I had a long way to go before I was a police recruit, but I now had a purpose.

*

I ran out of money, except for the silver coins, just outside Midland, TX, which was more than half way. Yes, I was stopping every couple hours and adding oil. After I left El Paso, it was more often, a lot more often. The engine finally blew just as I was entering the Dallas city limits. I pulled off on a ramp and that was it. I hiked to a phone and called Uncle Earnest. He would come to get me within the next hour.

We both knew the VW needed a new engine and he knew a garage we could have it towed to, but it would be a while. We loaded all my belongings into his vehicle and proceeded to Mesquite. Home sweet home.

My cousin, Christine, brought an application home with her and we spent a couple days completing it. I brought all the papers I thought would be pertinent in completing the process—birth certificate, etc.

*

I called Jody and told her I arrived OK, but the Carmen Ghia didn't. I had no idea how I would pay for the engine overall or how I would get around to the appointments I knew would be forthcoming if I were to be accepted into the various phases for the academy.

Jody seemed elated I had made it and wanted to know how she could correspond with me by mail so as not to run up a huge phone bill, or so I thought. She sounded gleeful, exuberant, but would not let me talk to the girls. Those warning bells should have been puncturing my ear drums at this point.

I was at my cousin's home about the middle of my third day in Dallas when someone arrived at the front door to see me. I had submitted my application just that morning so I did not think it could be reference to that. It wasn't. It was a process server serving me my divorce papers for my court appearance in Mesa in just a few weeks. She had me.

I felt like I had been kicked in the groin. I knew this was something a long time coming and I knew deep down that I deserved this and more. She wasn't asking for much, just everything I did not have with me. I knew I couldn't possibly appear in court on the appointed date. No car, no money and no job. And, in the near future, no family.

Jody got everything except the Carmen Ghia and the personal items I had with me. This in its totality didn't amount to much, but she also was awarded $350 per month in child support. This was all unprotested to me as I would have to appear in court or have an attorney represent me, both of which I did not do. She was to get married a few weeks after our divorce. Who got to who?

*

My application with the police department was proceeding at a snail's pace. A few things had slowed my application. The first were some inconsistencies in my time at Goose Air Force Base in which I could not explain and the other was my scheduled child support payments which were eventually worked out with Jody.

I missed the deadline to becoming part of the Dallas Police Department Academy Class 95 and would have to wait for the next class scheduled to begin in September 1967. I had no job and everything was relying on my application for a police officer position.

Fortunately, I had a place to stay as long as I needed at my uncle and aunt's house. I also now had a Carmen Ghia with a rebuilt engine paid for by my uncle. I insisted on a promissory note from me to him that he said was not necessary. But, I insisted on it.

Fate turned in my favor when all the necessary paperwork was completed. I had been accepted into Class 96 with the Dallas Police Department. When I went before the oral board after being accepted to the class, I was asked what my immediate future was. I told then, honestly, I did not know what I would be doing between now and the start of my academy class.

Deputy Chief B.B. Smith, who was in charge of the academy asked if I would like to work for him as a records clerk until Class 96 started. He added that I would start at cadet pay. I started the very next day as a records clerk for the Dallas Police Department with the distinction of being the No. 1 hire for the upcoming class which was to start in about five weeks.

My duties were to purge old Dallas Police Department files stored in the basement of the academy. Hundreds of boxes of old files were to be reviewed and recommended for destruction. The most notable amongst these files were those of the notorious bank robbers Bonnie and Clyde.

These were the original files including pictures and articles about them, including tons of investigative reports. I saw the pictures of the vehicles they had been driving when apprehended or what I thought at the time, slaughtered. I saw them laid out on slabs in the morgue with their bullet-riddled bodies. They were ugly people, really ugly.

What I did not see was any records at all of the JFK assassination. Not a solitary piece of paper. I guess the Feds collected almost every thing the Dallas Police Department couldn't hide.

What I did find in abundance were old test papers with answers for prior academy classes. Did I look at these in order to get an advantage once my academy classes started? No. Maybe I was turning over a new leaf since I had gotten a new lease on life.

Deputy Chief Smith asked me about this very thing one day as I was watching Class 95 tactical firearms training while having lunch in what I liked to call the backyard of the academy.

It caught me by surprise when he came and sat by me before asking me how things were going even though I had to give him a weekly report or more often on my activities and suggestions for purging the files. He asked me what I thought of the test questions and if I had any suggestions.

It felt good when I responded that I could not make any suggestions on those matters because as I had relayed in my note on the boxes to be purged, "Not for my eyes, you make the decision."

I told him as I'm sure he already knew that I did not do well in high school, but better in college courses I had taken because it's something I wanted. Whatever happened when I started the academy would be on me and not from anything I was doing in the basement.

He thanked me for my candor and seemed pleased. But it wasn't like I didn't see him everyday and report to him. There was a modicum of respect, which I had earned and deserved. I was ready for the academy to begin.

Chapter 8

Working for the Dallas Police Department

On the first day of Academy Class 96, I was elected vice president of the class. I'm sure it's because by this time I had become an "old salt" around the academy, having worked the prior class, albeit in the basement, out of sight for the most part.

The class was a whiz as I graduated second in my class with an average score of 92.059. Again, I want to emphasize, I did not review the tests I had purged although I could have done so very easily.

A couple things that I thought was humorous then, but not so much today.

First, during our firearms training, i.e. the Thompson machine gun. We had a very large tree, I believe it was an elm or cedar, at the range. A recruit would climb up the tree via steps that had been constructed. A pulley system holding a lime-filled sack would be released downward as a recruit would use the machine gun to shoot an "x" number of rounds as it descended. The sack then would be retrieved via pulley and replaced or sent back down for the next recruit.

Second, was the driving range for defensive driving which was only about a quarter of a mile, give or take for acceleration, defensive moves, and braking before leaving the parking lot of the academy. This was a hoot because if you lost control and veered right, you would collide with a chain-link fence. If you veered left, it was a ditch and then the academy walls. The fence had seen numerous repairs.

Every academy class had to attend an autopsy done at the county coroner's office. I guess this was to help prepare you for being around death. The gentleman being autopsied was a homeless person and cause of death was unknown. As a class, we hovered around the body, close enough to see everything the autopsy had to offer.

After all the measurements and preliminaries were done came the first cut, straight down the chest to the groin area. Then came the cross cuts to open up the interior, exposing the internal organs. I might add at this point this was done right after lunch. If you have never attended an autopsy, you cannot be prepared for the sickening, gross odor a dead body emits. It's worse than atrocious and more than a few classmates immediately lost their "cookies," and started vomiting.

I was not new to death, but the smell was bad. The internal organs of the deceased were pulled out and dissected. As for the brain, many cringed as the coroner used an electric saw to cut through the skull in order to expose the brain. To make a long story short, it was determined he had died of black lung disease or lung cancer.

Becoming sick at an autopsy was not going to keep you from completing the academy, but those who had lost their "cookies" were talked to afterwards. Death is a constant in police work, either from homicide victims, accident victims or suicides.

*

At this time, I still lived with my aunt, uncle and cousin in Mesquite. After graduating on Nov. 10, 1967, I was assigned to the downtown Dallas area. My training officer was Luther Dennis. Luther was about 5-foot-5 tall and 5-foot-5 wide. Hell of a nice guy and very informed on police procedures as long as it was his way. In just a couple weeks, I was getting paid on a regular schedule and the only thing I had to supply personally was my service revolver. I purchased a Smith and Wesson .38-caliber revolver and I thought I was in heaven.

My first priority after the academy was to get my own place to live. I had a few feelers out at various apartment complexes, but, because of child support payments, I had to have a roommate in order to make ends meet. I got a call from a Mr. James Brown, not the singer, who was looking for a roommate at the time. This apartment location was at 1288 N. Bagley, Apartment 10. This was one of the areas I was interested in so I called and set up a meeting with Mr. Brown.

Mr. Brown was about my age and was a vice president of loans for Dallas City Bank which was within walking distance from the apartments. He was not home much and needed an overseer for when he was gone, We seemed to kick it off and then I met the apartment owners. They were also younger people and very nice. They welcomed me as a new tenant and we signed the contract.

I had been in the apartment for just a few months when the Dallas City Bank began calling for Mr. Brown. This went on for a few days. I had been working nights and one morning after a night shift, two men dressed in suits were waiting for me along with the apartment owner's wife. They wanted to talk to me about Mr. Brown.

As our apartment was furnished, I thought Jim and I were only missing each other because of my shift, mostly nights. I also knew there were nights when he never came home.

They informed me they were with the FBI and that Mr. Brown had embezzled a considerable sum of money and securities prior to leaving Dallas. They wanted to look around his room and so I let them in. All his personal things were gone. A felony warrant was subsequently issued.

Because of my short-term relationship with Mr. Brown and the long-term embezzlements, I didn't think I was in any way a person of interest as they say.

But the totality of the incident left me in a dilemma as the location was nice, the apartment was exceptional, but expensive. It was an ideal location for me, but if I had to pay the total amount of the rent, I could not afford it. The FBI was very adamant about no one knowing their involvement for at least 90 days, so they could keep a watch on the apartment should Mr. Brown return. They were not, however, willing to keep paying one half of the rent.

*

I talked to the owners of the complex. Although it never led to anything, I should mention I was daftly in love with the manager's wife who was a former Miss Dallas winner in a beauty contest and seemed to spend a lot of time around me. Nothing ever happened, but they seemed to like me and offered me an opportunity I could not turn down.

The Dallas Black Hawks ice hockey team, a farm team of the National Hockey League's Chicago Black Hawks, had just rented a bunch of apartments in the complex for their players who, for the most part, were single and pretty rowdy. The owners would let me have a one-bedroom apartment next door to the one I was in rent free if I would provide security during their absence. I jumped at this chance as I had heard other officers were also getting discounts on their units in other complexes. It also wasn't in violation of any code of conduct at the Dallas Police Department.

The swimming pool was directly below my second-floor apartment. The pool was the landing party area for the team after their home games and these post-game affairs could get rather loud. Since this was the farm team and not the renowned Chicago Black Hawks, I felt I had a little more leeway and control of their activities.

After one of their games, the noise woke me up and I figured it had awaken other tenants as well. I got dressed and went down to the pool. I identified myself as a Dallas police officer and complex security guard. I talked to them about the noise and laid down my terms of behavior. They were very apologetic and appreciated the way I handled it and we came to terms then and there.

They supported me with free passes to their games. They also invited me to share with their women which there was an abundance. At this time, I was dating a stripper who worked at a club within walking distance. She was frequently out of town on various "assignments."

*

Back to some of my police experiences while still on probation, the first year.

Luther and I were prone to eat at the same all-night diner when on the midnight shift, or third shift. We had one particular waitress we liked and always sat in her area. One night, in the wee hours of the morning, we got a call regarding an accident, vehicle vs. tree, in the area of the diner. The vehicle had rammed the tree at a relatively high rate of speed. The female driver was not wearing a seat belt, thus went through the windshield, or at least her head had.

She was decapitated and the head had rolled under the front of the vehicle. Because I was the rookie, I had to retrieve the head. To my horror, it belonged to our favorite waitress from the diner. I know I vomited, and I pretty sure Luther also did.

Another incident involved a dead Native American (Indian) in a roach coach, a fast-food service van. When we got to the parking lot, Luther completed all his vitals and declared the person alive. He broke open an ammonia inhaler and shoved it up one nostril of our victim with no response. Luther then broke open another ammonia inhaler and shoved it up the man's other nostril. For a few seconds, there was no response, then pandemonium. It took Luther, me and four of the drivers who had reported the "dead" Indian to subdue him. He was arrested for entering a locked, secure area, even though he only wanted the heat, that cold winter night, generated from the hot water lines in the back of the vehicle.

Luther was not without a warped sense of humor. On numerous dead body calls, he would become quite a "contortionist" with our victims to surprise the ambulance units sent to pick up said dead body. Once rigor mortis sets in, Luther learned you can manipulate the arms in some very grotesque manners.

We had to write reports on every thing we did during the course of our shift. We wrote the reports and would go to the nearest fire department. All fire departments afforded us with a room and a phone. Filing a report was as simple as a telephone call. We would call a police department report line and read off our forms—i.e. Line 1: Bike Theft; Line 2: Owner; and etc., ending the report with name and badge number. No going into the office and doing reports. Everything was done via telephone to a central office where it was typed up and returned to you for your signature. Some reports weren't typed and returned, but not many.

One night or early morning, we were cruising around White Rock Lake. I was driving and Luther was finishing some reports we had yet to submit. I braked and asked Luther, "Did you see that?"

He said he hadn't as he had his head in his reports. I backed up and a young girl was standing at the edge of the water. Just standing there. Luther got out and confronted her and I saw her point to a house across from the lake. She was wearing a long white gown or dress that appeared wet.

Luther led her to my side of the patrol car and had her sit in the back seat. He then got in the passenger seat so he could face her while instructing me which house to drive to. I drove up the carport of the house and Luther said he would handle this. He went to the front door and knocked. Eventually, a light came on and an elderly female answered. The woman and Luther approached the driver's side rear door and he opened it.

While Luther was talking with the woman at the door of the house, I had busied myself looking at Luther's reports and wasn't paying a lot of attention.

Luther then said, "Ken, did you let her out?"

I couldn't comprehend what he was talking about until I turned around and there was no one there. Nothing where she should have been. The elderly woman was very affable when she said not to worry, this has happened a few times since her daughter drowned in White Rock Lake.

If we didn't want to report it, she would understand. We couldn't get out of there fast enough. We parked, took a couple of deep breaths and decided no report was a good report. I asked around and learned that a girl had indeed drowned. I also learned other sightings had been reported. There were also a couple of articles in area newspapers reporting the sightings of the young girl's spirit.

If you are wondering whether I am a believer in the after-life and so-called sightings, the answer is yes—always have been and will be. You can also probably put UFOs in this category of beliefs. Remember Payson?

*

I am writing this section in a rather disjoined way in order to touch on the highlights of my short career with the Dallas Police Department.

After about eight months partnering with Luther, I was patrolling on my own as they felt I could handle a solo unit and so did I. We worked rotating shifts, one month days, one month evenings and one month late nights. I liked the late night shifts the best because I didn't have to work traffic control in the downtown Dallas area.

*

While with Dallas police, I was involved in three accidents, all in departmental vehicles, and two the result of icy conditions.

The first occurred while I was still working with Luther. I was stopped at a stop sign on a side street in the dead of winter. Black ice was covering the roads when a female driver of a vehicle, coming from my left, was traveling at a speed much too fast for the icy conditions. The woman, unfortunately, tried to make a right turn. I knew if I sat still her vehicle would ram the driver's door of my fully-marked patrol car. I tried going forward, but basically just spun my wheels. However, I did get far enough forward where she impacted the rear quarter panel, instead of the driver's door, of my police cruiser.

The second occurred in the parking garage at the main downtown police precinct. I want to elaborate a bit about this parking structure. If anyone remembers or has seen pictures of Jack Ruby shooting Lee Harvey Oswald, this was our entrance and exit to the holding facilities located at the basement level of the station.

To enter, you would drive down a fairly steep ramp past the doors where Oswald was shot. This was our parking area. Normally, you parked pretty close to each other. One of our regulations was that when you started and ended your shift and if you had hauled a prisoner, you were required to check under the rear seat for contraband—knives, guns, dope etc., anything that may have been stuffed behind the seat by the prisoner. I have a pretty cool collection of knives and even a set of brass knuckles.

I had pulled my marked vehicle out of the parking place far enough to open the rear door in order to access and lift the back seat to conduct my cursory inspection. I was doing so when I heard a horn blaring. When I looked up, I saw a marked unit sliding down the ramp right at me. Remember black ice? Because of black ice, the ramp was quite slippery and within seconds, we had two police cars "conjugally" united. Speed was not a factor in this one and the impact was minor. No injuries, but mountains of paperwork awaited.

However, due to the shortage of marked police vehicles, it was decided I could continue on and submit the vehicle for repairs at the end of my shift. Unbeknownst to me at the time, my patrol car would endure a lot more damage by the end of my shift.

*

Here's how this story unfolds.

While on patrol later that morning, dispatch issued a report reference an armed robbery in my area at a Cabell's, a convenience store similar to today's 7-Eleven and Circle K. The dispatcher also issued descriptions of the suspect and his vehicle.

I didn't feel safe driving an already damaged vehicle, but as luck would have it, a vehicle matching the description and its occupant passed by my location. I pulled out and got close enough to get a license plate number. I called it in and asked for assistance. The dispatcher said not to expect a quick backup response as most units were working accidents.

About this time, the driver of the suspect vehicle had gotten quite nervous with me on his tail and decided to bolt. The chase was on.

Although I can't say it was high speed, it was exciting. As we approached a "T" intersection with no traffic to speak of, it became apparent we weren't going to stop. He made the left turn. Unfortunately, I did not. I slid hard into the curb which caught both my right front and rear tires, causing my vehicle to roll. After rolling once, my vehicle ended up on all four wheels again, but the car was not running.

Upon coming to rest, I noticed the suspect's vehicle had made the next right and was heading towards a nearby neighborhood bar to my right. I let dispatch know I would be out of my vehicle in foot pursuit of the suspect, possibly going into Del's bar. It could have been Delbert's, but I knew it to be a quiet neighborhood bar that never gave us any trouble.

I ran as fast as possible across a small field in time to see the suspect exit his vehicle and head for the bar. The bar's door was shut, but just as he opened it two people rolled inside—me and the suspect I had tackled. As we scrambled to get up, I pulled my S&W .38-caliber revolver and put it to the suspect's head when we were both basically in a sitting position. There wasn't many people in the bar nor was there any other cops, at least for a few seconds. My backup was there, however, before I could blink twice.

The suspect was arrested and taken away by our robbery unit detectives. Someone drove me back to my vehicle which still didn't have a lot of visible damage, but let the paperwork begin.

One shift, I was partnered with a young black officer about my age. We were working a high offense area for burglaries and robberies. I was driving as we pulled up to a bar pretty much by itself in a field, something similar to Delbert's. It was in the wee hours of the morning and at this time all bars are supposed to be closed and locked. After reaching the building, we started checking doors making sure they were locked. As I looked through the front window, I noticed a pool table with a bag lying on it along with cigarettes and change.

The front-door hasp and lock seemed to be OK so I had my partner walk the perimeter to see if there were any windows broken or any other signs of entry. As he was doing this, I decided to check the front door again. I gently pushed against it and to my surprise it opened. I put my head just inside the door to see if there was any movement. Just to my left, I heard something hit the floor and slide away.

After jumping back, I called my partner and then radioed for backup. We then decided to enter the establishment without backup. As I pushed open the door, a tall thin black male appeared from behind the doors with his hands raised. We would later learn that this individual was a three-time loser. He could have killed me and received nothing more than a life sentence. As he told me while we were waiting for transport that when I stuck my head inside the door, he saw my hat and badge and knew I was a cop.

He dropped his gun and kicked it into the kitchen area where it was eventually recovered under a refrigerator. It was an old break-down single shot revolver. The bullet in it was as crusted as the pistol itself. I still wonder even today if it would have worked had he decided to pull the trigger.

I guess he just didn't want to kill a cop which was unusual because such a misdeed would have gotten him much more respect in prison where he would remain the remainder of his life.

*

A while later, I was placed on what I thought would be a "kick-ass" detail. I was to lie in ambush for parkers, neckers, etc. at a point on Trinity Lake in east Dallas. We had received complaints about littering, loud noises, etc. from residents of a new residential sub-development. I was issued an unmarked vehicle, but still had to be in full uniform. The two of us would work about two to three miles from each other.

The first few nights we ran off a few romantic souls, but there were no really loud noises or parties. I think it was on the third night that I observed a vehicle pulling into an area extremely close to the river. Just after it stopped, the driver turned off the vehicle's lights. I was parked about 40 yards away at an angle away from the river. I couldn't see into the vehicle that had just arrived so I waited a few minutes before exiting my vehicle to sneak toward some low trees between me and the suspicious car.

I had only been in position for a few minutes when the driver's door opened. The male walked around to the passenger side, opened the door, reached in and pulled the passenger out. The passenger's body, a female, was limp. It was like she was asleep or drugged or both. Anyway, he pulled her from the seat began dragging her towards the nearby river.

He had to pass within touching distance of me and was almost to the lake when I stepped out and identified myself as a Dallas police officer. While holding onto the limp body, he froze. I shined my flashlight on him and when I pointed the flashlight down to her, I noticed she had a "third" eye, right in the center of her forehead, about the circumference of a bullet.

Very little blood had escaped the wound where she had been fatally shot right between the eyes. Now, it doesn't take a mental giant to know what's happening here, he was about to dump her body into the river for the fish and other carrion-feeding animals to dine on.

*

Back to my social life. The social part was going very well, but my stripper was spending all her time traveling, mostly to Las Vegas where she was contemplating moving. My Dallas Black Hawk friends seemed to have other interests besides hockey and girls and that was gambling.

I had been invited to some of their social gatherings, gambling parties, all of which seemed to get rather rowdy and not a place I needed to be. After a few of these sessions, I offered a proposal. Those who wanted to gamble—poker, black jack etc. and enjoy quiet drinks while they did so—I would organize a gathering once a week in my apartment. I would furnish the beverages, food (pizza and subs) and I would be the table.

I would pull 25 cents from each hand dealt and I would be the dealer. I also would let them know what games were going on and if they had more than seven players, I would hire a second dealer, which was usually a good friend of mine, James Whiteley also a Dallas police officer.

These games went along without incident. Some nights, when my stripper girlfriend was in town, we would have live, hands-off, entertainment.

My social life was going nowhere until a female friend of mine in the complex invited me to meet Patricia Glasscock, a girlfriend of hers who had just drove in from Michigan shortly after breaking up with her fiancée.

Patricia was only going to stay a few days before moving on to Temple, TX, where her family was. At least, that was her plan. Shortly after meeting Patricia, I was assigned to a downtown walking beat in a different precinct area. This was quite a drive in my Carmen Ghia from my apartment. Consequently, I decided to relocate to a different apartment closer to my beat area. I was given a written referral from my apartment owners to present to the owners of the new complex I was looking at with Pat. Yeah, I had turned up the charm and not only did she stay in the Dallas area, she even was going to move in with me at the new complex.

I was given a 50-percent reduced rate for a real nice two-bedroom apartment and a part-time job as a security officer. The security part was simply driving or walking the parking area of the complex, in or out of uniform—a piece of cake.

The walking beat basically was the main drag in the downtown area where the bars, restaurants and movie theaters were located. While in uniform, I never paid for a meal, coffee or anything. When I was off duty and showed my badge in my beat area, I couldn't pay for anything—movies, drinks, dinner or whatever. It was free. I can't say I was comfortable with this and normally I left rather large tips, but it was what it was.

*

I only worked this assignment a short time as a new unit, new concept for policing, was being implemented by the department. In implementing this program, the department was looking for six sergeants, six dog handlers and 24 of the best officers Dallas police had to offer. Their verbiage, not mine.

It was to be called the shotgun squad and each unit would be comprised of one sergeant, a dog handler and four officers. We were to patrol high-offense areas as a squad and each area was to be a square mile. Our shift would be from 7 p.m. to 3 a.m. or later. Prior to embarking on this assignment, we were required to go through two weeks of tactical training and then we would be assigned unmarked cars.

I applied and was accepted as only the "elites" were chosen. I was assigned to the Oak Cliff area of Dallas which was primarily Blacks and

Hispanics with a high rate of crime from homicides to armed robberies to burglaries. You name it and it was going on in Oak Cliff.

We drove older unmarked cars with all insignias and top lights removed. Otherwise, they were regular beat vehicles. We wore full police uniforms except for hats. Also, always, always, had to carry our shotguns in our laps, instead of in the front seat mount. Not having a shotgun in your lap was grounds for immediate transfer if caught by your sergeant or higher authority.

We worked all holidays and weekends. On major holidays and some weekends, we would encamp so to speak in liquor stores and area Cabell stores. We would sit in the refrigerated coolers wearing parkas that were supplied to us. In case of an armed robbery, we were instructed to come out shooting, with the shotgun of course, and ask questions later. The coolers had one-way windows which overlooked the cash registers. The clerks on duty had been notified to hit the floor after giving the money to the bad guy.

The sequence of events that happened to me while on this squad are not in order, but I want to relate an event that happened to me, that could have went a completely different way.

Our sergeant would drive us to our locations where we sometimes would set up until 3 in the morning. This was our so-called unmarked vehicle which would not be in the parking area for hours on end.

On this particular night, Dec. 8, 1968, I was assigned a stakeout at a Cabell store with my partner, Officer Floyd A. Knight, assigned to the liquor store right next door. We were told that under no circumstances were we to leave our stations unless it was to shoot an armed robber.

It was well into the shift when I heard what I thought was a gunshot, but couldn't really tell where it had come from. About an hour later, my sergeant entered the store and walked directly back to the cooler area. My partner, Officer Knight, had just been killed at the liquor store and the investigation was under way. They did have a description of the shooter, but I had not seen him in the store.

From what information provided by the liquor store clerk, she was approached at the counter by the suspect who told her this was a robbery. He then had her go with him to the cooler. After opening the cooler door, he shoved her down. She said she then heard a shot. It is still unknown what my partner was doing. He was shot under the chin the bullet lodging in his brain. He was only 23.

A description of the suspect was put out, but it was a few days later when it was determined the suspect had already been arrested the night of the shooting by Dallas County sheriff's deputies for DWI. So he was already in jail by the time we had a description of the suspect. Such great communications amongst agencies. The cop killer eventually got a life sentence for killing Officer Knight.

*

We were not supposed to write citations for traffic offenses, but I had been following this vehicle, driven by a black male, for a while. After he busted about every stop sign in my area, I pulled him over and was talking to him when I heard something whiz by my head followed by a loud ping in the top window panel of his vehicle.

I immediately ran to the passenger side of my vehicle where my radio was and called for backup. Within a minute, numerous units responded, including a sergeant and dog handler. The sergeant made the deduction that the shot had come from the top floor of a nearby building, directly across the street from our location.

A 13-year-old black male was taken from the roof of the building as well as a .22-caliber rifle. He just wanted to kill a cop. Had the old black man in the vehicle led me into an ambush or was this just random? I will never know.

A few weeks later, I was working an area where there had been a increasing amount of burglaries. In the wee hours of the morning, I was cruising past a stand-alone laundromat, free of any adjoining buildings. As was the norm, I was doing maybe 5 mph with no lights on when I decided to check the rear of the building. The solid glass door had been busted inward. I exited my vehicle, left my shotgun on the seat and shined my flashlight, held an arm length away from by body, into the interior of the building.

I had already called in the situation, told them I would check the situation and report back. I did not see anything within the laundromat and was thinking that this would just be a report about a missed burglar. In situations like this, we called the owner. He or she would then come to the scene and together we would assess the damages inside and document the items stolen or missing.

All of a sudden, I heard a loud sound of breaking glass before seeing an individual run out the building, going left. I ran to the left of the building, actually only a few feet from the broken door, and saw the person running. I yelled for him to stop which only caused him to speed up.

I pulled my trusty .38-caliber Smith and Wesson and leveled it on him. My first shot missed, but I heard something loud shatter. My second shot, I was aiming at his head, struck home and he went down. My backup was coming and I was starting to shake a bit. I advised that the subject was down just on the other side of the Laundromat near the street.

My squad was there and had the subject lit up with the headlights of their vehicles. As I approached the subject, he got up on his hands and knees and started shaking his head. He appeared to be in his teens. Two of my squad members jumped on him and he was handcuffed. He was a 16-year-old black male. My bullet went in above his left temple and exited out the top of his head, never penetrating the skull.

The bleeding was ferocious as it is with all head wounds, but no other damage. As per the doctor at the hospital, this kid was living a charmed life. I told my sergeant about my first round and the shattering I had heard. We eventually learned the bullet had went through a phone booth, impacting the coin holder before flattening out.

*

Back to my social life.

I married Patricia Jeanne Glasscock in a ceremony at a Catholic church in Temple, TX, on June 22, 1968. The next few months were rather uneventful. In December, Pat and I decided to fly to Arizona so she could meet my family. My brother had a 1968 Datsun (today's Nissan) 1600 sports convertible that he was going to sell. I was still driving my Volkswagen Carmen Ghia and if I liked his Datsun, I would buy it.

Everything went fine the first day home. I only took a week's vacation because the busy time for my squad, Christmas, was approaching and I wanted to be back in time for the action.

I loved the Datsun and bought it. I signed the papers and Ron said he would file them. The same day I signed the papers, Pat and I met up with John Allen and his girlfriend. We decided to have a picnic at Canyon Lake. There was a nice, paved winding road getting to the lake presenting an opportunity to really test my new car.

John and I were in the Datsun with the girls following, with the beer and food, in his brand new Volkswagen Beetle.

I was really getting a feel for the Datsun when I entered a curve a bit too fast, hit some gravel on the road and went into the ditch just before I would have impacted with a rock culvert. I did some major damage to the undercarriage. After a casual inspection, I knew it would not be drivable. The front wheels were sitting kind of funny, sprawled out.

We were only a couple miles from the lake and I knew they had phones and a concession stand there. The girls went ahead and called the Highway Patrol. We had an hour wait or so before the patrolman would get there giving John and I ample time to concoct a story, a lie, that would be believable, maybe.

The patrolman took the report about the phantom vehicle that had come around the curve somewhat on my side of the road. As I tried my best to avoid it, I hit the gravel and it took me into the culvert. No, I had not been speeding. I actually was doing a little over 60 mph in a 30-mph zone, but he really didn't need to know that. I did not get a citation, but I did deserve at least a warning.

The vehicle was going to be towed. We were really close to the lake and somewhat hungry so we decided it was time for a beer or two. We loaded into John's new car with John and I in the backseat, providing security for the cool chests on our laps. The girls were not happy campers at this point and they wanted to go home. There was some arguing going on and not much attention paid to the road. As we rounded the last curve before you could see the lake, we were not totally in the right lane when we saw an approaching van.

Two crashes within a period of hours, who would have thought, and we hadn't even cracked open a beer. John's VW was totaled. The van had some damage, but no injuries in either vehicles. "God Is Great."

I called Ron and told him what happened. He got a vehicle to come get all of us. The same Highway Patrol officer investigated and wrote John's girl friend a citation. His vehicle was towed to the same place as my vehicle had been. The girls, of course, were much beyond livid.

Ron had not filed the paperwork for the sale of the Datsun and was agreeable to changing the date of sale as his insurance would pay for the repairs to the Datsun. I paid all insurance deductibles as I was an approved driver thus his rates would not increase.

It was going to be a while before the repairs would be completed which meant I would not be back at work in time. I called my sergeant and commander while they were conducting a briefing and explained the situation. They agreed to give me a few additional days off.

*

When I reported back to work almost a week later, I had been conditionally terminated. Fired!!!! I appealed this and won when several of the officers at the squad briefing testified that they had heard my supervisors grant me additional days off.

On March 10, 1969, I resigned from the Dallas Police Department to go into business with my parents. My brother and Dad had built the small lawn business into a full-fledged landscaping company, third largest in the valley area. They needed help and I knew my career with the Dallas Police Department was going nowhere.

*

Before leaving the subject of Dallas, I should say something about the Kennedy assassination, Lee Harvey Oswald, Jack Ruby and 1963.

These are not first-hand accounts, but a much of this information comes from my cousin, Christine who recruited me to the Dallas Police Department. The rest is from numerous books written on the shooting or assassination.

In 1963 and prior, Dallas was a hateful, spiteful place. Confederate flags flew right-side up while U.S. flags flew upside down.

The Oswalds lived at 214 W. Neely Street in the Oak Cliff Section in an upstairs apartment. At the time, this was a terrible area—transients, run down homes with no grass front or back yards, just weeds penetrating through God's natural dirt. It was not much better when I was there a few years later.

Jack Ruby owned the Carousel Club, located just west of the downtown police station. Just about everyone at the police department had at least a passing acquaintance with him. He handed out free passes to his club and bought all the cops entering the premises free drinks.

It is believed Oswald shot the president after setting up a sniper's nest on the 6th floor of the Texas School Book Depository on the southeast corner on Elm Street in Dealy Plaza.

After the assassination of President Kennedy and Lee Harvey Oswald's capture, Ruby arrived at the police department on Saturday, Nov. 23,1963, with a concealed .38 Colt Cobra on his person. He fully intended to shoot Oswald that day, but the room was too crowded so he gave up.

The next day, Sunday, late in the morning, Ruby wandered down to the police department again, believing Oswald would have already been transferred to the county holding area. Ruby was surprised to see a big crowd of reporters and other people. He hurried into the garage area where he said hello to some cops who allowed him to walk down the ramp toward the double doors between the jail and garage.

A few minutes later, a national television audience watched as Ruby calmly walked up to Oswald and shot him in the stomach, igniting a series of assassination conspiracy theories that remain rampant today. Oswald died at Parkland Memorial Hospital shortly thereafter. Ironically, it was the same hospital where the 35th president of the United States was taken and where he was pronounced dead at about 1 p.m. Nov. 22, 1963. Oswald's last breath came 48 hours and 45 minutes later at 1:45 p.m., Nov. 24, 1963.

Chapter 9

Post Dallas, Prior to DPS

My father, mother and brother had built a small lawn service business into the third largest landscaping business in the valley area. Ronnie did not want a partnership in the business and was satisfied as a working supervisor. However, I bought into a 50/50 partnership with my parents.

Pat and I purchased an 8x35-foot trailer house and moved it onto my parents 5-acre lot on Signal Butte Road, just east of Mesa. It wasn't a large trailer, but adequate as we took most of our meals at my parent's house, maybe 100 feet away.

The business had numerous contracts with new home builders for landscaping and planting. Mastercraft Homes was one of our largest contracts and Dad was also bidding on remodel projects, swimming pools, as well as some commercial projects.

I was paying for my partnership out of my wages. We were getting tractor-trailer loads of plants out of California and I thought with some more help, they already had the land, we could grow most of what we needed ourselves. So we started a nursery and eventually we were selling our products to both retailers and wholesalers.

Finding and keeping good help was practically impossible. The job was a six, sometimes seven, days—a-week endeavor. Our social life was non-existent. Hell, my best friend John Allen thought we had moved. I had two crews going, leaving one individual in charge while I was at another site. One day after work, I decided to stop and have a beer with John at a pub close to the construction site.

The guy I left to finish the house we were working on was going to finish then load the tractor behind the dump truck and take it to our property on Signal Butte Road. This was our start-and-stop point each day. The workers all reported there. He had to call Dad because the battery on the dump truck was dead and there was no way we could jump it.

As Dad was responding to the problem, he saw my Ford pickup parked in the bar parking lot. He went to the site and got things right. When he came back by the bar, I was still there. When he entered and saw me sitting with John, he absolutely lost it. Did I mention neither he nor Mom liked John and that both of them were on the wagon and not drinking alcohol at all? I had probably just started my second beer when he came in.

I was driving my own personal pickup and would in no way drive while under the influence. I could not convince Dad I was not camped out at the bar all day. We took the argument home where I had to stew while driving home.

Before I got home, Dad had convinced everyone I was drunk, been in a bar all day and shouldn't be driving, etc., etc. Everyone started unloading on me when I noticed the guy I had left in charge was walking to his car. I asked for his help, took him inside and asked him one question. "How long had I left before you called Dad?" He said, "probably 10 to 15 minutes," as he was cleaning up the site to take off.

This cooled the situation somewhat and my claim of two beers also sounded about right to Mom. Dad was a little harder to work with and proclaimed I should have stayed at the site until things were cleared and everyone was gone. He was right. I was wrong until he said I'll give you one more chance.

I looked at him and said that I thought we were partners. He stated not yet because I hadn't fully bought into the partnership and the way I was going, I wouldn't make it. That was it. I needed to move on so I asked my parents if Pat and I could stay in our trailer on their property for at least 30 days while I looked for another job. I let them know that they were probably right and they had enough personnel to choose a good supervisor. The didn't really need me because I had no intention of changing my ways.

*

Revlon Cosmetics was hiring and I applied for a position as a line mechanic. I took the test and got the highest score ever at that time. I was hired immediately. Pretty good pay with good benefits.

My job at Revlon was pretty interesting. I set up various high-speed fittings and assembly lines for products such as Aquamarine shampoo and conditioner, Flex Balsam and various after-shave and colognes, Norell perfumes and others. I met some life-long friends such as Richard and Bobby Hubbard while working there. Sometimes, I supervised 20 to 25 people working on the lines. I feel I did an exceptional job while working there some four years and three months.

At Revlon, I also was elected as a union steward and met with management on numerous occasions, including contract negotiations. The days were rather long, at least 10 hours, and sometimes I had to work Saturdays. I had to come in an hour early to set up my line and stay an hour later to clean up.

Pat and I moved our trailer to a trailer park at 3437 W. Buckeye Road, the Lazy T Park. We stayed there for a few months before purchasing a home at 821 W. Paseo in South Phoenix, just north of the Phoenix Police Department Academy.

Within a few months of purchasing the house on Paseo, which was in my name only because Pat didn't have a work or credit history plus she didn't want her name on the title, Pat got a job at Arizona Feed and Seed Co. in order to have something to do as I was working long hours.

We were not having a lot of problems, but what we were having seemed to stem around John Allen and me doing things together. She was invited to be with us, but she didn't like him or his wife. As I had told my parents earlier, I informed her, I did not intend to change.

In August 1971, I became worried about her one evening and called her work place. The night watchman was the only one there and I told him I was worried about Pat because she should have been home by now. He said he didn't even know she was married, but he knew the bar she and her friends hung out at.

After hanging up, I drove to the bar on South Central. She was sitting in a booth next to a guy, who as it turned out was a driver for Arizona Feed and Seed. She really didn't look surprised to see me. I was in a fighting mood, but quickly calmed myself down. It was early evening, probably around 7 p.m. when I told her if she wasn't home by midnight, her stuff would be boxed and sitting outside. She wasn't and it was.

I started packing her things as soon as I got back home. I used all the boxes I could find at the house and then I went to the 7-11 at the corner of 7th Avenue and Dobson and got some more out of their dumpster.

Just about anything I could think of hers went into the boxes with her clothes on top. I wasn't very good at folding her clothes, but I did try. While packing, I had a few beers from a six-pack I had purchased at the 7-11. Hell, I had to have some reason to spend money there if I was going to take their boxes.

The next morning when I looked outside, the boxes of clothes, etc., were gone. But something in the driveway was still there—her 1965 Ford Mustang convertible. No note, nothing. The keys to the Mustang were not in view, but I already had a set of my own.

I filed for divorce on Aug. 13, 1971. I claimed the house as my own personal property and all of its contents which I had to document. As an afterthought, I claimed her Mustang. The lawyer looked at me like I was from another planet. We decided it had been abandoned at the time she recovered her belongings and included it as abandoned property. I was granted an uncontested divorce on Oct. 7, 1971. The settlement included the Mustang.

*

In January 1972, through my good friend, John Allen, I met my soul mate. I use that term because if I had not met Beth Ellen Kindred when I did, I would not be writing this. I'd probably be in prison or dead. John was dating a friend of Beth's, Bonnie Shideler. He knew I was in a downward spiral funk and asked me to at least ask Beth out. Beth was married at the time, but separated from her husband. She also had a 5-year-old son, Travis.

I asked her to a movie and a drink. We talked, but really had nothing in common. She told me about her marriage, her son and her being a teacher in Avondale. I think I told her a little about myself. Before I realized it, I knew I had to see her again. I actually wanted to meet her son and see where this might go. A few days later, I had them over to my house. Her son was completely the opposite of what I expected. I guess I was thinking of a little rug rat who had to have his way with everything.

I knocked his tooth out that day. I guess that showed him who was boss. No, I simply threw a football up high and he unfortunately caught it with his face, Well, I knew this was probably our last date as I had man-handled her son. I don't remember if I asked him if he believed in the tooth fairy.

After meeting Beth, times were really good for me around that time and I remember waiting for Beth's calls and to call her.

*

Sometime during this romantic interlude, I was playing softball for the Revlon team. I hit a ball and started to run to first base and felt a rip in my right groin area. I went to the emergency room and was diagnosed with a hernia in my right groin area. I elected for immediate surgery as I was already at the hospital.

Within a couple hours of surgery and being located in my own room, I decided I felt good enough to leave and go home. Narcotics are great. I dressed, went down to my vehicle and was driving home oblivious to all kinds of red lights behind me. At some point in time, I slid sideways, stopping just before hitting a concrete barrier at 24th Street and the Salt River bottom. Those policemen "pursuing" me weren't very happy with me.

I remember being pulled from my 1600 Datsun convertible and handcuffed. Because of pain in my groin area, I was taken to the hospital to be checked out. I was also bleeding through my pants where I had broken the stitches. I was charged with DWI, pending toxic results. I was not drinking, but was high on pain killers of some sort and they were rapidly wearing off.

I was admitted back into the hospital and remained strapped in my bed for the next 24 hours. I was never charged with escape or DWI or anything. Being stupid was not a crime at the time, or I would have been charged.

*

Beth and my relationship continued to the point where and when and if she ever got divorced, I would be there for her. Towards the end of 1972, our relationship had progressed to a point where we were looking for a new home for when we got married. We chose a new Continental built home at 7520 W. Cambridge, just south of Thomas

Road. We had not moved in together as I was maintaining the residence in south Phoenix when Beth and Travis moved into the house on West Cambridge.

Beth and I were married on Nov. 17, 1972. We were married at Brooks Memorial United Methodist Church by the Rev. Dennis Ramsey. Beth's sister stood for her and a co-worker from Revlon and a great friend, Richard Allyn Hubbard, was my best man. I was baptized at this church about a month earlier on Oct. 15, 1972.

A side note on this church. Today this church is now Brooks Mortuary. Is there a message here?

*

I resigned from Revlon in November, 1973, to go into a franchise restaurant business, "The Golden Skone Sandwich Shop." Ron had been operating one quite successfully in the Mesa area and I was to open mine at McDowell and Scottsdale Roads in Tempe.

Within a couple weeks of completion and opening, I was at the point where I needed to get my food handler's permit. I had to go to the Maricopa County Health Services to get my chest x-ray which was a requirement for the permit. I remember walking into the lab in perfectly good health, so I thought. I felt great. I had the x-ray taken and was told the results would take awhile and they would call with the results.

That afternoon, I received a phone call from the Health Services Division wanting to know who my personal doctor was and advised me the results from the x-ray would be sent to him immediately. I also was told to go see my doctor ASAP.

I called my doctor and made an appointment. The doctor had already seen the x-rays and advised me to go straight to Good Samaritan Hospital where I would see a Dr. Lewis Brown. I had a collapsed lung and needed to have an emergency pneumothorax.

I went to Good Sam with Beth and Travis. Dr. Brown was there and he immediately had another x-ray done on my chest. My lung was collapsing so fast that the doctor did not even wait for me to get a local anesthesia to deaden the area. In an attempt to save my lung, he performed the pneumothorax by inserting a large stainless steel hollow rod, with a rubber tube inside it, into my chest cavity.

I remember he had to get onto the gurney with me in order to get enough leverage to insert the rod through my chest just to the left side of my sternum. This, I was told, was to relieve the air that was escaping from my left lung into my chest cavity causing my lung to collapse.

I remember lying in John C. Lincoln for about five days thinking I would die if they could not save the lung. I didn't know you could live with only one lung.

The procedure worked by taking the captured air out of my chest cavity thus allowing my lung to inflate. When it was time to extract the rod and tube, the doctor told me I might have a some trouble getting my breath. I wasn't prepared for what happened next.

The doctor withdrew the rod and what seemed to be an accompanying several yards of tubing. I was fighting for breath. I couldn't breath and thought I would pass out. It was very painful. I finally caught my breath and realized there was a God. My lung had been saved.

There was no explanation why my lung collapsed other than the possibility of the bursting of a cyst or other weak spot in the lung. The doctor advised me that if I hadn't been treated at that precise time, within minutes my lung would have folded onto itself and the sticky fibrous materials within the lung would have reacted as Velcro, eliminating any chance of recovering it.

*

Because I was laid up for a few weeks, I was going to miss the opening of my own restaurant. Ron volunteered to let his manager run his shop, he would come over and open mine. This brought into play some of the fine print of the contract agreement between the Golden Skone owners and myself. The store had to be opened by a certain date and I had to be the opener/operator or I would forfeit my franchise. The owners, the Smiths, would not authorize Ron to open my store.

This began a lengthy lawsuit in which I eventually prevailed with an out-of-court settlement for the return of all of my franchise expenses. I had received less than half of my investment when the Smiths filed for bankruptcy. I was left holding the bag so to speak.

The Smiths ultimately won out on the opening of my store. They had told me on many occasions that they wish they had kept it as a company store, not franchised, because of its nearby location to Arizona State University and the thousands of potentially young customers.

*

Sometime during my recuperation, Beth, Travis and I had moved in together and things were good. Beth worked as a first grade teacher in Avondale and Travis was going to school in Avondale. She had extremely long days and was taking care of me when she was home.

Jennifer Lynn Haw was born on Nov. 12, 1974, at 1:53 a.m. at St. Joseph's Hospital, Phoenix. Beth went to the hospital early on Nov. 11 and was having a long labor. I was going to school at the time and was studying for tests while waiting at the hospital. Dr. Kirchner came out about midnight and told me Beth was OK, but she would not be having the baby that day. I did not even think about it at the time, but thought Beth was having a false labor and I would have to bring her back later. It wasn't more than a couple hours later when Dr. Kirchner returned to tell me Beth and our daughter were doing well. Another gift from God.

*

During most of my time with Revlon and the Golden Skone fiasco, I had served as a weekend warrior with the 161st as a National Guardsman. I had a chance in August 1974 to become a full-time technician for the National Guard. I would be doing the same thing as I had done in my five years of active duty, Base Supply—technical order compliance (TOC) for refueling a fleet of C135's.

My supervisor was Sgt. Art Denkler. I quickly promoted to E-5 as a staff sergeant as my work reports were superior. But I was not happy sitting behind a desk reviewing material or ordering parts for TOC maintenance, an annual maintenance all the refueling birds had to undergo.

My previous military experience helped tremendously as I already knew how to correspond with the various issuing agencies and how to research items in the tech books. While on this job, I initiated a new card filing system and location system for the numerous manuals we used. I continued to feel I was becoming stagnated especially when it became apparent that promotions were practically nil in my field.

On several occasions, I had told Beth about my Dallas police times and experiences. I also had told her I would never return to any type of police work. Ha, ha!!

It also was around this time that I decided to never let anything get in the way of my relationship with Beth, even if I had to start distancing myself from several of my long-time friends, including John Allen.

Les Miller, Terry O'Connor, Me, James Heimer
and Marvin Whittier

Haw's caravan 1940's

Camp set up Haw's and Brown's

Grandma and Grandpa Haw

Dad, Maggie, Aubrey, Valle, Earnest and Reba (the Haw's)

Grandma and Grandpa Brown (Moms parents)

Mom and Dad's wedding photo

Mom, Dad and I (march 1945)

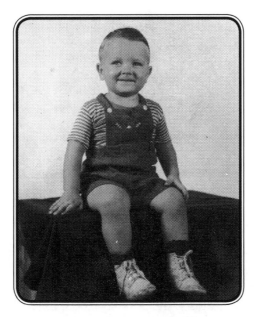

Me (unknown year)

Grandpa Brown and Mom (1949 mercury)

Mom and Dad (1950 mercury)

Cotton scales right side is Aunt Reba

Queen Creek Tunnel (Superior, Az.)

Sunflower General Store (Stubby servicing a vehicle)

Ron and I with Randolph Scott (Jamestown, Ca.)

Ron and I (First day of school)

House on Southern Ave. Mesa, Az.

House at 1362 W. 6th Ave. Mesa, Az.
Mom sitting on planter box (1962)

Christine Haw and I

Mom, Ron, Dad and I (1962)

Les Miller, Terry O'Connor, Ron, Me, James Heimer,
and Marvin Whittier (1962)

Me and Marvin Whittier (1962 Senior Prom)

Me and Al Bishop, my fight manager (1962)

U.S.Air Force photo (1962)

John Allen with his wrecked VW bug

Dad circa 1940

Great Grandmother Callie Ward
(Robert lee Haw's mother)

Chapter 10

The Arizona Department of Public Safety

History of the Arizona Department of Public Safety

Executive order 69-3 mandated the establishment of the Arizona Department of Public Safety, effective July 1, 1969. The governor was Jack Williams while Wesley Bolin was the secretary of state.

Arizona Highway Patrol Superintendent James J. Hegarty was appointed the first director of the newly-formed department. The formation of the Arizona Department of Public Safety brought together three existing state police agencies: Arizona Highway Patrol, Department of Liquor License Enforcement Division and the Department of Law Narcotics Division. DPS also assumed responsibility for the state crime laboratory, law enforcement training and the Criminal Identification Section.

The primary responsibility of DPS was upon request to supplement local police agencies that did not have necessary resources to provide a professional level of services desired by the citizens of Arizona. Prior to the formation of DPS, there were no first-class records or central filing systems. Many criminal records were kept by trustees within the state prison. See a problem here?

Prior to the formation of DPS, training was minimal for law enforcement officers, especially on the local level. Funding simply wasn't available to justify "cop trainers." But, even if the funding had been available, there weren't enough people qualified in this area to work throughout the state.

Progressive people at the state level agreed with the DPS bill. However, an almost immediate cry of "State Police" sprang to the forefront. It also didn't help when Sen. John Conlan, the prime mover for the bill, told *The Arizona Republic*, the largest daily newspaper in the state, "we don't have a state police now, but we may evolve toward it." He added the newly-formed law enforcement agency had the authority to investigate anything and everything.

In the very early stages of DPS, Phoenix Police Chief Lawrence Wetzel said he saw a unique capacity of DPS to cross jurisdictional lines to be effective in fighting organized crime, narcotics and gambling. In today's world, the Department has the ability and resources to conduct all of these types of investigations.

The Department also investigates police corruption upon request and has its narcotics and liquor units at various state and county activities.

During its early years of formation, DPS employed 800 men and women both sworn and civilian. Today, there are about 2,000 sworn and civilian employees. During its first year of existence, DPS also introduced an air medical evacuation program which still exists today with helicopters stationed in Phoenix, Tucson, Flagstaff and Kingman.

Since its inception, the Department has had nine directors, including one acting director. The directors in order are: James J. Hegarty, Lloyd Robertson (acting), Vernon Hoy, Ralph T. Milstead, F.J. "Rick" Ayars, Joe Albo, Dennis Garrett, Roger Vanderpool and Robert Halliday. The director is appointed to a five-year term by the governor. The appointment is confirmed by the state senate.

If it had not been for the foresight of the legislators, both Republican and Democrat, and their willingness to work with each other in 1967 and 1968, Executive Order 69-3 would not have survived.

After more than 40 years of service, the Department has remained the top law enforcement agency in the state and among the best in the country. Throughout its history, the Department has been in the forefront of such progressive programs as DNA, automated fingerprint systems and traffic safety.

*

With that said, let's get on with my life at the Arizona Department of Public Safety.

Although I had said I'd never go back to police work, I began having second thoughts as I reviewed my career choices. Simply put, I didn't see much of a future with the military or Revlon, so I turned my attention to the Phoenix Police Department and the Arizona Department of Public Safety as both were hiring.

I applied for the DPS Highway Patrol academy in June 1975. I went through a written examination, physical agility test and oral interview. After successfully completing this, I was placed on a waiting list. Within weeks, I had a home interview. An officer came to my house and talked to my wife, Beth, and I about the Department. I was accepted to begin the academy on Aug. 10, 1975.

I arrived at the DPS Training Academy bright and early that August morning. I soon learned the next 18 weeks were going to involve all my mental as well as physical abilities. During the academy, we studied accident investigation; Arizona geography, city government and history; communications, oral and written; counseling techniques; defensive and pursuit driving; firearms maintenance and training; first aid; various general police subjects; Breathalyzer school; judicial, legislative and executive forms of government; criminal law; public relations; report writing; basic math; and extensive traffic accident-related math, physical training.

Along with the classroom work, we spent many hours in the field working accident problems, completing investigative reports and drawing scale diagrams.

*

During my first 14 months on the road, I investigated numerous accidents and made numerous felony and misdemeanor arrests. Two months after working the road, I was involved in a major traffic accident which killed one person and critically injured another seven people.

This probably was the most traumatic experience in my life and one, in which for the grace of God, I wouldn't be writing about. I was subsequently awarded the Valor Award, the highest award offered by the Department, on May 28, 1976. I also received the Rotary Club's Officer of the Year Award on Feb. 18, 1977, for my performance during this critical event and my overall job performance in 1976.

*

More on this later. Back to the academy.

Two weeks before the final week of the academy, cadets were assigned to work in the area they would eventually be assigned. My first choice had been Gila Bend and I was assigned to that area. My training officer was Joel Barnett and he was on a short list to make sergeant.

On Thanksgiving Day 1975, we were working just west of Gila Bend when we received a call concerning an accident involving injuries on Interstate 8 about 10 miles further west. We responded Code 3 (red lights and siren), arriving within minutes. The vehicle was down in a wash. As we arrived, there were numerous vehicles stopped near the scene.

This accident involved a family of five. The crash occurred when the vehicle gradually left the roadway, traveled a couple hundred feet before going over a wash, impacting a concrete bridge supporting wall. The father and his 2-year-old son were pinned inside the vehicle. The son was sitting in a child carrier strapped in next to the father who was driving.

Upon impact, the mother and two daughters had been thrown from the vehicle. I determined later they had folded the rear seats down and were lying on a bed of blankets in the rear of the vehicle.

As the first officer on the scene, I quickly determined the father and son were dead and that the mother and two daughters had suffered massive injuries. Two of the females were unconscious and the third was moaning, about to go unconscious. I knew I needed a helicopter and an ambulance. Upon examining the woman, I believed she had various broken ribs, a shoulder fracture, a broken or fractured pelvis, broken right foot and broken left femur.

About the only thing I could do in an emergency care situation was to splint her leg to prevent movement and monitor her respiration. The 5-year-old daughter was conscious and crying. She had a broken right femur and bad facial lacerations. I splinted her leg and monitored her breathing. The worse was a small 16-month-old infant. She was unconscious and apparently had several abdominal injuries as evidenced by the bruising on her chest, lower abdomen and her raspy breathing.

I quickly learned much more than I was prepared for. In checking her head, I observed the entire right side of the scalp was mushy. While checking her pupils, they were uneven, signifying serious brain injury. She died four days later.

Various people were at the scene, offering assistance and I had them monitor the breathing of the victims for me while I hopped around, like the proverbial Energizer bunny. Others were stopping, looking, getting sick and leaving.

If a person has never seen death, it is an appalling sight the first time. For those who have seen horrific death, many are able to hold it within while protecting the dead lying in the moonlight. But after the job is done and the crowd gone, it's tough to keep holding it in. I was one of those who could and did hold it together.

It was tough to hold it together due to the nature of these untimely deaths and the people involved, especially the young. If you didn't shed a tear, you weren't human. I learned on this day that my sergeant and lieutenant were human.

The rest of my two weeks of OJT (on-the-job) training was pretty much tied up with paperwork. But, I did have a story to tell upon my return to the academy. Everyone in my academy class had to tell at least one story of what happened to them during OJT. Mine, by far, was the most eventful.

*

After graduation from the academy, we moved to Gila Bend, a remote-duty assignment where we would receive relatively cheap housing along with a boost in salary. Joel Barnett, my training officer, had been promoted to sergeant and transferred. So, we moved into his house. These houses were actually modular homes, 24 feet wide and 48 feet long. All were three bedrooms with good size front and back yards. There were nine of these homes within a fenced compound and all were quite nice.

Our full contingent consisted of eight officers and a sergeant. Our office was rather small, just a shed set up near our gas pump, but it was sufficient because we could always do some paperwork at our houses.

I was supposed to be with a training officer for six weeks, but because of my prior experience with the Dallas Police Department and my maturity, I was only with one for three weeks and it was not always the same one. The Gila Bend officers patrolled a rather large area of Interstate 8 (west from mile post 150 to mile post 74) and State Route 85 (north about 15 miles from Gila Bend, south from Gila Bend for about 35 miles). High-speed driving was normal, 100 plus on numerous occasions.

While on patrol, accidents and motorist assists were our two biggest responsibilities and they occurred regularly. The Gila Bend Herald, our weekly newspaper, called constantly to get updates for the paper as the newspaper took to heart its slogan which basically said, "The only newspaper that gives a damn about Gila Bend."

I was asked to be the liaison between our offices and the paper. In this capacity, I wrote a weekly update for the newspaper. I kind of liked this as I could keep track of what was really going on in our district as well as building a rapport with the newspaper and its editor Janice Haynes.

*

I investigated numerous accidents, including several fatalities in 1976. It seemed we were having two or three accidents per day, sometimes more. You always dreaded the phone call when you were the early-morning person.

There are a couple crashes I am going to elaborate on somewhat. What follows is an edited report I submitted in February, 1976.

"I was eastbound on I-8 at about 1210 (12:10 p.m.) hours when I observed three motorcycles and a beige-colored Oldsmobile parked in the west-bound emergency parking lane. I observed a female sitting in the passenger seat of the car while five other males were up against the right-of-way fence urinating. I turned around in the median, turned on my rear-deck lights and pulled in behind the Oldsmobile and then turned on my top-mount red lights.

"After exiting my vehicle, I stood by my patrol car until the five had finished their business. They then noticed me and came over to where I was standing. I asked all for their driver's licenses and all provided valid licenses.

"I advised them of the hazards of parking in the emergency lane without there being an emergency. One motorcycle rider, Mr. Boles, told me that a bolt had worked its way loose on his bike and they had stopped to fix it. I observed no tools in the area.

"I then related an incident that killed two people a few weeks earlier when a vehicle rammed into the rear of another vehicle parked in the emergency lane. I issued Mr. Boles a citation for no motorcycle license. I then advised that I could write all of them citations for being parked

149

in the emergency lane. I told them I wasn't going to and told them to get on down the road and the next time either find a rest area or a wide place to get off the road to take care of their business.

"We started back to our vehicles and Mr. Palmer, driver of the Oldsmobile and I were walking around the front of his car. Mr. Palmer was to my right.

"I looked up to my left and saw a tractor-trailer rig coming straight down the emergency parking lane at a very high rate of speed, about to strike my patrol car. I observed the driver and he seemed to be slumped over the steering wheel. I estimated his speed at 65 to 80 mph.

"I remember yelling, "Get off the road!!" As I turned to my right and struck Mr. Palmer knocking him and myself into a shallow ditch. I remember seeing my vehicle go by in a burst of flames with the truck on the back of it. My vehicle struck the Oldsmobile, knocking it off the right side of the road.

"I saw bodies being knocked off the road into the dirt. I observed an object come out of where the vehicles came to rest. At first I thought it was part off one of the vehicles, but then I realized it was a person completely engulfed in flames. I knocked him to the ground and attempted to extinguish the flames.

"I noticed another person had arrived (I later learned he was Mr. Heck, the truck driver) and I told him to strip off his clothes and use them to help smother the flames. I had taken off my shirt and t-shirt in an attempt to smother the flames. Mr. Heck stripped off his shirt and trousers and assisted me in extinguishing the flames. Another person arrived with a small fire extinguisher and sprayed what flames we couldn't cover with the clothing.

"I looked up at the truck and noticed it was carrying Class A and B explosives. I advised all who could move that we had to get the injured people out of the area. I told them we had explosives on the truck. We moved the victims about 150 feet east of where the vehicles had come to rest and were burning.

"There was a loud explosion, the ground shook. We then moved the victims another 400 to 500 feet down the way. The first motorists to arrive, after all the injured had been moved to safety, were placed about one-half mile in each direction to stop traffic.

"I used an east-bound tractor-trailer rig's CB radio to call for help on channels 9 and 19. I told the driver to keep trying and I then had the first car in the east-bound lane turn around and go to Gila Bend for assistance. I told them to go to the first place they could find and report I had a burning truck with explosives, multiple injuries and that there was a Highway Patrol vehicle involved.

"I returned to the injured and started administering first-aid as best I could with handkerchiefs, pieces of clothing, etc. I put out the word that I needed some blankets and water in a bad way. It was only a few minutes when a motor home pulled up to where we were working with the injured and provided blankets, sheets and water. I doused the burned victim, Mr. Simon, with water and layered the sheets, more water, blankets, more water, etc.

"Officer Greg Eavenson arrived, observed the situation, called for the necessary emergency equipment and began administering the necessary splints, bandages, etc.

"We were administering first-aid, waiting for the helicopter and ambulance to arrive when an off-duty registered nurse arrived and helped stabilize the situation somewhat. At 1345 hours (1:45 p.m., about 90 minutes after the crash), the truck driver and myself were transported to the Ajo hospital by Highway Patrol Officer A.V. Moore in a patrol vehicle.

"I advised Mr. Heck of his Miranda rights at 1350 hours. He waived these rights, but did not want to talk about anything. After we arrived at the hospital, I overheard Mr. Heck's conversation with his employers. He stated he just didn't remember anything until he felt the heat from the fire and exited his vehicle. Officer Moore overheard the conversation also.

"Mr. Heck again was advised of his Miranda rights at the hospital by Officer Moore. We told him we wanted to get a blood sample for alcohol and drug tests. The subject refused. The subject had earlier been asked if he would submit to a blood-alcohol test and he indicated he would. Later, when advised it would also be used for drug analysis, he declined the test.

"On our return trip to Gila Bend, Mr. Heck told me and Officer Moore that he didn't remember anything, not even the impact, until he felt the heat coming up around him. He then exited his vehicle and attempted to get to the fire extinguishers which were engulfed in flames. He stated he did not see my vehicle or any of the other vehicles. He did not remember rounding the curve some three-quarters mile east of the accident scene."

The tractor-trailer rig was later found to be loaded with four large dromedary boxes containing Class A and Class B explosives. The tractor also had a large dromedary box on the tractor frame mounted directly behind the cab. The driver had stated that he also had some dynamite caps, jet propellant and some bombs in various boxes. Later it was discovered he had two 155mm howitzer rounds and five rocket pods unknown in size.

When I got home that evening from the hospital in Ajo, KOOL news was in my front yard. I had on my pants, a jacket borrowed from Arwin Moore who had driven me to the hospital. Beth was near hysterical as one of the stories she had heard had me dead in my burning vehicle along with a myriad of other stories related to the incident. She really didn't have a clue of what had transpired. But, all was good at the end. I was home with Beth and the kids and every thing was OK.

On May 28, 1976, the Department presented me with its Valor Award, the most prestigious honor the agency grants, for my "heroic actions and conspicuous valor above and beyond the call of duty, disregarding risk to my own life." In actuality, I just did what I could do in an extreme situation.

Soon, I became a training officer for a new Highway Patrol cadet James Brockway. After some interesting times, I finally passed him.

*

The second incident I want to elaborate on happened on Nov. 25, 1976.

I was on patrol at about 6:30 a.m., east of Gila Bend, when I observed a vehicle approaching from behind, about a mile back. After seeing the headlights of the vehicle go off, I slowed down, thinking the vehicle had run off the road. Within a minute, the vehicle passed me, traveling 62 mph in a 55-mph zone, with only the its front fog lights on.

What follows is the report I submitted to the Department (with some minimal editing).

"I attempted to stop the vehicle, a silver-grey 1975 Dodge van, by utilizing emergency lighting. The subject was very hesitant to pull to the right side of the road from the high speed lane. The subject weaved quite badly and almost came to a stop in the high speed lane before moving to the emergency parking lane.

"I approached the vehicle and asked the driver for his license and vehicle registration. The subject opened the driver's door. The subject fumbled through a brown leather wallet in an attempt to find his license. He then reached up onto the dashboard and handed me a temporary motorcycle driver's license with the name Charles Michael Turner.

"As he handed this license to me, two cards fell to the ground. As he exited the vehicle to retrieve the dropped cards, he came very close to me and I smelled the odor of marijuana.

"After the subject retrieved the cards, I asked him if he owned the vehicle and he said yes. I asked him for the vehicle registration and he stated he had left it at home. I asked him where home was and he said Ohio. The subject told me he was in the military and handed me a military ID card with the same name as the temporary license. This ID card had Mr. Turner's picture on it and listed him as having blond hair and blue eyes. The subject I stopped had brown hair and brown eyes. He definitely was not the subject of the picture appearing on the ID card.

"I noticed a large brown paper bag between the driver's seat and myself. Upon looking inside the bag, I found it to contain three brick-shaped packages of what I believed to be marijuana. I read the subject his Miranda warning from a card I carry and placed the subject under arrest for possession of marijuana, failure to use headlights during darkness, speed, and possession of marijuana for sale.

"After handcuffing the subject, he asked me if I was a good cop. I said yes, I think I am. He then asked if I'd like to make $1,000. I said wouldn't anybody like to make that kind of money. I then asked him what he had in mind. He stated he would give me $1,000 to let him go, that he had to go home.

"I asked him what the hurry was and he said he was on leave, going to Ohio. He said please take the $1,000 and let him go. I asked him if he had the $1,000 on him and he said yes. I then advised him that I was also going to charge him with bribing a police officer. I then placed him in the right front seat of my patrol vehicle and seat belted him in.

"I requested a stolen-wanted check on the vehicle and subject Turner. The check came back on the vehicle as being stolen and involved in a homicide. Having already advised the subject of the Miranda warnings, I asked if he was involved in a killing. The subject said that if he was he would get only one to 10 years with time off for good behavior.

"I requested assistance from another unit to transport the suspect's vehicle to Gila Bend. Officers Greg Eavenson and Arwin Moore were called to assist. They arrived at about 0710 hours. Officer Moore stayed with the suspect while Officer Eavenson and myself searched the vehicle.

"We found a brown pipe full of what appeared to be marijuana in the glove box. We later found a black leather wallet inside an AWOL-type bag with markings CCH on the side of the bag, in the rear of the vehicle. This wallet had ID belonging to J.G. Clagett. Also found inside the bag with a U.S. Marine ID card belonging to Mark A. Wilczynski. This card also had a picture of the subject I had seated in my patrol vehicle.

"Also found in the vehicle was a registration card to the vehicle with the name John Gilbert Clagett of San Diego and a checkbook belonging to Cycle's West of San Diego. We also observed dried blood on the passenger seat left arm rest.

"When I returned to my vehicle, I asked the subject if his name was Mark Wilczynski and he said he'd take the fifth and then refused to talk to me. I noticed the suspect had a bandage on his right hand forefinger and also some blood spots on his blue coveralls. I confiscated the suspect's brown billfold found in his left rear pocket.

"I transported the suspect and Officer Eavenson drove the suspect vehicle to Gila Bend. On the way to Gila Bend, I asked the suspect whose brown suitcase was in the vehicle and he stated it was his. I asked him if all the contents were his and he said yes. As I started to write this information down, he quickly said not all of the contents were his. I asked him which of the contents were not his and he refused to comment.

"On our arrival at the Maricopa County Sheriff's Office (MCSO) in Gila Bend, I started booking procedures on the suspect while Officers Eavenson and Moore did a complete inventory of the vehicle. I received a call from Mr. Breen of the San Diego County Coroner's Office in relation to the subject I had in custody. He advised me that he had the bodies of a Clagett and Turner in the morgue and that they were homicide victims. After talking with Mr. Breen, I had the suspect strip off his clothing so we could package it as evidence. The suspect still would not give us any information.

"During inventory, we listed, among other incidental items, 15 $100 bills that had various blood stains on them. Almost all items collected were held for San Diego police detectives.

"I also observed the suspect had a fresh cut on his back about four inches long, bruises on his right shoulder, scratches on his left arm, cuts on his left elbow, and scratches and bruises on his chest.

"The suspect was left at MCSO and the vehicle was taken to the Gila Bend DPS office where we contacted the San Diego Police Department in regards to what they wanted us to do with the vehicle. I talked to Detective Shively of the SDPD and he advised me to hold the vehicle until it could be dusted for fingerprints. Detective Shively also advised he had been called to the residence of J.G. Clagett in San Diego on Nov. 24, 1976, to investigate a double homicide where the suspect apparently stole one of the victim's vehicles. He also told me warrants were being drawn on the subject I had arrested.

"The suspect's vehicle was taken to and stored at Posey's Motors in Gila Bend. I talked to Bobby Posey and told him what I had and that detectives from San Diego would be over to check the vehicle and absolutely no one was to be around the vehicle until that time. He had me park the vehicle under a shed and secure it.

"I talked to Mike McCloy of the U.S. Navy who ran the suspect's information through a computer. He advised me this subject was also wanted as a deserter and that the suspect had been a student at the administrative school in Camp Pendleton, CA. They did not have information as to the next of kin."

Some evidence was retained for the San Diego police detectives while other items were sent to the DPS Crime Lab in Phoenix with a copy of the suspect's fingerprints to check for latent prints and analyzing of items. During the next few months, Greg Eavenson and I spent a few weeks in San Diego assisting San Diego police in the investigation.

A few months later, the Rotary Club of Phoenix selected me as its officer of the year for the role I played in the arrest and subsequent investigation. Beth and the kids attended the ceremony held at the Adams Hotel in downtown Phoenix.

Eventually, the San Diego Police Department accepted a plea agreement on Mr. Wilczynski. He would spend a minimum of 20 years in prison before being eligible for parole. Then the Feds would have a go at him for charges brought up by the military His chances of getting out of prison after 20 years, state or federal, would be almost nil.

*

Cadet Class 31 was due to start in September 1977 and I applied to be a class counselor, not thinking in a million years I would get it. My lieutenant and sergeant both had to sign off on this as it would take me away from my area for more than four months. After trying to talk me out of it, neither of them thought I would get chose so they signed off on my request.

Surprise! I became a class counselor on Sept. 5, 1977. There were five counselors, each responsible for eight cadets and we were to oversee their every move so to speak. We had to complete all the same physical activities required of the cadets, have daily meetings with them and help them with problems they may have reference classroom assignments. Each counselor took considerable pride in what they were doing as the loss of a cadet for whatever reason would reflect on us.

Apartments were rented for the counselors and cadets at the Greenway Sheraton, Greenway and Interstate-17 in north Phoenix. These were all two-bedroom apartments in the extended-stay area. We were given per diem for food and were doubled up in the apartments. My roommate was from Tucson and he always went home on weekends. Beth and the kids would come up from Gila Bend on the weekends. Time went by fast for me, but I could tell it was sometimes a real grind for Beth.

The cadets had two weeks of OJT (on-the-job training) towards the end of the academy. My cadets were strewn from Tucson to Holbrook and I had to meet with them and a field trainer at least twice to evaluate their performances. I knew I was going to lose one cadet because he just couldn't comprehend the things he was supposed to do and was a real liability to himself as well as others. After his OJT and reams of documentation, he was called in by the class sergeant and captain. He resigned before he could be terminated.

*

I finished the counselor assignment on Jan. 20, 1978 and returned to Gila Bend. It should be noted that I was continuing my education, attending a Phoenix-based campus for Saint Mary's College of California. I traveled to Phoenix from Gila Bend at least two nights a week and, occasionally, on weekends. This was a real drag, but something I wanted to do. The college accepted what they called an experiential portfolio that would possibly help me earn enough credits so I could finish in a little more than a year.

Thank God, Beth was a good typist and as I wrote, she typed, literally a couple hundred pages, many hours of key pounding on her part.

Again, an education was something I really wanted as there was no one on either side of my family who had ever received a college degree. Hell, there wasn't a lot of them who even went to high school and graduated.

I received my bachelor of arts in Public Management from St. Mary's College on Oct. 24, 1977. This was a big deal for me. Beth and I both were elated and she deserves more credit than me, not only for her typing but for her guidance and support as well.

*

Before expounding on some of my DPS experiences, I will state that I received numerous awards and attended many, many advanced training courses. Instead of trying to affix them into the proper areas, I will list them as attachments at the end of my book and will also try to place them in chronological sequence.

I finished the counselor gig and returned to Gila Bend. While in Phoenix, I had occasions to learn more about the various aspects of DPS. It not only includes the Highway Patrol, where everyone starts, but also includes state narcotics, state liquor and the crime lab, among many other things. All these support divisions handle complaints and requests from other agencies.

As a counselor, I met Sgt. Jim Madison who was running the night squad for the Liquor Division. He was trying to recruit me to put in for his squad as he was going to be in need of a person in March. I was already in pretty deep doo-doo with my sergeant and lieutenant with the patrol. I knew they were going to require some sort of commitment from me after I returned. They did and they told me in no uncertain terms I was theirs for at least one more year. In other words, I couldn't put in for a transfer for at least another year.

I told Sgt. Madison this and he said there were at least 40 applicants for this slot and he would see to it that I was one of them. Sgt. Madison had spent quite a few years with the FBI and had some pull somewhere. I believe it was with the director, Vernon Hoy. My sergeant relented and allowed me put in an application for the Criminal Investigation Bureau's Liquor Division. I felt for awhile that I was persona non grata and not very well liked by my supervisors.

As proof, I offer an interoffice memo written by my lieutenant, Richard Landis, to Major Tom Milldebrandt, Highway Patrol Southern Division commander.

"I wish to go on record as opposing the transfer of Officer Ken Haw, #1750, from Gila Bend.

"I feel District Four made a sacrifice in allowing Officer Haw to be a class counselor. This sacrifice was made by the District to allow Officer Haw to further develop his talents. Now, I am being asked to allow him to transfer from the District. If he were to transfer now, District Four would not have a chance to benefit from the experience this man has gained in training.

"Officer Haw has been one of the best officers in the Gila Bend area. He has talent and he has experience. Both are commodities sorely needed in an area like Gila Bend. District Four has a great deal to gain by Officer Haw's presence in Gila Bend. New officers must be properly developed and Officer Haw's abilities, particularly with his recent experience as a counselor, are desperately needed. Gila Bend is a remote area duty station with a relatively high turnover of personnel. As a result most officers there are relatively new and in need of good direction. This need, along with the excellent abilities of Officer Haw, lead me to conclude that a transfer of Officer Haw at this time would seriously short-change District Four. I am a firm believer in developing our people, but I am concerned about the lack of return to the District for our efforts expended in providing developmental tools and programs to our people.

"My opposition is against transfer at this time. I would be satisfied with keeping Officer Haw for at least six months. Six months of his talent will be a reasonable return on our investment. I have explained my position to Officer Haw and am sure he does not agree with me."

Hey, you gotta do, what you gotta do so off I went to work liquor control.

While working the road as a patrolman, I made numerous arrests for DWI, stolen vehicles, narcotics, etc. I also had investigated more fatal crashes than anyone in Gila Bend, this despite the fact, I was gone for about four months as a counselor. I had a pretty rounded background when I applied for the position in Liquor.

*

On March 5, 1978, I started working for Sgt. Madison in liquor investigations. We primarily worked complaints on various liquor establishments, complaints that were called into a central telephone number or hand written. My work area was Phoenix west to Yuma, east to Show Low and everything north of Phoenix.

Tucson squads handled the rest of the state. The complaints would be anything from serving an underage person, over serving intoxicated patrons, opening early or closing late. A compliant is a complaint and the complainant deserved to be notified of the findings, or at least being kept appraised. I didn't necessarily agree, but that was our policy at the time.

I cannot believe the state was paying me to go out in an undercover capacity, pay for my drinks and sometimes food. Plus, pay me per diem while I was out of town after so many hours. This is something I might have done for nothing. You are probably saying why food. Some of our complaints were reference to so-called restaurants either not serving food or not selling enough food, 40 percent, to qualify for a restaurant license.

In 1979, businesses could not serve or sell alcohol before noon. Some complaints were about various, usually really nice, restaurants that started serving champagne at 11 a.m. on Sundays for their brunches. I even got to take Beth out to eat a few times on the state. I traveled extensively, all over the northern part of the state. Usually, two officers would go, depending on the complaint.

*

I read, re-read and then studied state liquor laws and believed some were in need of rework. These laws are done legislatively and not by little old me. But, I could make written suggestions to the state Liquor Board which I did. A few were accepted and some others rewritten.

One of the major problems at that time and still is today, is the serving or selling to an underage person, a minor. The liability after the fact came back to the person on the license. They were the ones I wanted to cite, not the cashier or server. Maybe both if the situation warranted it.

Phoenix police had its own liquor enforcement squad and I assisted them on a couple occasions. They would dress up an 18-year-old, male or female, to make them look older and send them into an establishment to purchase alcoholic beverages. Sometimes these 18 year olds would look to be in their early 20's at least. I thought this was wrong.

I talked to Sgt. Madison about this particular situation and he asked me to write up some guidelines we could use and present them to the state Liquor Board for Certification. It took a long time and some trials and errors before I finally came up with guidelines for what I felt was a very innovative program called our "CUBS," Covert Undercover Buyers. As far as I know, it's still being deployed today.

Instead of making an 18 year old look older, we were using 16-, 17- and 18-year-old high school students, with parental permission, as a key ingredient in our operation. If anything, they looked their age or younger. No makeup, no facial hair and no dressing up. They looked their age. We photographed them at the start of the shift and again after, just to be on the safe side.

We watched them enter the establishment. If it were a bar we would have at least one officer in there before they entered to observe who waited on them. If we were at a Circle K, 7-Eleven, Fry's Food and Drug, etc., we were observing everything. I even came up with the idea of writing letters of appreciation to those establishment employees who refused to sell our minors liquor and asked for an I.D. The letter went through their supervisor to be placed in their employee file.

The experience I had in Liquor Enforcement was great. I held seminars for Circle Ks, 7-Elevens and any food store or liquor establishment wanting the training. I even did some of this on my own time because overtime was eating us up. Beth even accompanied me on some of my out-of-town seminars.

*

There was one situation that hit pretty close to home, not directly involving me as an investigator, but rather a distant family story. It happened in July 1978, shortly after I moved from Gila Bend to state Liquor Enforcement.

Remember, I spent some time during my youth in Casa Grande, AZ. My Aunt Valle (Dad's sister) and my uncle, Rob, lived across the street from us. One of their daughters, Dorothy, married a guy by the name of Gary Tison. I never liked Gary even though I only had met him a couple of times. I felt he was destined for jail or an early death. How little did I know. Dorothy and Gary had three sons—Donald, Raymond and Ricky, in that order. I never really knew the boys, but they were pretty much raised by my aunt and uncle in Casa Grande.

Gary, like I had predicted, spent time in jail and then in prison for various charges. In an escape attempt, in the late 1960's, he killed a prison guard. He was sentenced to spend the rest of his life in prison. Because the prison in Florence, AZ, is only about a 20-mile drive from Casa Grande, AZ. Dorothy and the boys were able to visit Gary quite often.

I believe the boys were actually brain washed into thinking their dad did not deserve to be locked up and he only did what he had to do. Right! I also think Dorothy had a lot to do with this as I am not sure she was capable of knowing right from wrong. Love is truly blind when it wants to be.

On July 30, 1978, Tison and another inmate, Randy Greenawalt, were working in the trustee annex at the prison. Tison's son, Raymond, arrived for a visit at about 9 a.m. A few minutes later Tison's other sons, Ricky and Donald, showed up carrying a cardboard picnic box. Inside this box were sawed off shotguns.

A few minutes later, with the help of the three boys, Gary and Randy escaped. As a get-a-way vehicle, they used a 1969 Lincoln Continental recently purchased by one of the sons. They made it to Quartzsite, AZ, in Yuma County, when they apparently had car problems. A family of four, a Marine sergeant, his wife, infant son and the 15-year-old niece of the Marine, were traveling in a 1977 Mazda when they stopped to render aide to the Tison gang.

Their bodies were found the next day, off the highway, stuffed into the Lincoln Continental. The 15-year-old was not found at this time and authorities assumed she had been kidnapped by the fugitives. She was found dead a couple days later, however, within a few hundred yards of where the family had been slaughtered. She had been in the Lincoln, but apparently not killed. She crawled into the desert where she bled out from her wounds.

I was called in to help on Aug. 2, when the Tison Gang was supposedly hiding out at a mobile home near Flagstaff that was owned by a girlfriend of Randy Greenawalt, who was serving time for the 1974 murder of a truck driver. The primary investigators knew I was a relative and that my aunt and uncle were like parents to the Tison boys. They wanted me to ask my aunt and uncle to tape record a plea asking the boys to surrender.

I was hesitant, but thought if it could save even one of the boys, it would be helpful. This visit with Aunt Valley and Uncle Rob was probably the hardest thing I ever had to do as a police officer. I tape recorded their pleas to the boys. I shed more than a few tears while they were making these pleas. This was done at their house in Casa Grande. Immediately after finishing the tape, I took the recording to two investigators in the backyard.

It was rushed to the Flagstaff area via helicopter. Their pleas was played over a loud speaker to the occupants of the trailer house later that night. After no response and with no one answering the phone in the trailer, owned by Greenawalt's girlfriend, Kathleen Ermentraut, it was raided. Ms. Ermentraut, the lone occupant of the trailer, said the Tisons had been there earlier, but were now gone. She had supplied the money and two of the Tison boys went into Flagstaff to purchase a pickup truck. As soon as the boys returned to the trailer—one was driving the pickup another the Mazda—everything was loaded into the pickup. They left shortly after.

The manhunt continues.

On Aug. 8, a newly-wed Texas couple were reported missing in southern Colorado along with their van. As the case unfolded, it was determined that the Tison gang had murdered these young adults before stealing their van. Their bodies of the honey-mooning couple were found by hikers.

On Aug. 11, road blocks were set up just south of Casa Grande because of a reported break-in at the Border Patrol office in Gila Bend. A few hours after the reported night-time break-in, a van attempted to run the first roadblock and was successful.

But at a second road block a few miles away, Donald Tison, who was driving the van, was killed by gun fire as he attempted to crash through the barricades. After the van crashed and came to rest, Ricky and Ray

Tison, along with Greenawalt, were taken into custody. Gary Tison, however, had escaped into the desert.

The bloated body of Gary Tison was found a couple days later when a worker at a nearby power plant smelled something foul and called in a report. It was Gary Tison, he had died from exposure and dehydration. Fitting?

Greenawalt, Raymond and Ricky were all found guilty and sentenced to death. Greenawalt's sentence was carried out. Eventually the Tison boys' death sentences were reduced to life in prison without possibility of parole.

Although I could write a book about the Tisons, I won't because it's been done many times. Also, a movie starring Robert Mitchum as Gary Tison was made in the 1980's. The books and movie portray these events relatively accurately, but many things were omitted because of time constraints.

Ironically, the break-in at the Border Patrol office in Gila Bend was later attributed to illegal immigrants looking for food. It had nothing to do with the Tisons, but did lead to their demise.

*

Back to my story.

On Aug. 1, 1979, a new undercover squad was being formed, "Organized Crime and Racketeering." Sgt. Madison was to be in charge and he wanted me to join him. In hindsight, I wish I had not gone to the new squad. It was an experience that would catapult me into the state limelight and not in a good way. I'm getting ahead of myself so let me write about what happened in a very, very condensed form.

This case, I believe, was the first the new squad was assigned, but I would not swear to it. It certainly was my first case with the newly-formed squad.

The FBI field office in Phoenix called DPS on Aug. 2, 1979, and reported that a couple of their agents were at the Prescott Downs horse race track in Prescott. They were requesting agents proceed to that location reference to possible felonious racing violations. Sgt. Madison grabbed me and said, "We're going to Prescott."

When we got there, we met with two FBI agents who told us about an individual they had arrested for using a hand-held shocking device to fix races. The FBI was under the impression that these were state violations and wanted to turn what they had over to DPS. After a lengthy conversation, Sgt. Madison agreed it was probably more of a state matter than an FBI concern. The investigation was relinquished from the Feds to DPS.

Now, what I knew about horses and horse racing, I could write in one sentence. A very short sentence. In other words, nothing. I had never been nor did I want to go to any horse races. I was the man for the job. My first racketeering assignment.

The individual the FBI had apprehended was willing to talk with me, but not work with me as a "CI" (confidential informant). The information I received varied from using electronic devices on horses during a race to samples of the winning horses urine being switched at pee stations or barn tests to drugs being administered to the race horses prior to the race which would necessitate switching urine samples, plus a number of other potential crimes.

I knew I was in over my head and needed help. Sgt. Madison and I talked about the situation, which according to my jockey source, was rampant at all state fair circuits. If this was true, "Oh, Shit!!"

At the time, there were 14 counties in Arizona with county fairs. A 15th county, La Paz, would come into existence in 1983 after separating from Yuma County.

It just so happened that one of the applicants to come into our new squad, who was transferring from the Highway Patrol, was a horse owner in Show Low and he appeared to be very knowledgeable about horses and horse racing. If we could get him onto the squad, he could go undercover (UC) so we had Officer Chuck Spooner come to Phoenix to talk with us.

We would need equipment we didn't have, but some equipment was available. We needed at least UC receivers, transponders, etc. because Chuck would have to be wired and we needed a van that could be positioned close enough to capture the transmissions. Plus, we had to wait for Chuck to get to the squad. That part didn't take long because he left his wife, Linda, in Show Low to ready their property to sell which hastened his transfer to Phoenix.

Within days, we were "ready." We were given a van that was just about a step away from state surplus. The van had a curtain behind the front seats that could be pulled for privacy which meant I could sit back there for hours monitoring Chuck's conversations. The tapes were all labeled for posterity or possibly court. We still had a few racing days left at Prescott Downs and then at other county fairs, but we didn't have any idea of where we were going or to what depth this investigation would take us.

The state Racing Commission had also been mentioned as an area of concern, but one individual we heard good things about was one of its investigators, Bruce Denneny. We also had heard that the Racing Commission may be getting a new executive secretary. That rumor became fact on Jan. 16, 1980, when Bill Billings became the new Racing Commission executive director. He immediately hired Denneny as his chief investigator.

Now, we had someone we could possibly confide in which wasn't the case previously and we were floundering. We were gathering information, but didn't have any idea of the inner workings of race tracks.

Shortly after Billings' selection, Sgt. Madison and I made an appointment with him and Denneny. When we met, we outlined our investigation as much as possible, leaving out Chuck Spooner. At this point, we didn't know who to trust. At this time, our investigation indicated widespread dissatisfaction by many people within the horse-racing industry. The primary cause was the lack of control and regulation by the Arizona Racing Commission and their employees who were mostly seen as "good ol' boys" who could be bought.

We brought up the use of electronic shocking devices and drugged horses as well as other violations occurring at county race tracks throughout the state. Mr. Billings agreed with our findings and said that Mr. Denneny had observed some of the same things going on, but the reports he had written had been overlooked. We felt we could all work together with someone working undercover who could possibly make an impact.

Mr. Denneny met with Chuck and me and showed us copies of the majority of his reports. He also indicated that one name kept coming up at all county race tracks—that we might be able to catch and turn into an informant. Rumor had it that this individual spent considerable time around race tracks throughout Arizona. He owned race horses and we were told by various sources he supposedly drugged horses. Our investigation also revealed he was paying off a test barn official to switch urine samples.

Thanks to Mr. Denney's reports and some of our investigative work, we now had a target, or so we thought.

We met with a prosecutor with the Arizona Attorney General's Office to get an idea on how to proceed being these violations crossed county lines. It was decided the charges would be filed in county courts and not city courts. We also decided that this individual should be our first target and that the investigation should run at least one full year so we could investigate other possible horse race track wrongdoings at all county fairs in Arizona.

It didn't take long to reel-in our possible informant on at least two felony counts. One for the doping of race horses and another from bribing a state racing official. In an undercover capacity, Chuck had gotten close to the informant and watched when the informant actually drugged his horse just prior to the race. He used a common narcotic called "Ritalin," a drug widely used on hyper-active children and adults to calm them down. However, it has exactly the opposite effect on horses. Chuck then watched the informant arrange for the purchase of four $10 win tickets, betting on that horse. This purchase was done by an unidentified individual and the tickets were given to our informant.

After the race, when the informant's horse won, he and Chuck went to the test barn where Chuck saw him hand the test official the four winning tickets. The urine test from the informants's horse was switched with a clean sample before it was sent to the lab.

Shortly thereafter, my report was prepared and presented to the Attorney General's Office for presentation to the grand jury for possible charges and indictment. Or, so I thought. The prosecutor for the state thought more good come out of from this if we could turn this individual into a "CI," confidential informant.

This suspect entered into an agreement to work with us as a CI. How could he not, and stay out of prison? Sniches or informants aren't very well liked in the state prison system. He also was told when he finished his written contract with us, he would immediately resign from his current position as a city employee and could no longer race horses, The suspect agreed to this and signed the contract.

Our investigations continued for about 18 months before we started winding it down. We had about 13 solid felony counts on different individuals when our informant approached me and said he was not going to testify against some of these people because they were his friends and he knew he would be killed if he did. He was advised that if he did not testify, his agreement with us would be null and void and he would be prosecuted also.

Our first court case was scheduled for October, 1981, in the Yavapai County Courthouse in Prescott, but all hell was breaking loose. The attorney for one of many defendants had learned that Chuck Spooner was one of our undercover officers. A charge was made that Chuck also was doping and betting on horses to fix races and that a second DPS officer possibly was also involved. Guess who? This crap was in all the newspapers. The direct link to leaking this stories to the media? Our confidential informant.

Meanwhile, two of the three defendants we were going to prosecute in Prescott pled guilty. The third, a good friend of our informants, was re-indicted by a grand jury. You see where this is going. All of a sudden Chuck and I are pulled from the investigation and given administrative assignments as we were now being investigated for doping horses, betting on horses and bribing the test barn official. The same damn charges just about everybody we were investigating faced. The defense attorneys were now making us out to be the bad guys.

This hit the newspapers throughout the state on Oct. 8, 1981. Our informant's name had not yet come out as being our confidential informant. If it did, he would be a dead man.

Next problem.

Our transfers to administrative assignments lasted five months. DPS never gets into much of a hurry when investigating one of its own. I think Chuck took the transfer better than I did. We were not allowed any communication with any of our squad members or sergeant. We had no idea what was really going on behind the scenes. We just knew that each and every day was the same hell. At least twice a week, I had to take my colonel's car and have it washed. It should be noted when assigned to my administrative position with Lt. Col. Ron Hoffman, I never ever thought he perceived me as possibly being innocent of the charges.

I lost so much respect for him, I can't begin to describe it. Let me describe one incident while on administrative assignment to him. This incident was highly publicized in newspapers and television news throughout the state and left me feeling like I was hung out to dry.

I had been subpoenaed to go before the state legislature. This subpoena was directly involving ongoing criminal charges and findings reference the State Racing Commission. As we were going to the hearing—Col. Hoffman, my major who was driving and me—they were telling me I could not divulge any information on ongoing criminal investigations even though I was appearing before the entire state legislative body at the state capitol building, in their chambers.

Rep. Burton Barr, R-Phoenix, the House majority leader, was leading the questioning. I was the only one scheduled to be interviewed, My major and Col. Hoffman sat directly behind me and were so slumped down in their seats, I had to look twice to see if they were still there.

During my testimony, all the television stations were there as well as a myriad of newspaper reporters. I was asked at least three times to elaborate on my findings in the horse-racing investigations. Each time, I responded I was not at liberty to talk about an ongoing investigation.

After the third time, a gavel hit so hard it startled me. The person who had struck the gavel said, "Son do you know who I am?"

The chamber was so quiet you could have heard the proverbial pin drop. I looked at him for a short while and stated that if he was sitting in the right chair, he was Rep. Burton Barr. I reiterated I could not speak reference to an ongoing criminal investigation. This did not get me any points, but did get a lot of news coverage much to the chagrin of my major and Col. Hoffman who about a year later was demoted to captain for allegedly trying to trade state property to Mexican law enforcement authorities in an effort to retrieve a friend's stolen boat.

On Feb. 12, 1982, Chuck and I were exonerated of any wrong doing pertaining to the investigation. We were both reassigned to our divisions.

About half of those we investigated pled guilty to lesser charges. As for the others, the charges were dropped. Chuck, me and our informant met with the Attorney General's Office and we were waiting to go into the office, the informant told me that if he ever had the opportunity he would kill me. I smiled and said, "Vice versa." There was no need for each of us to ever cross paths again. It would not be good for at least one of us if we ever did. Our informant went on to retire from the the city job he worked at. He never was officially charged.

Chuck and I frequently discussed what to do when everything was over. We had both been libeled, slandered, you name it. We sued our informant and the city he worked for and various city officials for slander, libel and anything else we could think of. This wasn't for the money, although that was OK, but to show we were right. We won.

Chuck died on June 22, 2011, from cancer. A better friend I could never ask for. I miss him.

About five months later, on June 1, 1982, I transferred into ILED (Investigations, Liquor Enforcement Division). This was a great assignment as we worked all kinds of investigations—street-level narcotics, liquor enforcement, auto theft, etc. In this capacity, I traveled extensively throughout the northern portion of Arizona, assisting other agencies with various investigations. I also was responsible for my own case load. On many occasions, we worked with a partner or as a squad.

*

Early in 1985, we received information about the owner of an ice plant in Gila Bend making moonshine and selling it to Indians on the Gila River Reservation, north of Gila Bend. Supposedly, he was conducting a business that not only sold ice, but had a license to sell beer and wine as well.

Working in an undercover capacity, I stopped at the ice house on a couple occasions and bought beer. I never saw the suspect, but did meet his wife who was at the business each time I visited. I had put Nevada license plates on my vehicle and told her I owned a few bars in the Las Vegas area. On my third visit, I mentioned I was looking for someone in the area I could buy a large amount of homemade alcohol from. I told her I wanted the moonshine to water down my good liquors at my bars in Vegas.

She was very leery and asked when I would be coming back through the area. I said I made frequent trips because I was looking at purchasing a couple bars in Phoenix and Yuma. She said the text time I was through to drop in and ask for her. A few days later, I stopped by during the late evening. She was on duty and said she knew someone who could possibly set me up for large purchases of moonshine.

I explained to her my greatest fear was the moonshine would be "shit" and I would be caught which would result in my licenses in Nevada being revoked. She assured me the product was good and had a quart sample for me. I had absolutely no idea what I was buying into when she asked me to sample it. I told her beer was my thing. She insisted and I tried a little, about a thimbleful. She was right, it tasted like a very good tequila and the smell matched the taste.

She also told me if this would work for my bars, I could meet her husband and work out the details for a bulk purchase. I told her I would return in a few days and let her know. I had the sample moonshine tested and analyzed by our crime lab and it came back as a high grade alcohol.

I set up a meeting with her husband who was also the licensee of the ice plant. I had absolutely no idea what was to confront me within the next few weeks. I was given a tour of their property located within five miles northeast of Gila Bend.

At some point previously, this subject applied and was given a license certifying his place as an Arizona Grain Fuels experimental plant. He had a sign, a rather big one, posted in his front yard. His property set on at least 10 acres and included a pig farm. He was raising hundreds of pigs and when I saw the deplorable conditions, I knew the Arizona Humane Society would have a field day. These pigs could not even stand because they were being fed the refuse from his so-called fuels, which was nothing more than fermented grains with a very high-alcohol content.

He asked if I would help him make 500 gallons of alcohol, he would discount my cost per gallon. I told him I would have to see what my time was like and get back with him. I ran the situation by Sgt. Rich Basso and he agreed I should spend as much time as I could helping to actually make the product. I felt at this point I should be wired whenever I went to the moonshiner's compound. We then got the Bureau of Alcohol, Tobacco and Firearms (ATF) involved, along with the Arizona Humane Society.

The only job, I really had during this investigation involved putting the water into the tanker that held the grains. The grains were put in by the suspect and he didn't trust me with the recipe. For the next few days, I added water, then more water until the suspect felt the ingredients were right. I used a garden hose and spent hours on top of the tanker. He occasionally took me into the ice house where we would have a couple beers and sometimes to the Dairy Queen for a hamburger. He also owned this establishment.

After a few weeks, the fermentation was complete and the suspect thought the product was ready. He only had to procure the 5-gallon water jugs to complete my order. The ATF had already supplied me with a few thousand dollars for the operation and I doled this out when necessary. Because of the trust the suspect had in me, the bulk of my payment would be upon delivery. I told him I had put in so much time, I wanted to be there when the product was bottled. He agreed and after the third 5-gallon bottle was pumped, I went to my vehicle and called in the troops.

I had taken a sample to drink when I went to my vehicle. Using this sample, I determined, via a field test kit supplied by the ATF, this was indeed a high-alcohol content liquor. Standing in wait at the DPS Highway Patrol compound in Gila Bend was our take-down squads. Included in these squads were DPS Liquor Enforcement (my squad), ATF agents, members of the Humane Society and members of four Phoenix television stations as well as our departmental video unit and our in-house monthly newsletter, the Digest.

Now, I was not aware that the news channels would be there or I would have worn some "nicer duds." Most likely, they were there primarily because of the inebriated pigs.

My squad, as well as a couple of the ATF units, spent the next two days demolishing the moonshine units. Everything was photographed and video taped. This was the largest moonshine bust in Arizona state history and probably will never be outdone.

My suspect died of cancer before he could be tried. All his properties and assets, however, were seized by the state.

*

We also spent considerable time in Lake Havasu. Lake Havasu was a hot spot for us during the summer months and especially around holiday weekends. We assisted the lake Havasu Police Department in undercover liquor and narcotics enforcement.

I believe it was during the summer of 1985 when I was working with Verne Watson in the Lake Havasu area. We had used my vehicle to drive from our motel room to the parking lot area near the London Bridge. We had both been pretty busy writing liquor citations and after midnight we were done. After walking to my vehicle, a 1976 Chevrolet El Camino, I approached the driver's side when I noticed there was a pickup truck parked beside my vehicle with its interior lights on.

Looking into the truck, whose only occupants were a male and female, I observed the male as he poured two lines of white power onto a CD holder. I whispered to Verne that we had narcotics. He joined me at the driver's side of my vehicle and observed the same thing. We decided at the count of three we were going to hold our IDS to the windows, announce we were police officers, open the doors and arrest the pair.

I don't really know who came up with this stupid-ass approach. Both doors were locked, but neither Verne nor I had heard the engine running. The driver, who had seen Verne, slammed the vehicle into reverse and was turning my way. I could only attempt to get out of the way by jumping into the bed of my El Camino. The driver's window of the suspect's pickup was down enough that Verne was trying to break the window to reach in and grab the keys. The vehicle, however, was continuing to go backwards, dragging Verne along the way.

When the driver straightened the vehicle and put it into drive, Verne let go and went down, rolling on the pavement. When he got up, I was just getting into my vehicle to start pursuit. Verne jumped into my vehicle as we began the chase. While traveling at high speeds for the conditions, about 45 mph, the driver of the fleeing pickup was holding his driver's side carpet out the window and shaking it.

A few miles later, the driver pulled into a service station, your typical everyday fill-up during a pursuit at your local AM-PM station. Right. We were on him like stink on an inebriated pig. We cuffed him and then cuffed his wife.

We asked him later why he tried to run. He said he thought Verne was trying to rob them as he did not see Verne's badge. Verne's badge had been plastered to the driver's window. I saw it from the passenger side. We moved both vehicles out of the gas lanes with Vern moving the suspect's pickup.

We knew we probably were not going to get enough of the cocaine residue to get a sample, but Verne continued to search the vehicle while I talked to the subjects. While we were doing this, responding officers from the Lake Havasu Police Department were just standing there watching us professional investigators go about our job.

I forgot to mention that we were working in civilian clothes, in an undercover capacity. This was our typical dress attire, usually Levis and t-shirts. Maybe those LHPD officers really weren't sure who the bad guys were.

The subject identified himself and said he worked in a high security position at an Air Force base outside Las Vegas. Verne came over and pulled me aside and told me he wasn't having much luck in his search. I asked if he had looked behind the seat as this was a standard pickup truck, not a two-seater. He returned to the vehicle and within a few seconds, he gave me a thumps up, meaning he had found something.

I had the police officers stand over the subjects and went to see what Verne had. He had found two large baggies of marijuana taped behind the seat and a box of empty smaller baggies. We arrested the subject for possession of marijuana and possession for sale. We confiscated the pickup and when we released his wife, we told her there may be charges pending on her.

I never did find out exactly what position this guy had, but it must have been somewhat important because all charges against him were dropped a few weeks later. This was done via the Mohave County Attorney's Office and the Office of Special Investigation (OSI) for the Air Force.

*

The next morning, I couldn't get out of bed. I yelled at Verne and woke him. He helped me out of bed and with extreme discomfort, I got dressed. We met with Sgt. Basso a short time later for breakfast and I still could hardly walk. It was decided I should return to Phoenix to be checked by my doctor. I made the decision that I could drive myself to Phoenix.

After pulling into my driveway, I had to honk the horn to get Beth to help me out of my vehicle. She ended up taking me to emergency where it was determined I had suffered a herniated and fractured disk. This was to be my first major back surgery, but certainly not my last. I do believe, however, this was the catalyst for all my future back surgeries.

*

On June 21, 1988, the sheriff of Hot Springs County, AR, requested the Arizona Department of Public Safety to assist his agency in a homicide investigation after a young woman was found murdered and buried in a shallow grave. There were no viable leads or evidence and the possibility of an arrest was remote.

Frank Shankwitz and I were assigned to assist and through "persistence, dedication and outstanding investigative techniques," (these are words from our commendation), we were able to positively identify the murderer. Based on our investigation, Arkansas authorities obtained an arrest warrant on Roger Hammond, a long-time Arizona resident. Our investigation went even further as we also tracked Hammond to Lawrence, KS, where additional information was developed and obtained implicating Hammond to the Hot Springs County homicide. Hammond was eventually sentenced to 20 years in prison.

ILED received a Director's Unit Citation for its work in 1988. The citation stated that the division was an integral part of vital drug interdiction efforts. The Phoenix unit, my unit, had distinguished itself as a jack-of-all-trades group because of our involvement in liquor and narcotics enforcement and in responding to requests from agencies throughout the state and nation.

*

While with ILED, I began to study for the sergeant's test whenever I had the time. Eventually, I passed the written test with an 89-percent score and had done well on the oral boards. When all was said and done, I was ninth on the list. I was asked if I wanted to participate in a two-month temporary cross-training assignment with the Highway Patrol Bureau as this would probably be where I would transfer to as a sergeant. This was a new program and I was the first trial officer/sergeant to volunteer.

*

On April 24, 1988, I was assigned to the Highway Patrol Bureau in Goodyear and began working for Sgt. Jim Grant. On the second day of my assignment, I was on my own. I was advised by Sgt. Grant that any advice I wanted to offer to any of his area officers feel free to do so. Sgt. Grant also said if I thought I could glean any information from these officers, feel free to be on site to observe and ask questions. I was assigned to the 1800 to 0200 (6 p.m. to 2 a.m.) shift.

There were numerous areas I felt deficient in such as DUI arrests. All the forms had changed since I left the road 10 years ago. Booking procedures, Intoxilyzer, Radar usage (which I was not certified in at the time), commercial vehicle enforcement and accident investigations were all areas I had not worked in 10 years.

I spent considerable time assisting officers in a sincere attempt to get myself up to speed. This, however, wasn't a one-way street as I had a lot to offer these officers as well. I taught them what I had learned from my narcotics experiences such as recognizing the smell of marijuana, the various packaging methods drug runners use and methods that could be used to identify drugs and other contraband.

I also informed them how beneficial the Department's Criminal Investigation Research Unit could be to them, especially when trying to obtain prior arrests records on narcotics offenders. This was of great assistance when it came to writing search and arrest warrants. On one occasion, use of CIRU led to the arrest of a hit-and-run suspect.

It wasn't long before officers working my shift started responding to my traffic stops to see what I came up with. I made numerous narcotics arrests from traffic stops. The only negative with this assignment was that our Data Processing Unit had no way to track or document my data or activities. Every time they input my badge number, it could not be retrieved because I was still assigned to Criminal Investigations, not the Highway Patrol Bureau.

Numerous conversations between Sgt. Grant and our Data Processing Unit proved futile. They would not or could not change its program because it was still in its trial stages. The only way around this was to give my statistics to a Highway Patrol officer for him to enter under his or her badge number, which I did. Many officers enjoyed coming to my traffic because they would get statistical credit while picking up some pointers on how to search for narcotics.

As Sgt. Grant wrote in his July 11, 1988, memo to his commander, Lt. Don Miller, "The temporary assignment of this CIB (Criminal Investigation Bureau) officer to the area was very enjoyable. The officer did an excellent job and was well received by all of his co-workers. I believe this concept is very workable and results in an improved officer."

As far as I know, this cross training went no further and I was the only officer to participate.

*

On Aug. 14, 1988, I promoted to sergeant and was assigned to the Highway Patrol Bureau holding area, awaiting a transfer to somewhere in the state. A sergeant from Phoenix Property and Evidence took the next open road position, thus I had an opportunity to assume his position which I did.

With Lt. Steve Roethle as my commander, I began supervising four civilian employees at Phoenix Property and Evidence. We were responsible for receiving evidence from agencies throughout the state, including DPS. Although Flagstaff and Tucson had their own Property and Evidence Units, I was also responsible for the Flagstaff unit and its two civilian employees. When Lt. Roethle traveled to either Tucson or Flagstaff, I went with him.

I traveled at least once a week to have meetings with my civilian employees in Flagstaff. This was a busy job with tons of paperwork. We also took in evidence from other agencies that did not have their own units. We had to store all evidence we received plus maintain the chain of evidence with law enforcement agencies, crime labs and courts.

The Phoenix Property and Evidence Building was located in a two-story building directly above the Phoenix Crime Lab. We had a dumb waiter, a quite small elevator, which allowed us to promptly transport and receive evidence from the Crime Lab.

We also had a remote site, about five acres, on West Buckeye Road in Phoenix where we kept evidence that was too large or bulky to store in our upstairs unit located on the Phoenix DPS compound. The Buckeye facility was for autos, auto parts and other large containers. There was a 60- by 150-foot warehouse at this facility and everything was crowded. Our Auto Theft and Chop Shop squads were doing a bang-up job and this is where we stored most of their evidence as well as vehicles seized during narcotics seizures.

All my employees were scheduled for call outs which were numerous, especially at the Buckeye facility. The smaller items could wait for regular business hours.

We had our own incinerator as did Tucson. We incinerated tons and tons of marijuana as well as bales of cocaine and heroin. This necessitated volumes of paperwork and a supervisor to be present at all burns. On at least two occasions, we took semi-trailers full of narcotics to the Arizona Public Service power plant just west of Holbrook, near Joseph City. This process required considerable security and at least two Highway Patrol vehicles along with Lt. Roethle, myself and another officer from Phoenix. The job was rewarding, but it involved a tremendous amount of paper work and corresponding busy work.

During Tucson visits with the Southern Property and Evidence staff, I met a number of officers and supervisors charged with various functions in Southern Arizona. One of these was Lt. Bill Breen who was in charge of the Southern Narcotics and Criminal Investigations units. He had a sergeant in Sierra Vista who had a squad of officers. This unit was currently assigned to the Border Alliance Group (BAG). BAG handled all narcotics investigations east of Tucson to Willcox and everything south. This sergeant was ready to retire and Lt. Breen asked me to put in for the position. It would mean moving to Sierra Vista and I was sure I could talk Beth into this as I saw it as a good career move for me. How wrong I was.

*

In 1986, we purchased a home at 15285 N. 64th Ave. in Phoenix. We really loved the house, the area and had really good neighbors. Travis was going to Arizona State University which was great and Jenny was doing good in school, but she was a handful for Beth. Beth was still somewhat recuperating from throat cancer surgery she had in 1991.

She was very hesitant in uprooting the kids from school and being away from her doctor. Moving to Sierra Vista would mean the nearest medical facility of any worth would be about 70 miles away in Tucson. I finally agreed with her reasoning and wholeheartedly sided with her. Why not? She was right.

I was being selfish, but saw this as an opportunity to further advance myself within the Department. In other words, move up to lieutenant, a promotional process I had already began to study for.

My daughter, Debbie (from my first marriage to Jody) lived in Sierra Vista with her husband, Greg, and her two daughters, Ashley and

Valerie, my grand kids. While contemplating my transfer, I visited with them on a couple occasions. The lived in a large mobile home on three acres and had an extra bedroom they would let me or insisted I stay if I transferred.

In talking with Lt. Breen during the formal interview process, I thoroughly laid out the situation reference my family. I advised him I had a place to stay, but my family probably would not be moving. I told him I would have my private vehicle and would commute to Phoenix on days off. I didn't feel good about being accepted because a few other sergeants were also interviewing and I knew at least one would make the commitment to move to Sierra Vista.

On Feb. 2, 1992, I was assigned to Sierra Vista and I moved in with Debbie and her family. This assignment was rather convoluted as not one of my officers seemed to know who they were working for (me) even though we had an office in Sierra Vista. This became clearer the more I got my feet wet.

Although my office was in Sierra Vista, we had officers stationed in Bisbee and Douglas where most of the other agencies and my guys reported. No paperwork I ever found assigned my officers to directly report to another sergeant who was actually the district BAG unit supervisor.

What the hell? I am a sergeant with no officers reporting directly to me? I wanted to be where they were, assisting them. I talked to the sergeant in Douglas, who was running the unit, and told him I just wanted to be included in whatever my officers were doing. I didn't want anything to change, I just wanted to be kept up to date on things that were happening.

Well, come to find out, he wasn't even the primary one calling the shots. Two federal officers, one from U.S. Customs and one from the U.S. Border Patrol at the Douglas office, were the lead officers and pretty much set up scheduling for all BAG officers. I said, "Well, shit, just schedule me also then. I would be an extra officer for them."

That really didn't work out all that well as I had tons of paperwork to write reference weekly activities as well as receiving the paperwork and evidence submitted by my officers. I then had to deliver said paperwork every Tuesday morning to lt. Breen in Tucson. No it could not be mailed. So every Tuesday, I was in the lieutenant's office in Tucson giving an account of weekly events as were all of his other sergeants. This shot the day.

I started to get into some of the all night surveillances, drug arrests, etc. I have to say that the U.S. Customs and Border Patrol had some very neat toys, especially their night-vision equipment and the sensors they had placed all over the county at known and supposed crossings into the U.S. from Mexico. The border crossing directly across from Douglas was Aqua Prieta and another entrance was at Naco (the name comes from the last two letters in Arizona and Mexico), a few miles west of Douglas. They primarily worked confidential informants or snitches as you might know them.

I soon got into a routine that was well received by my officers. Every week, I would travel to Bisbee and then Douglas to pick up their paperwork, especially their weeklies which are required of all personnel. They did not have to travel to Sierra Vista and could spend that time at BAG meetings and operations which were also held weekly. Some BAG meetings I made, most I didn't.

My days off were not always the same, but when I had at least two days in a row, I would go home. I could tell my absence was growing on Beth, but she was doing a great job on the home front. She very seldom complained about anything.

*

On the morning of Aug. 22, 1992, a Saturday, I got up and made my rounds picking up paperwork to prepare my monthly report. At about noon, I was in Tombstone for one of their weekend events and also to see who was campaigning, handing out fliers for the upcoming county elections.

*

I had lived with Debbie and Greg for about a month when my secretary at the Sierra Vista office told me of a friend of hers who was looking for a roommate. This friend of hers owned a large mobile home on acreage just south of Sierra Vista and only occupied the master bedroom suite at the rear of the trailer. The remainder of the trailer, she said, he had opted to rent. This included two bedrooms, family room, kitchen, laundry room and a bathroom.

The owner was in his seventies and living alone. When we met, I explained to him I kept irregular hours, had two vehicles and he would probably be better off renting to a young couple as I didn't need nearly that much room. My secretary had already informed him about me and my shift work so he already had his mind made up. He wanted me to rent, so when he quoted me a price per month, I was shocked. I told him, I couldn't agree to such a small fee, but if he also let me pay all utilities, I would consider it. We reached an agreement and I moved in later that day.

*

Sierra Vista's elevation is about 5,000 feet above sea level, about the same elevation as Prescott. But because of its location being southernmost in the state, it was still high desert country, instead of forest land as many might expect. The Huachuca Mountain range is huge with numerous hiking trails. I loved to hike and did at least three or four days a week.

On June 18, 1992, I was hiking in Lutz Canyon, just off Ash Canyon Road, about a mile past a residential area. From where I parked the vehicle, I had gone about a mile up the trail when I smelled something different, a rather strong musky smell. I was concentrating primarily on being quiet and to be on the lookout for rattlesnakes. I was dressed in shorts, t-shirt and tennis shoes.

As I rounded a slight curve, I noticed a movement and observed a black bear about 100 feet from me and coming my way. The bear abruptly stopped put his nose in the air and apparently gathered my scent. He shook the water off him as a dog does after getting wet. The bear then lumbered up a hill to my left. I could hear it busting brush for a good couple hundred yards.

I measured the distance from where I stood. It was 33 yards or 99 feet. The interesting part of this is I was never scared nor do I think my pulse rate even spiked. However, I was more leery about bears and less attentive to the snakes afterwards.

I could write story after story about my hiking experiences, but I will leave you with just this one.

*

I had been studying my butt off for the upcoming lieutenant's test and finally took the written portion in Phoenix. My heart wasn't totally into it because if I did make lieutenant, I knew I would again be transferred to wherever the position was open. I passed this test, with a score of 87 percent.

The written test comprised 40 percent of the overall score. The remaining 60 percent was the oral board. I was in the top 10 going into the oral portion and knew if I aced this portion, I would be on a short list to be promoted.

The day I was to take my oral, I called and cancelled. I told them I had other priorities in my life and this wasn't the time for me to be getting promoted and transferred. The Law Enforcement Merit System Council, which oversees departmental activities, never had anyone in the top 10 call in and cancel an oral board.

The LEMSC business manager, Capt. Coy Johnston, called me at least two times and told me that my time could be switched if that was a problem. He then told me he had it on good authority that if I passed as everyone thought I would, I would be on a very short list, maybe as high as third for promotion. I told him thanks, but no thanks.

I learned later from a friend who would know as he was one of the three on the oral board that it had been discussed sending me to Holbrook as a lieutenant and Highway Patrol District 3 commander. I probably would have declined this position anyway as I cannot stand Holbrook and besides, it was as far away as Sierra Vista which now seemed like it was 10 hours away instead of four.

*

I wanted to go home, no, I needed to go home. The distance between Beth and me was increasing and we are not simply talking miles. Lt. Breen was aware of my family concerns and said he would keep an eye and ear open for anything coming up in Phoenix, but not in the Highway Patrol as per my request.

An acquaintance of mine, Sgt. Roland Cole, was working as an administrative sergeant for Capt. Mike Denny in the Intelligence Division. Roland was thinking retirement and the captain had asked him to pick out a possible replacement before leaving. Capt. Denny and Lt. Breen were friends and it became known I was looking for a position in Phoenix because of my needs and my family needs.

I only knew Roland Cole as the sergeant in charge of the internal investigation pertaining to Chuck Spooner's and my involvement in the race track investigation years earlier. Now, I don't know why or even if he did put in a good word for me to Capt. Denny, but the captain decided to take a chance on me.

I started working for Capt. Denny, most likely in early 1993. He was in charge of the Intelligence Division, which consisted mostly of civilian employees. Now, I knew we had such a division, but that was as far as my knowledge went. My duties were to monitor the division, assist the Intell people with whatever and submit reports to the captain.

*

I had slightly more than two years to go before I could retire with 20 active years with DPS. This was one of my goals when I started with DPS in 1975. Under a special program, I was given an opportunity to "buy back" up to five years of my military time to go towards my DPS time. In essence, if I purchased my military time, I would have enough time in to retire. I bought back 3½ years at a considerable expense to me. Your retirement pension at the time in DPS was based on an average of your highest three earning years, including overtime. I knew I could build on overtime by possibly returning to liquor enforcement as an officer and I was strongly considering this.

*

After working for Capt. Denny for about six months, I approached him and asked for a sit-down on a rather personal issue. I was granted the time and had all my ducks in a row when I met with him.

I started by letting him know I appreciated the chance he gave me to be his administrative sergeant. I told him I just wasn't an administrative person and felt he could do better with someone else. I also said I was thinking of resigning my commission as a sergeant if it would allow me to get back into the Liquor Division so I could be more active and productive.

Capt. Denny, if anything, was known as a straight forward person. He told me I was doing a good job, but he felt my uneasiness. He also said he didn't even particularly like what he was doing and there was something going through the state legislature that might benefit us both.

He would not or could not elaborate, but he just asked me to sit tight for a few more months and things could change for both of us, for the better. He said if things worked out the way he expected, we were both transferring. He said he wanted to tell me earlier, but couldn't. He also said he didn't know I was so willing to take such drastic measures in order to become more active and productive.

Again, he advised me to be patient and to wait. Perhaps, it was some of the best advice I ever received as I was about to embark on a very challenging and exciting assignment.

*

In 1993, Arizona Gov. Fife Symington III asked the Department to develop a comprehensive approach to deal with the escalating gang problem in communities throughout Arizona. In response to this request, the Gang Intelligence Team Enforcement Mission (GITEM) was conceived. Capt. Denny was the primary force behind the Department's plans to conceptualize and develop a state-wide gang task force.

Our mission:

1 To impact gang related criminal activity wherever it occurs in Arizona;
2 To increase awareness and skills of law enforcement in dealing with and documenting the existence of gangs and their members throughout the state.

GITEM was the first model of its kind in the nation to bring together law enforcement agencies from all levels to share information for a centralized purpose—the elimination and eradication of gangs in our state. In 1994, the legislature appropriated funding for GITEM. GITEM became reality on July 1, 1994.

Letters were sent to almost every police agency in the state in regards to this new program. In these letters, we asked all agencies for assistance, some for manpower and all for intelligence involving gangs in their areas. Officer Charlie Ruiz and I traveled often to meet with police chiefs or their representatives to gather the intelligence.

Credit needs to be given to two officers who are probably the foremost authorities on gangs in the state of Arizona—Charlie Ruiz and Shannon Lewis. They both worked gang intelligence with our Intelligence Unit for a number of years. To this day, they continue to be among my closest friends. They were known statewide for their intelligence work on street gangs. Shannon was also an instructor to other agencies on gang identification. At times, all three of us would travel to various parts of Arizona to work together with local law enforcement agencies in street gang matters.

*

Literally, reams of paperwork were gathered regarding various gang problems throughout the state. These documents were turned over to our Intelligence analysts and technicians who made up a very important part of GITEM. Squads were formed in September 1994 and serious training began led by Shannon and officers from the Phoenix Police Department.

I was assigned 10 officers—three from other metro departments as well as Shannon and Charlie. Shannon was the designated instructor for GITEM and Charlie was my squad's designated Intelligence officer. Each squad had an Intelligence officer whose job was to primarily select our work areas.

Our statistics were phenomenal as the gangs had no idea what was happening. We worked two-man units. The only problem I consistently had involved scheduling. Some officers were not compatible working together and it took a while to get the right ones together.

*

During this time, for the past few years, I went on regular week-long house-boat trips to Lake Powell with Dick Roberts, a friend and a partner with Travis in an investment group. This particular trip occurred during the week of Oct. 21-27.

Usually, we could get a group of at least four or five people for this trip. Dick had a time share on a very luxurious 16- by 66-foot houseboat named "Dream Catcher." Who wouldn't want to go? We usually towed a couple of our fishing boats behind the house boat, up the lake to the San Juan River. Once there, we would find a nice spot to tie off the house boat and use that location as our base camp.

This particular outing, however, it was just Dick and myself. We met at the house boat on the 21st and motored up the lake, towing my boat. Just past the mouth of the San Juan River, we found a likely camp spot and tied down the house boat, no easy task as we had to have at least two good areas to place our stakes "iron poles" for the tie downs.

We secured the houseboat and unloaded the two jet skis, via a power winch from the top deck of the houseboat. It was getting late after we putted around for a while on the jet skis. We were going out on my bass boat early the next morning and we tied off the bass boat to the rear of the houseboat. I might add I tied it very securely. It was a beautiful 18-foot, 4-inch Champion bass boat with an Evinrude 150 outboard engine.

During the night, I felt some strong winds and went to look at the boats and the jet skis we had run ashore about five feet up onto the sand. Everything looked OK. At about 4:30 a.m., I heard a loud snap and felt the houseboat rapidly shift. Before I could get dressed and respond, the houseboat was sideways to the shore and my bass boat was banging on rocks.

Dick went to start the houseboat engines to get us away from the rocks. He was just backing up as another huge wave hit the boat and my bass boat flipped upside down and under the rear of the houseboat. One of my tie downs for the bass boat had snapped, but one was still tied to the front rung. We had no choice, but to move to a more secure area, out of the direct winds and waves.

Music Temple Canyon was about 2.5 miles away and if we could get there, we could get out of the winds. My bass boat was capsized, but I thought we might make it at a slow rate of speed. I was wrong. The last line to my bass boat snapped and I watched as the winds took it back to the shoreline. Only about 12 inches of my boat was visible above the water. For our safety, our only option was to seek shelter.

Because of the safety hazard of my bass boat being capsized, floating aimlessly, we broadcast an SOS and proceeded to Music Temple Canyon to get out of the winds. At about 8 a.m., U.S. Forest Service rangers located us and took the necessary report. Dick was given a ride back to the area where we had beached the jet skis. He was wearing a wet suit and took a gas can and tow line with him.

About noon, I heard Dick coming into the canyon at a slow rate of speed. He was driving one jet ski and towing the other. Jet skis are not made for towing and it took Dick forever to get back to the houseboat. Dick said the jet skis were 12 to 15 feet onto the sand so it took a while to get them back into the water. We were actually three miles away from where we had been moored. He also said he had seen my bass boat and he thought we could tip it upright by using the jet skis and some rope.

When we drove the jet skis back to the area, my bass boat was last seen, there was a large fishing boat in the area. Those aboard were very helpful in helping right my boat. Jet skis would never had done the job. We got my bass boat in shallow enough water to where we could start bailing water out of it in hopes of getting it to float.

I had the brilliant idea to try the bilge pumps. They worked. Can you believe that? The batteries were still good after being in the water for hours. Guess that's why they are called marine batteries.

As our saviors in the larger fishing vessel watched us, they offered to tow the bass boat to where we were in Music Temple Canyon. We left the bilge pumps running. Dick and I followed on the jet skis.

It was already getting late and we decided to get my boat as far up on the sand as possible and try to get it running the next day. We cussed and discussed what we could have done differently. We decided, eventually, it was all Mother Nature's fault.

The next morning, we got up and my boat was pretty much under water again. I had not left the bilge pumps on overnight and thought this might be the case. I knew the gas tank, at least, would have to be drained and new gas put in before we could even attempt ignition. This took a couple hours. When I attempted to start the Evinrude, a wonderful motor, it kicked over. I drove the boat around the canyon we were in and when I got back to the houseboat, I told Dick I was going to try to drive back to Wahweap Marina and load it onto the trailer.

This was about 60 miles away, but if I wore a life vest and stayed as close to the shoreline as I could, I felt it could be done.

While draining the gas from my boat, we winched up and secured the jet skis as we knew we were going into the marina the first chance we got. Dick said he would be behind me and if I had problems, he would be looking for me on his way in.

It didn't take long to determine the best speed to keep on plane was full-speed ahead. It took a little over an hour to reach the marina with both bilge pumps working full steam. I left both pumps working and the engine running as I ran to my vehicle and backed it down the ramp.

I had no problems loading the boat and getting out of the dock area. It was only when I got to the top of the ramp and was tying down my ties that I saw the damage that had been done to my boat's underside.

Apparently, when my boat was underwater, it came into contact with one of the engine props from the houseboat. At least a 12-inch hunk of fiberglass was missing. All compartments holding all my fishing poles, tackle, life vest, etc. had come open and every single item was gone. Fortunately, I had put my wallet containing my ID, badge and money in the glove box and it had not come open, but everything was quite soaked.

Dick arrived a few hours later. After reviewing the damage to my boat and discussing the situation, I told him I was heading back to Phoenix. He said he would stay for the remaining few days in the marina dry docked.

The insurance company considered my boat a total loss. After estimates were obtained, including the cost of my lost equipment, I settled with the insurance company.

*

I returned early to GITEM and found they had gotten along very well without me. The year 1995, however, was a very difficult one for my squad as we were involved in three shooting incidents within one week.

The first occurred when a passing motorist, in the early morning hours, fired three shots at Officer Kevin Jex of DPS and Officer Lupe Davila of the Goodyear Police Department. They immediately turned their vehicle around to pursue the suspect who turned out to be a juvenile. I also responded and arrived just after the suspect was taken into custody. The suspect was a 16-year-old from Iran who just wanted to shoot somebody. He had a chrome-plated Colt .38 special that worked well.

During the pursuit, he tossed the weapon, but it was recovered. Another 16-year-old who was also in the vehicle gave us a close proximity of where the weapon was tossed. This second suspect was not charged.

My officers did not return fire and the suspect offered no resistance after stopping.

In the second shooting, we were working a detail in an area just north of Casa Grande when an Arizona National Guard helicopter pilot spotted a vehicle on a desert road traveling without headlights. The pilot informed us the driver would turn out his headlights, travel a short distance and then turn them on again. A couple of my units caught sight of the guy and began pursuit. After rounding a curve, the motorist stopped his vehicle and bolted into the desert.

I was rapidly approaching the scene and listening to the radio traffic while this was occurring. I came to a fence on the road began my foot pursuit. I could see the helicopter and listened to the radio traffic as I started my version of a foot pursuit. The other officers had the luxury of lights from the helicopter as I had only my flashlight. I was bushwhacking it in almost total darkness while trying to parallel my officers' pursuit from across a wash about a quarter-mile away.

The suspect would not stop, but often slowed and reached into his pocket as if to retrieve a weapon. At one point, Officer Jerale, one of my officers, expended a full can of pepper spray on the subject, almost at point-blank range, but it was of no effect. During this, the suspect with a knife in one hand, used the other to knock the pepper spray from Jerales' hand.

Following the deployment of a second can of pepper spray, the subject probably ran another half mile all the while threatening the officers with the knife, saying he was not going back to jail.

I was close enough by now to hear Officer J.D. Freese command the suspect to drop the knife. Instead of dropping the knife, he raised it in a threatening manner. From about 10 feet away, J.D. shot him once in the stomach. The suspect took one step before falling. The helicopter pilot video taped the entire episode and this would be made available to the administrative investigation that follows all police-related shootings. I was on the scene within a minute of the shooting and some other officers were still en route.

After the suspect was "air-evacted" to the Maricopa County Hospital jail ward in Phoenix, we went to our respective vehicles some 2½ miles away. Then we met at the DPS compound in Casa Grande. I had to relieve J.D. of his weapon and wait for our lieutenant and captain to arrive.

A few days later, we learned that the suspect was a 27-year-old resident of Casa Grande. The reasons he ran were numerous. There were four outstanding warrants for his arrest—three misdemeanors and a fourth for probation violation. He also was involved in a domestic altercation and kidnapping that occurred the previous day. Ironically, he was not a gang member.

The third shooting occurred while we were working in the 1800 block of Alta Vista in Phoenix. We were assisting our undercover squad in an arrest when someone shot at us. No one was hit, but a toilet bowl was shattered when a round went through a home in the area. The shooter or shooters were hiding in an alley in the vicinity and fired numerous shots at us. No arrests were ever made.

*

During my time with GITEM, we implemented a bike squad. I was the first GITEM sergeant to receive this training and the same held true for most of my squad. Having bicycles would give us greater mobility in congested or highly-populated areas, i.e. community events, county fairs, parks, etc., as well as greater accessibility and visibility to the community.

This training program was taught by Officer Keith Otts, a Glendale police officer assigned to my squad. This was a two-week course and very demanding. At one point in our slow maneuvering drills, I dumped my bike and when I tried to break my fall, I dislocated my little finger on my left hand. It hurt like a son-of-a-gun and also looked kind of funny. J.D. Freese pulled it back into place, not 100 percent, but enough I could finish the training. It still looks a little funny even today, but functions fine.

We all were issued top-of-the-line Raleigh off-road bicycles retrofitted with headlight, taillight, saddle bags and extra inner tubes. Our vehicles were fitted with bike carriers and we were ready to get after it. The bicycle unit was very well received in almost all communities. Because it was a high-profile unit and an unusual function at DPS, it garnered considerable media attention.

GITEM was housed on the fourth floor of a high-rise commercial building located on the southwest corner of Thomas Road and Central Avenue. We had garage parking, and at least twice a month, conducted advanced training in the garage emphasizing such tactics as vehicle stops and suspect take downs.

From July 1, 1994, through June 30, 1995 (the state's fiscal year), GITEM responded to 228 gang suppression details at the request of 72 law enforcement agencies, including 12 from other states. GITEM arrested more than 3,200 suspects for offenses ranging from illegal possession of a firearm to homicide. Of those arrested, 44 percent were juveniles and nearly all were documented gang members. We seized more than 470 firearms with about 40 percent of these in possession of juveniles.

Officers Charlie Ruiz, Shannon Lewis and I were responsible for setting up GITEM squads in Mohave County (Bullhead City), Coconino County (Flagstaff), Navajo County (Show Low). We contacted the respective police chiefs, interviewed the prospective officers and then supplied training for the officers and sergeants selected for gang enforcement.

Our undercover squad, supervised by Andy Vasquez, selected the best officers it could to work within this elite squad. All squads within GITEM were elite, but it takes a certain type person with the right personality to work undercover in gang-infested areas.

In 1995 and 1996, cop programs seemed to be the trend on national television. "Real Stories of the Highway Patrol" and "Cops" covered activities involving GITEM Metro Phoenix squads. It was a privilege to have cameramen ride along with us on numerous assignments. Consequently, I was on local and national television on a few occasions.

GITEM was probably the most exciting assignment I had with DPS, although my ILED assignment ranks right up there.

*

During the latter part of 1996, I started having some tingling and then numbness on the right side of my face. It actually felt like bugs crawling on my face. I underwent various medical tests, including an MRI (magnetic resonance imaging). All came back negative. During the last week of December 1996, it was recommended I have an MRA magnetic resonance angiogram) to look for aneurisms in the brain. This was done and on Dec. 31, New Year's Eve, Dr. Sandly called to advise me concerning the MRA.

I had an aneurism on the right side of my brain and he wanted me to see a neurological surgeon as soon as possible. Even though they discovered the brain aneurism, it would have nothing to do with the numbness on the side of my face. But for having the tests done, I wouldn't have known about the aneurism. The funny thing, not really, about brain aneurisms is you usually hear about them after the person has died and an autopsy performed. At least, I was in a pre-autopsy stage.

Beth and I did a considerable amount of research in regards to surgeons for the procedure and decided on a Dr. Carrie Walters. When we met with her on Jan. 9, she showed us the MRA negatives and explained that the aneurism behind the right temple area was located on a major artery leading to the brain. She said we were very, very lucky to have found this before it burst because very few are diagnosed prior to rupturing. Only about a third survive and those usually entail some sort of paralysis. She also stated that God must be watching over me, for what reason I don't know, but with my past history, I'm sure he will let me know in time.

She went on to explain that I would be off work at least eight weeks, possibly longer. I would be in the hospital at least five days after the surgery. She would have to go in and remove a portion of my skull to clamp off the aneurism with a titanium clamp. She would then aspirate the aneurism with a very fine needle, replace the portion of my skull with titanium plates and suture me with staples. She scheduled the surgery for Jan. 30, 1997, at Good Samaritan Hospital.

After leaving the doctor's office, I returned to work. I was going to meet with my lieutenant, Wendell Grasee, and went to his office. He was in the process of moving his belongings to the captain's office. At the time, the totality of the situation impacted me and I couldn't talk with him. I knew, although I had not been told, that I would lose my squad and possibly have to finish my career in some sort of an administrative position, possibly the training position.

I decided to meet with Sgt. Ramon Figueroa who was working administration at the time. I stated my position and asked if he would switch positions with me when the time came. I did not have the authority to pull this off, I was only trying to lay the groundwork to possibly keep my squad. He agreed if we could arrange it. I took the rest of the day off. Ramon agreed to keep our conversation confidential until I could speak with Lt. Grasee.

After arriving at work on Jan. 11, 1997, I advised my squad members and the other two sergeants of my situation. I then called Lt. Grasee and left word for him to call when he got home. He was out of town at the time.

I felt a sense of helplessness because I knew I had a time bomb in my head, ready to explode. If it did, I also knew I had about a 25-percent chance of survival, and then only as a cripple.

On Jan. 13, 1997, I finally got to talk with Lt. Grasee. He had not heard anything and was quite shocked by the news. He readily grasped the idea of my flip-flopping with Ramon. I felt an immediate sense of relief because I truly wanted to stay with GITEM and maybe even get my squad back.

I continued to work, hoping to finish the week, and I did, but I couldn't concentrate much on work. On Thursday, Jan. 16, 1997, my squad left to work in Yuma. I wanted to go, but realized I would only be a liability and if anything happened, I needed to be close to the hospital. The next week, I worked and got a lot done, but had lapses where I couldn't even think of work.

*

On Jan. 23, 1997, I had all my pre-ops done which were extensive. My last day at work, Jan. 24, 1997, I received a phone call from Major Bob Halliday. He was very concerned and supportive. He told me that after the surgery, if I felt like I could return to work to take another week off and go fishing. I laughed and told him I might hold him to his word. He said he was serious and he would sign off on it.

As a side note, Major Halliday would later retire from DPS and then come back a few years later as director of the Department.

I have always felt like I had an extended family at DPS and if anything were to happen to me during or after surgery, Beth would be looked after with her best interests at heart.

Beth and I were up at 5 a.m., to head for Good Samaritan Hospital. I was scheduled for an angiogram at 6:30 a.m. which would last about eight hours. They went into the groin area with the catheter and I wasn't much help as I kept trying to look at the screen to watch the procedure. They finally had to strap my head down to keep me from moving.

I was given morphine. I love this drug and another drug they fed into me through an IV. The IV probably was more painful than the angiogram. The IV was left in for seven hours.

At about 3 p.m., Dr. Walters came in and spoke with us. She again explained the procedure in detail and told us the most common after effect was extreme tiredness which could last up to a year. She said I would be able to do anything I felt like as far as my progression went. She also said I would be almost pain free as far as surgery effects because the brain does not have any nerve endings.

On Jan. 28, 1997, about noon, I returned to Good Sam for the last of my pre-ops. This was an EEG (electroencephalography) of the brain. The technician who completed this test was Mary Mitchell, a sister of Bob and Dan Mitchell, two sergeants I had occasionally worked with at DPS.

*

Next came a long day of waiting and getting things together for my admittance at 6:30 a.m. on Jan. 30, 1997. I was ready for the surgery both physically and mentally, I had given Beth the power of attorney for my health care and I was sure if anything out of the ordinary occurred, she would make the right decision. Charley Ruiz, Ramon Figueroa and lots of family and friends were there for Beth. I felt I was handling things better than Beth and thanked God for the people who would be with her.

I went under the knife at about 8 a.m. and about 1:30 p.m., Dr. Walters informed the family everything went OK. I was in ICU for 24 hours before moving to a regular room, just around the corner from ICU on the same floor.

The next day, Jan. 31, 1997, a Friday, Dr. Walters came to see me. She said I was coming along great, adding that I could possibly go home as early as Monday if I kept progressing as well as I was. This really surprised Beth as she was concerned about going home being way too soon and probably with good reason as I looked absolutely grotesque with both eyes almost swollen shut and my head shaved, even though there really wasn't much to shave.

Enhancing my look of demise were the staples. I had assumed the staples would be like paper staples. They were humongous which made me look like Frankenstein. Now, some may say it was an improvement, but I still would wear a baseball cap when friends and family came to see me at home.

Following the surgery, I was hoping for some sort of a headline in the newspaper blaring, "DPS Sgt. Ken Haw Survives Knife Attack." Oh, well, I can dream.

*

On March 14, 1997, I had been away from work for about seven weeks. I was released to drive and return to work, but only allowed to work half days. I was on heavy doses of Dilantin and wasn't real sure of the driving part, but I did go to work. I would stay on Dilantin for at least eight more months to combat the possibility of a seizure. I was real shaky, nothing I thought resembling a seizure, but it still scared the hell out of Beth. I also developed a problem with my right eye as it would drift somewhat out of focus, but Dr. Walters assured us this would pass. Guess what? It never has.

I was assigned as Lt. Grasse's administration sergeant. This was a great fit as I had very little to do because the lieutenant was a real hands-on person and liked to do everything himself.

Around mid 1998, GITEM had a slight organizational change and I got a new lieutenant, Jamie McGuffin, who had just been promoted. Previously, Lt. McGuffin was a sergeant in Wickenburg where he had spent his entire career with the Highway Patrol.

The next few months, I felt like I was a training officer and enjoyed every minute of it. The lieutenant, never having been in Criminal Investigations, relied heavily on me for information and input. We got along great and he was a quick learner.

After a few more months, I felt I had given as much as I could. I discussed this with Beth and after several lengthy conversations, I submitted my letter of retirement to Director Joe Albo.

It went like this"

"After 26 years of police work, 23 plus with the Arizona Department of Public Safety, I have decided to hang up my guns, so to speak. I have developed quite an extended family while with the Department, many of whom I will maintain contact with. I've heard it mentioned a few times that there is no 'I' in team and I am indeed leaving a great team. It is with great honor and a smidgen of trepidation that I tender this letter of retirement, effective Sept. 30, 1998."

*

My retirement party was to be at the Fraternal Order of Police building at 24th Street and Devonshire, starting at 6:30 p.m., Friday, Sept. 26, 1998. At 3:30 p.m., I received a phone call from Mrs. Kris Horseman informing me her husband, Tom, had passed away at their home the day before. Tom had been laid up for about 10 months with stomach cancer. He had been a big part of my life and career since I was investigating horse racing. Tom was one of the good guys and had supplied me with lots of solid and credible information. His heart was always in the right place even to the end. Kris said he never gave up hope or lost his faith, dying with a smile on his face.

About 6:30 p.m., Beth, Travis, Jenny and I arrived at my party. There were already about 50 people there. I won't mention all by name. Lt. Frank Calligari and his wife were there from Tucson as Frank was to be the master of ceremonies. Lt. Grasee presented me with my parting gift, a hand-sculpted and hand-painted largemouth bass. I still see this everyday in my study at home.

Lt. McGuffin presented me with a plaque from GITEM. Director Albo read my retirement letter written by Lt. McGuffin. Lt. McGuffin presented me a certificate signed by Director Albo and Governor Jane Dee Hull. Director Albo also presented Beth with a certificate of appreciation for being by my side the entire 23 plus years. Director Albo also presented me a nice plaque with my original Highway Patrol badge affixed to it.

Sylvia Lopez, founder of Mothers Against Gangs (MAG), presented me a plaque from the MAG group. I was introduced to Sylvia in 1995 by Charley Ruiz and Shannon Lewis. Sylvia had lost her son to gang violence and as a result, founded MAG, now a national organization in which she became chairman.

Donna Neill, president of NAILEM, a cooperative neighborhood anti-gang group, presented me with a t-shirt for the work my squad and I had done in the Westwood-Simpson neighborhood in central Phoenix.

195

Donna is a red-headed, fiery, feisty-type person who got things done. With more people like her who care about their neighborhood the way she does, we probably wouldn't have a gang problem.

*

Two days before my effective date of retirement, my daughter Karen (Dee Dee) and Jody called and wanted us to come over and visit with her and Debbie. Debbie had entered a program in Chandler and had been there for about a week. When we arrived on the evening of Sept. 28, 1998, Debbie, Dee Dee, Valerie, Ashley and Greg were all in counseling. This session was being mediated by Dee Dee and we could hear the yelling coming from the counseling room as we sat in the waiting area.

Valerie and Ashley came out first. Beth and I had a short talk with them until Debbie came out. Debbie was visibly upset and told us she was leaving Greg as he would not support her in dealing with her problems. Dee Dee came out and spoke with us. She said Greg did not understand why Debbie was taking this approach to getting help.

I had drawn my own conclusions over the years and thought the primary problem with Debbie was not necessarily her issues, but with Greg. Dee Dee agreed with me. The end result was this was going to divide the family in a big way.

*

On Wednesday, Sept. 30, 1998, I turned in all my DPS equipment and actually became unemployed for the first time in a long time. I said my goodbyes. I already had turned in my departmental vehicle so I was in my personal vehicle when I decided to stop by Glen Lakes Golf Course at 55th Avenue and Northern to say "hi" to an old friend, Roland Cole.

Roland, whom I had replaced as an admin sergeant when he retired in 1993, was now general manager at Glen Lakes Golf Course. I sat in his office and told him I had finally pulled the pin and retired. We talked a bit and he asked me what I was going to do. I told him Beth was climbing the walls wondering the same thing, but I really didn't know. He told me he was looking for an outside services supervisor to work part-time and if I was interested, the job was mine.

This job would entail supervising and scheduling, picking up range balls, washing said balls. This job also would involve cleaning and detailing golf carts and as much free golf as I could play. He told me meals would be half price at the snack bar and free non-alcoholic beverages for me and my immediate family.

Wow, how could I say no? They also were going to pay me $8 an hour and I could set my own schedule as long as there was coverage at the course.

Glen Lakes was managed by American Golf Corp., who owned or operated some really nice public and private courses. I could play at any of them, nationwide. I am not a great golfer, some would probably say not even good. But when I did play, I gave it my all. The drinks coming around the courses via the beverage cart girl didn't hurt either. I liked the game, but because of back surgeries, my mobility was hindered. More on the surgeries in an attachment.

I went home and talked this over with Beth. She was surprised I wanted to do anything so soon. I said I had already been without a job for about a day and it was time to for me to start looking. I know my surgeries and full-time disabilities would be a hindrance to any full-time position. But with my DPS retirement, we could make a go of it.

Shortly after my retirement, Beth's mother, Marge, passed away on Nov. 17, 1998, at her house with Beth, Kathy and Bob present.

Chapter 11

Life after DPS

Just on a whim, I placed a call to the Social Security Administration, reference the possibility of getting disability income because of the condition my surgeries had left me in. I remember the gentleman I talked to, when I explained my physical situation, stating, "How come you haven't applied sooner." He sent me the paper work and told me to start gathering copies of my medical reports and all documentation I could find to support my request.

My job at Glen Lakes was great. I was able to work outside as much as I wanted, but I was again having back pains which kept me from overdoing it on the job. I was almost sure I had another herniated disk, but kept putting off going to the doctor because I knew the doctor would probably recommend surgery.

*

I need to elaborate a little on this surgery because it was a precursor for the above call to the Social Security Administration.

On Jan. 17, 2000, I had my second back surgery at Good Samaritan Hospital and what followed became an absolute nightmare.

Dr. Carrie Walters, who had done my brain surgery, also performed my back surgery. Following surgery, I was self-medicating with a morphine pump and was also taking other narcotics orally for the pain. When Dr. Walters came in to see me the next day, I told her even though I was on morphine and other pain-relieving drugs, I still had a stabbing pain in my lower back.

She said the surgery had went pretty well, but she had to pry the nerves away from the herniated disk and probably had irritated the nerves. She added this pain probably would pass in a short time. For the next two months, Dr. Walters prescribed various drugs for the pain—Propo-n/apap, Endocet, Dexamethasone, Diazepam, Prochlorper, Celebrex, Neurontin, and Amitriptyline.

She also recommended I go to a pain clinic. On Feb. 10, 2000, I went to the pain clinic and conferred with Dr. Nenad. After a lengthy consultation, he put me on massive doses of Endocet and took me off all the other medications. A week later, he added Paxil, Methadone and Neurotine and took away the Endocet. Two weeks later, he added Amitriptyline, Celebrex and doubled up on my Methadone.

I stayed on these until I had to go into CIGNA emergency on April 22, 2000, as I was throwing up, had bad stomach pains and also still had considerable back pain. I was treated by Dr. Soo. He put me on Promethazine as well as all of the above. He didn't want to override the pain management recommendations.

I went off all the pain meds except the Promethazine. Dr. Soo had told me this could cause me to go into a coma and was against going off the meds all at once. I felt I was already comatose, just sitting around the house vegetating.

On May 5, 2000, I had an appointment with Dr. Nenad. I told him about going into the emergency room and I thought all the meds were killing me so I had quit taking them. I was now very weak, especially down my back and legs, and had severe stomach problems. Dr. Nemad indicated if I did not want to stay on their program, he didn't know what else he could do for me. I thanked him and told him I thought the pain clinic already had done enough and that I was never coming back. A promise I kept.

*

On May 14, 2000, I went back to the emergency room with excruciating stomach, back and leg pain. Hell, by this point, I didn't know which hurt worse. I was admitted into Thunderbird Good Samaritan. I spent three days in this hospital where they ran every test imaginable on me. They even thought I was having a heart problem. They eliminated any heart problems.

Dr. Robert Enguidanos was my doctor at the hospital and when I left the hospital, he prescribed Prochlorper, Prevacid and Metoclopromin. I got these prescriptions filled and began taken them. On May 22, 2000, I had a follow-up with my family practitioner, Dr. Donald Spelhaug. We discussed all the tests that had been run in the hospital. I told him about the pain clinic and all the meds I was prescribed. I also told him I had quit all of them and was only on the three Dr. Enguidanos prescribed. Dr. Spelhaug scheduled me for a HIPA test, a test that is gall-bladder specific.

Beth and I had discussed the gall bladder in specific and we both felt this test would show a bad gall bladder.

On May 31, 2000, Dr. Spelhaug told me the HIPA test was normal and we could probably eliminate the gall bladder as the culprit. The gall bladder is one of those organs you can live without and is sometimes very difficult to determine with 100 percent accuracy if it is indeed good or bad. At this time, I felt as if my options were up. While still in his office, I had an attack of bad stomach pain, but I did not throw up. Beth was there and we firmly believed it was gall bladder-related. I think Dr. Spelhaug did too because when I asked him if he knew someone who I could talk to about taking gall bladder out, he said he would make some calls.

*

On June 5, 2000, Beth and I met with Dr. Thomas Strawn regarding gall bladder surgery. I had another mild attack this time, vomiting while in his office. By now, these attacks were very frequent. Dr. Strawn agreed to do the surgery, but was booked solid for a month.

On July 6, 2000, I had outpatient surgery at Thunderbird Good Samaritan. They took out my gall bladder and also repaired a belly button hernia I didn't know existed. Dr. Strawn prescribed Endocet. I got the prescription filled, but did not take any.

On July 21, 2000, Beth and I met with Dr. Strawn for a follow-up on my surgery. He said when he removed the gall bladder, it appeared normal, but as a precautionary measure, he sent it to a lab for analysis. The analysis revealed the gall bladder indeed was diseased and would have continued to give me problems. This was determined through the dissecting of the gall bladder and everything from within the gall bladder itself. None of this was evidenced on any of my previous tests.

I asked him if this could have been caused by the accumulative effects of the drugs I had been on for my back pains. He said it was possible. Since the surgery, I have had no stomach problems, but my back and leg pains continued. Because of the hernia, Dr. Strawn would not release me go return to work until Aug. 18, 2000.

*

I decided to complete the paperwork for Social Security disability and turned it in on Dec. 16, 2000.

I was granted these benefits shortly afterwards with them being retroactive to when I had first called a few months earlier. This benefit would enable Beth and I to make all our payments and secure our future. Anything I was to make at Glen Lakes would help, but was not absolutely needed.

Trav was a Godsend in helping us organize our income and recommended that I put my income from Glen Lakes into an IRA which I did. To this day, I have never touched a penny of this money. I have built up a nice IRA that can be pulled from it if it is ever needed.

*

Tuesday, Sept. 11, 2001, a day that will be in all history books forever. I awoke that morning and as usual put on my coffee, got dressed and went outside to retrieve the newspaper. While I was reading the newspaper, Beth went into the computer room to watch "Good Morning, America" on Channel 3, the ABC television affiliate in Phoenix at that time. I had sat only for a few minutes before Beth came out and said something catastrophic was happening in New York City. We turned the TV on and our day of horror began to unfold as we learned a commercial airliner had flown into one of the Twin Towers at the World Trade Center in New York City.

While we watched, a second airliner flew into the second Twin Tower. We both sat and watched in horror as the Twin Towers were going up in flames prior to imploding.

Our country was under attack, but the Twin Towers was just the beginning of four planned suicidal missions orchestrated by terrorists with intent to bring the United States to its proverbial knees.

While watching these ghastly scenes in New York City, it was reported a third commercial airliner was flown into the Pentagon in

Washington, D.C., our nation's capitol, resulting in massive deaths and casualties. And, it didn't stop there as we learned about a fourth commercial airliner that crashed in Pennsylvania, killing everyone aboard. It was later reported, the fourth plane was to target the White House and if it hadn't been for the heroic efforts of those aboard United Airlines Flight 93, the terrorists might have taken out the home of our president.

We immediately thought terrorists were responsible for these cold-blooded murderous assaults on our country as thousands of innocent people died that day. As we sat glued to the TV, within an hour both Twin Towers collapsed and imploded. We watched knowing the death toll had to be in the thousands.

*

For days following 9-11, I was unable to sleep and did quite a bit of writing. What follows are some of my writings at the time.

"Today is Sunday, Sept. 16, 2001. The reason I'm writing this now, as it is almost midnight, is I haven't been able to sleep at night. I go to bed around 10-10:30 and toss and turn. Unable to sleep, wanting and needing to do something, anything to help those who have given the ultimate sacrifices. Over 200 New York firemen have lost their lives and about 100 New York police officers. I feel their pain, suffering and hatred for the cowardly acts. I have lost friends and classmates while on the police department. I know the suffering.

"On Friday night, Sept. 14, Jenny brought Timmy over to spend the night. He's only been in kindergarten for a few weeks. Neither Beth nor I had any idea how much he had been exposed to this tragedy. I asked him what he had heard about what happened in New York. He was sitting on my lap and whispered to me, 'A plane flew into a building and a lot of people were hurt.' He had also been told that at 7 p.m. everyone should go outside and light candles to help the people because this night had been designated as a national night of mourning. At 7 p.m., we went down to our corner, 64th Avenue and Acapulco, and lit our candles.

"Timmy stated to Beth later that everybody would be OK now because we lit our candles for them. Oh, the age of innocence. He may never realize the totality of this tragic event until he reads it in history books or reads the newspapers we have saved for him.

"We have entered into the first war of the 21st century and God help and guide us in our endeavors to eradicate terrorism. Sen. John McCain made a statement Wednesday that I think is of profound importance to the way I feel. He said, 'May God forgive those who have done this, but we won't.' He was speaking of not only the suicide terrorists who died but to all the terrorists they are associated with."

*

As I write this on Oct. 10, 2011, about one month after the attacks on the World Trade Center and Pentagon, the United States has begun bombing in Afghanistan and much was going on in the world. We have kept all the "A" sections of The Arizona Republic newspapers since 9-11-01.

Around this time, Timmy came to stay with us because he had pink eye. I went to see Dr. Strawn, the doctor who removed my gall bladder and repaired my hernia. Now, he is going to take out a cyst in my left breast with surgery set for Nov. 23, 2011. This will be done in his office and he will send the cyst to the lab for analysis. He didn't think it would be a big deal and if I wanted, I could just leave it until it started to bother me. But, with my track record, I wanted it out ASAP and to be over with it.

*

I had a giant book sale on Nov. 10, 2001, with all proceeds going to the Fireman's Relief Fund in New York City. I started my book drive with the Glen Lakes employees and throughout my immediate neighborhood. I also asked two fire stations to help and Jenny solicited a couple hundred people from Discovery where she worked. Beth and I bought new leather furniture from LazyBoy on Bell Road and while speaking to our salesperson, I brought up the book drive. She thought she could gather quite a few books from the sales people. She said she would call and I would pick up the books.

*

Timmy went in for his first surgery the morning of Oct. 25, 2001. He was really excited as they were going to take his tonsils and adenoids out and put them into a jar. He did fine and was in the recovery room for about three hours before being released. The doctors said he was an excellent patient and came through the procedure really good. His tonsils were very big. Dr. Steven Traicovich said they were about as big as his thumb. The doctor said Timmy should breathe easier and feel much better after he recovers.

Two days later, Jenny called and said she was taking Timmy to emergency as he would not eat or drink anything at all and was very dehydrated. Beth went down to be with Jenny as she seemed very upset. About 12:30 p.m., Jenny called and said they would probably admit Timmy as he still would not eat or drink. I went down and he was happy to see me, but would not eat even a bite of a popsicle. I tried to coax him to no avail.

A nurse, Jody, came in and convinced him to eat a popsicle by telling him there were other little kids sicker than he was who needed his room. She fed him an orange popsicle with a spoon. He wanted another one and Jenny fed him this one with a spoon. A novel way of eating a popsicle. I cut this one with my pocket knife, but he didn't care and his whole demeanor changed. Within a half hour they discharged him Grandpa Jim and Sherry were just coming into the emergency room as we were leaving.

*

The day after Christmas 2001, Timmy and I loaded my boat to go to Lake Pleasant and I soon learned he surely had to do his part with everything. There's a $7 entry fee to get into the lake so I filled out the envelope, put the money in and sealed it, but he had to drop it in the slot.

This was one of the proudest days of my life. I couldn't have asked for a better fishing partner. I knew the catching would be very difficult at best. I figured us for a few hours on the water before Timmy would want to go home. Wrong as Timmy cast and cast and really enjoyed himself, never once complaining.

When we got out of the no wake area, I told Timmy to come over and sit on Papa's lap and drive the boat. He looked at me with the biggest smile on his face. His eyes were as big as silver dollars.

I shut the boat off when he was seated with both hands firmly on the wheel. I coached him on how to start the big engine, put the boat in gear and although he couldn't reach the foot throttle, I did this. I also showed him how to guide the boat straight into the plane and then how to turn to the right and left.

Each time we changed locations to go from one side of the lake to the other, he wanted to drive and he did. I even let him steer us into the main marina where we went into the store and we got a cup of coffee for me and a cup of hot chocolate for him. We walked around the marina sipping our hot drinks for about 30 minutes, then back to the boat where we sat and ate our sandwiches while feeding the ducks the crust of our bread.

We then went back to different fishing areas where I tried to show him how to use the trolling motor to get us around, but this was a little difficult for him with his short legs and little feet.

After a couple more hours of fishing or should I say casting, I finally asked him if he wanted to go home. He said not right now so we stayed a little longer. I finally told him we had to go so we could tell Nana about our trip.

I knew he was getting tired, I was, but he never complained about not catching a fish. On the way home, he wanted to play our travel game "My Itsy Bitsy Eyes See?" Less than two miles from the lake, he was sound asleep. For me, having a day on the lake with my grandson was a dream come true.

*

During a six-year period (1998-2004) of annual physicals, I noticed a steady, significant rise in my prostate specific antigen (PSA) numbers.

September 1998 1.6
September 1999 2.0
December 2000 3.2
January 2002 3.5
March 2003 3.6
March 2004 4.7

Following my PSA in March 2004, a urologist in Sun City asked me to consider having biopsies done on my prostate. He could not feel anything on the DRE (digital rectal exam), but was concerned with the rising PSA numbers. We discussed this and I decided on a wait-and-watch program where I would monitor my urinary flow and control and see where I was on my next physical.

We changed insurance carriers in October 2004, from CIGNA to Pacificare.

On Oct. 22, 2004, I went to see my new physician, Dr. Samuel Steirman. He had received my documentations/records from CIGNA and had concerns about the PSA levels. He set me up with a referral to see a urologist, Dr. Robert Lipson. Dr. Lipson did a workup on my urinary flow and control. He also did another DRE and said he felt a hardness on my prostate and it was a concern. He scheduled a biopsy for Jan. 31, 2005.

When I went in for the biopsy, which was done in Dr. Lipson's office, he took 12 specimens—six from each side. This was relatively painless and only took a few minutes. I was given a local shot for pain in the area of the prostate. Dr. Lipson said it would take a week or so to get the results back and he would call once he received them. I was pretty impressed with Dr. Lipson and his sincerity.

On Feb. 9, 2005, I was playing golf at The Legends when Beth received the call from Dr. Lipson saying I had prostate cancer. She probably had a while to shed tears, but when I got home, she told me she only broke down one time, just for a few seconds. Ever since the biopsy, I felt I had cancer, but wasn't positive.

Earlier that day at the golf course, I ran into a friend of mine from DPS, Bill Reutter. He was just getting over some complications from prostate surgery. I told him I had recently had a biopsy done and was awaiting the results. He told me to call if I had any questions. Never in my wildest dreams did I think I would be calling him back that same day.

I really didn't know much about my cancer except it was my uninvited guest. Dr. Lipson wanted to see me and Beth on Feb. 25 to discuss options. Meanwhile, I had to have a bone scan and a CT scan with and without contrast and with radioactive injections. These tests were both painless and quick. I hoped and prayed they would be negative. The results would be called/faxed to Dr. Lipson prior to my appointment on the 25th.

Reutter, a lieutenant colonel at DPS, recommended a book written by Dr. Patrick Walsh, a professor of urology at The John Hopkins Medical Institution, "Guide to Surviving Prostate Cancer." Beth and I went to Barnes and Noble Bookstore to purchase the book. There were numerous other books in the same section reference the same subject. During the period leading to the 25th, I would have time to peruse many of these books. It's a scary subject and a very delicate surgery, one in which you have to have total confidence and trust in your surgeon.

Beth and I put together a list of questions to ask Dr. Lipson. I thought the 25th would never get here, but before I knew it, we were sitting in Dr. Lipson's office while he was explaining my biopsy results. On a scale of 1 to 10, mine was a nine (4 plus 5 on the Gleason scale), according to Dr. Gregory Coon, a pathologist. The results also were reviewed by Dr. Brian McNally with Sonora Quest Laboratories.

This was not good news, but it does get a little better. The stage of my cancer was +2A, which means it could be felt on at least one half of one lobe of the prostate. This was the hardness felt during my DRE. Dr. Lipson believed the cancer was probably confined to the prostate, but was considered fast-growing because of the Gleason score of nine.

Of the 12 samples taken during the biopsy, only one from the right side of the prostate near the bottom, showed cancer—20 percent of the sample was cancerous. Dr. Lipson proceeded to discuss all surgical/non surgical options. Beth and I had discussed my options before meeting with Dr. Lipson, referring to information gleaned from the aforementioned book. If there was a chance, even remotely, that all of the cancer could be taken out with the removal of the prostate that was our top priority.

The continence factor was second and the impotence issue was pretty low on the wish list. Don't get me wrong, I was pretty proud of that little puppy and I didn't want to give up the ghost too early.

After Dr. Lipson explained everything, I asked what he thought would be the best option for someone my age, given my health status and the stage my cancer was in. He thought the radical retro pubic prostatectomy, where they go in and remove the entire prostate is what I should have. This is what we opted for, but we thought it would be a good idea to send the biopsy tissues to a different lab for a second opinion. Dr. Lipson agreed and he recommended Bostwick in

Richmond, VA. The results came back from Bostwick with about the same readings as Sonora Quest Lab.

Surgery was scheduled for Wednesday, March 16, 2005, at 8 a.m., Thunderbird Banner Hospital. Beth, Kathy, Trav, Jenny, Dwat and Dee Dee were all there when I went in. The surgery took about five hours and I was not an easy patient as my pelvic area was quite small which would not allow Dr. Lipson to work as fast as he wanted. I also had to have one unit of blood.

He told us he couldn't be 100 percent sure he saved the nerve bundle on the left side because of the bleeding, but he also told us the lymph nodes in the general area were all negative for cancer.

I don't remember much until I was taken to my third-floor room, No. 355. I could not have asked for better treatment. The only thing I would do differently is not have the morphine pump where I could self medicate. I believe this set me back a couple days and I was extremely grouchy and irritable.

I was released to go home on March 21, 2005, around 10 a.m., dragging my newest friend, "The Catheter," which wasn't removed until March 31. I didn't do much at all for those 10 days.

On March 31, I had an appointment to remove my "newest friend.". The nurse in Dr. Lipson's office performed the rather delicate procedure and when it was extracted, it burned like hell for a minute or so. But, this was the start of some new problems no one really had forewarned us about. Every time I went from a sitting to standing position, I would start to urinate. I had no control over it because my prostate and internal sphincter muscles were no more. The external sphincter muscle in most men is never used and it's really unknown until after surgery how strong this muscle may be.

I never had a major problem with leakage while lying down, but when I stood up I had to have a pee container right then. After about a week, I was able to stand up and make it to the bathroom before I started to flow.

On April 9, I got out of the house for the first time and went to Timmy's football game with Jenny. I stayed fairly close to the bathroom, but overall I did fairly well. Day by day it seemed to get a little better. Three days later, Beth took me to Barnes and Noble while she went to Target. It was a good break, but I felt extremely weak most of the day after returning home.

*

I quit Glen Lakes Golf Course in January 2011. I am now completely unemployed and probably unemployable. However, I have my hobbies to keep me busy. I collect coins and currently am buying/selling on E-bay and about once a month I set up a table at various locations to sell and trade coins.

I still fish a couple times a year, primarily at Alamo Lake. I do not have a boat anymore, but still catch fish from the shoreline. I enjoy this, but have to really watch where I go and what I do because of my health, which isn't bad for the shape I am in.

I walk at least once and sometimes twice a day with each walk covering up to two miles. While walking, I look for rattlesnakes and have seen quite a few over the years. I am totally in awe of them. They live in such desolate areas and survive on very little. To me, they are magnificent creatures.

Beth is very involved with her church, Shepherd of the Valley United Methodist Church, and is on the church prayer chain. With her father and sister both in failing health, she keeps pretty busy.

I know that pretty much all of my DPS career it probably seemed as if the family was second place because of all the traveling I did. The job necessitated this, but I knew without any doubt in my mind that the home front would be well taken care of by Beth. This peace of mind released me to do the best job I could for the State of Arizona. In hindsight, I know I could have done better on the home front and that is probably the only regret I have.

*

In retirement, I have re-established contacts with some of my closest friends from high school—Leslie Miller, Terry O'Connor, Marvin Whittier and James Heimer. They have prodded me over the years to finish this book and get them a copy. They do not appear in a lot of my writings and that is by design. Even though the statutes of limitations for most crimes have gone by the wayside, I don't want to take chances.

I do want them to know that they have been an inspiration to me over the years. But this book is about me, not them. I could easily write another book on my memories with them going back to my junior high school years in Mesa. Right, Terry, you still never beat me at the 1320-yard run we had in junior high. Did you?

Thanks to all of you for the weekend trips to Phoenix and Tempe when I went looking for fights or to play pool, buy beer, and cruise Central. There also was the Carnation Ice Crème Shop on Central Avenue, and let's not forget the movies where we sat in the balcony at the old Fox theater in downtown Phoenix, shooting water guns at the first floor patrons. Then there were the nights of stealing gas and hub caps just to have something to do. Remember, the old flipper hub caps. They were really nice, but now obsolete.

I know I am missing an awful lot, but I did have a brain aneurysm that could have diminished some portion of my long-term memory. You guys are and always will be the best. I want all of you to be pall bearers for me. It shouldn't require a much effort because I will be cremated. Cremation, I hope, is still many years away. Until then, we will, hopefully, continue our purple and gold luncheons, even more often God willing.

I have also left out all the sex because I know some if not all of my grandkids, and great great grandkids will read this. I could, however, possibly write about these under a pseudonym. I could write a novel, or maybe a novella or at least a memo, but all of them seem to escape me. I would like to think there was some, but who knows. Maybe a brain aneurysm is a good thing. You think?

Chapter 12

Letters to Mom, and a journal of her passing

Hi, Mom:

Remember me, Ken, your oldest living son, or am I? More on this later, Mom, as I am going to try to present this to you in some semblance of chronology.

Recently, I was told that possibly I could come to understand my feelings better and maybe try to understand your feelings towards your husband and kids if I wrote you a letter. I'm thinking, wow, this could be a lesson in futility being you passed away a couple years ago.

Then I got to thinking we never really talked, I mean really talked about the important things in life—family, love, trust and, maybe, we can add responsibility. What can it hurt to try and talk to someone you don't really know or understand even if it's post life? This letter may not be pretty, Mom, but it is going to be truthful from my aspect of 60 plus years.

I am sitting here looking at some pictures of a beautiful although somewhat overweight little boy. He seems to be happy, smiling and did I mention a really good-looking kid? Even when Ron came along, I didn't lose my smile as I had someone I could help, someone who would look up to me.

One thing I notice that there is a theme in most of the pictures, Mom, even though we lived in some pretty shoddy places—tents, transient housing, small really small trailer houses—it looks like we always had the best cars money could buy at the time—Mercurys, Buicks, Chryslers, New Yorkers. These were all back in the 40's/50's/60's when they were some of the most expensive vehicles around.

Kenneth Haw

I remember a time, I think it was in Jamestown, CA, or roundabout there, you, me and Ron went to visit someone. It must have been cold because I remember you left the vehicle running (I believe it was a 1950 Mercury). You left me in front and Ron in back. The car was parked on a pretty good slope in a forested area. It was nothing for me to slip it out of park into neutral. I didn't even get scared when the vehicle started rolling. I still didn't get real scared until it was heading for some trees and picking up speed.

Then you were there jerking the door open, hopping in and slowing the vehicle down just before it hit the trees. I don't really remember your exact words, but because someone else may read this, I'm sure I could not have printed them anyway. You were worried about the car!

I remember traveling an awful lot. Lots of different places in Arizona and California. I remember when we finally left the transient life of following the cotton, veggies and fruit harvests and bought a trailer house. I remember the approximate size was 8 feet wide and 30 feet long. It had a couch in front, a small table, very small kitchen and bunk beds directly behind the kitchen wall. The bathroom was across from the bunk beds and to the rear of the trailer was the large bed.

Now, we got to go pretty much wherever Dad could get work in construction through the AFL-CIO union hall.

I remember around Christmas in the early to mid 50's, we lived in Flagstaff. You and Dad had been out partying, Ron and I in our customary places under the table, out of sight, out of mind so to speak. When we left the liquor establishment, of which there were many in Flag at that time, you were driving.

You and Dad were arguing, shouting at each other. Then came the jolt, the sound of the crash. No one in our vehicle was hurt, but Dad switched places with you and told the police he was driving. He went to jail and the police took the rest of us to our trailer just east of downtown Flagstaff.

I was not always an Angelic little tyke as I'm sure you remember, Mom. But I've always wanted to ask you if you ever heard of the old saying "Double Jeopardy." This means to the best of my recollection, Mom, that a person should not be punished twice for the same crime, or in my case, transgressions.

You remember some times you had to take a belt, switch, paddle or whatever to remind me of my wrongdoings. This was OK with me,

212

Mom, if I had, in fact, deserved said punishment. But to tell me after rendering the punishment to "Wait 'till your dad gets home," I thought was a bit much. You knew when Dad got home you would immediately tell him of our daily or sometimes weekly, depending on where he was working/what he was doing, misdeeds or can I say our little fuck-up Mom. Every kid has them!

When I saw Dad coming through the door that evening or weekend, I would run because I knew as soon as you and he sat down and had a brewski, he would come looking for me with his cordial hello of "Where are you at you little bastard, get out here and take your punishment."

Now, those words may have intimidated lesser individuals, but not me, Mom, not me. By God, if Dad was going to spank or whip me, he was going to have to find me. He did and he did. Mom, those six words, "Wait 'till your Dad gets home," were the most feared out of your mouth to me.

Another couple words I wanted answers to were what I thought my name was for a long time, "Little Bastard." Just a side note here. Bastard referred to in the Webster's Dictionary as "one of inferior breed or stock" such as a mongrel dog. These words created anxiety for me for a lot of years. At least, I later learned it was not my name.

Mom, I know you and Dad had literally hundreds of fights and arguments. When I mention fights, I'm not talking verbal, I'm talking knock-down, hit each other over the head with something fights. Blood letting, black eyes, swollen faces kinds of fights. This was well before we had color TV and could see all the same shit on TV.

You had a few jobs. I remember especially when Dad was out of town. I guess you needed something to keep you busy and bring home some more money.

I remember when you worked as a nurse's aide at Mesa Memorial hospital, you would take Ron and me to work with you. You had to leave us in or at the general vicinity of the car which you usually parked at the curb on the street. We got to be pretty good friends with the workers at the Pete's Fish and Chips, just across the street, west of the hospital. The times have changed, Mom, I'm not bitching about a lot of these things. They may have been wrong by today's standards, some of them may even be criminal, but together they have made me the person I am.

The part about the "Little Bastard," after believing for many, many years that I was not Dad's, but a product of a fling you have had. I know this is not true because after years and years of reflecting, and believe me, Mom, after the upbringing Ron and I had, the tormenting you and Dad put each other through, I have reflected on it. Numerous times, I heard you tell Dad that if it wasn't for the kids, you would leave him. You hated him and wanted away from him.

Well, Mom, when I was 18 years old, graduating from high school, leaving home. You didn't say much, but Dad went ballistic on me. The only way I'm leaving home is to go through him. I knew he was serious and I looked to you for help. It's wasn't there. I had no choice, but to fight. It didn't last long, I just wanted gone. I broke some of Dad's ribs and came close to putting him in the hospital. Oh, such a small price he could pay for putting the whippings on me years before.

I guess what I was going through at that time was selfish. I never thought about Ron and the hell he would be put through when I left home. And he was. He related to me a few months ago that he wished I would leave the stones unturned and not pursue my autobiography. He said, "Ken, you have no idea what I went through after you left home."

Mom, Ron's now graduated from high school and left home also. He came out to Dallas, TX, and looked me up and he stayed with me for awhile. He never talked you or Dad down to me. He never mentioned you at all. A chapter best left closed in his life. I respect him for that, Mom, maybe in that respect, he's a better man than I.

You never left Dad. You stayed on, started a good business, expanded it into one of the biggest and most respected nurseries in the Phoenix metro area. Y'all kept drinking and fighting and probably would until one of you killed the other.

You had your chance, Mom. You and Dad were starting your weekend off like many, many others. Beers for the morning and when the clock strikes 12 noon, go to the hard stuff. Usually, whatever whiskey or vodka was on sale or the cheapest. You started fighting and Dad reached across the table and hit you. You went into the bedroom and retrieved the little .25 auto pistol you kept in the closet. You went back into the kitchen, sat back down, resumed drinking and told Dad if he hit you again, you would shoot him. Mom, Dad never had any education, except the hard knocks of life experiences. Right or wrong for him was whatever he could take care of by himself. That's why he reached over the table and hit you again.

The bullet went in about belly-button high and as Dad said, it burned like hell. Just a little lower and it would have done him grave bodily harm, a little higher would have put him in his grave. This is what the doctor told me when I went to visit Dad in the hospital.

Time is passing us by now, Mom. Dad passed away a few years ago. You were still living in Salome, AZ. You have had some heart problems, including a heart attack that required you be helicoptered to Phoenix from Wickenburg. We finally talked you into moving to the Phoenix metro area, actually in Peoria. You bought some land in a mobile home park and we picked out a really nice double-wide mobile home. These have come a long ways since we had ours in the 1950's and 60's. You were never really happy when you moved to Peoria, but I don't have to tell you this as you reminded us often enough.

I don't know when I finally realized, Mom, after many, many years of thinking, I was not Dad's natural son. I guess after hearing about "that little bastard," hundreds of times when I was growing up that anyone would get a complex and be anxious to some degree.

I always blamed Dad for these feelings, but your true self started to come to light when Ed Bishop befriended you and eventually moved in with you. As long as he could provide you with what you wanted, Mom, he was OK to hang around with. I'm talking about stuff like helping to split the rent money, pay for things like the storage shed, transport you to the casinos to gamble, even provide you with gambling money.

Once, he started to get in such bad shape and couldn't continue doing some of these things as frequent as you wanted, he became a liability. You couldn't get him out of your life fast enough. Hell, you even convinced me to help you get him out of your life.

Your health has really started to be of a major concern to all of us, Mom. We moved you in with us at our house for a while, but it got so hard on Beth trying to take care of you, we decided to try a home.

On May 18, 1999, we admitted you to Chris Ridge Retirement Home where you would have professional assistance. You didn't like this place and made everyone around you miserable. On June 6, 1999, you were released from Chris Ridge to go home with Ron and Kathy who lived in Queen Creek.

Mom, I won't even pretend to know the pain you were in or your thought processes at these times, but everything everyone was doing for you was in your best interest. There were no ulterior motives.

On June 21, 1999, only two weeks from the time you moved in with Ron and Kathy, you were back in Arrowhead Hospital. Kathy said she found you lying in your bed room in a fetal position with excruciating pain in your stomach. On July 1, 1999, your health became so bad that they wanted to do exploratory surgery on your abdomen area. They think your cancer has spread from your lungs into your stomach. Before they will do this, you needed to go into a rest home for physical therapy to strengthen you up. We put you into Life Care Center in north Glendale. This was only about two miles from where we, Beth and I, live.

Your health immediately started declining. Not only was your COPD and cancer of grave concern to us, now they tell us your dementia is worsening and you have no appetite. Beth and I visited you on a daily basis.

And now they're telling us, doctors and nurses, that they can no longer take care of you at this facility unless you're put on hospice. We do know something needs to be done soon. Mom, you will never know, well maybe you do know, but you never appreciated the many hours, the deep conversations I had with myself and ultimately others, talking about your prognosis, not good, dying from cancer, COPD and dementia.

On July 19, 1999, I signed the papers to release your care to hospice so they could commence immediately with your pain relief. You remained at Life Care Center in Glendale until Aug. 25, 1999, when you were transferred to Good Shepherd Care Center in Peoria. This in essence, Mom, was a life sentence for you as I'm sure you know as we all did that you would die in Room 47 on the second floor.

This was the beginning of many, many restless nights for me, Mom. You befriended a social worker named Jan Moore who worked in the facility. She began taking notes for you to transcribe into a letter to be given to Ron and Me after you are gone. She'd know when the right time was to give it to us.

Well, Mom, it's getting late and we are already into January 2005. I'll write more later. We have a lot to talk about, still. Don't we?

*

Mom, I'm back. It's July 2, 2007, a couple years since I last wrote you.

Beth and I finally got all the admission papers signed and you are scheduled for a pre-admission assessment on Aug. 23, 1999. They diagnosed you with malignant neoplasm and lung bronchi with severe abdominal pain, anorexia, depression and anxiety disorder along with pneumonia. They say you are confused and disoriented. Duh. As much as you have went through within the last couple months, who wouldn't be?

Mom, you're a strong woman, have been all your life. Independent as hell, but you are not going to lick this and deep in your heart, I think you know it. This is probably one of the reasons you're shutting out the ones who care the most.

They also tell me your pain is poorly controlled because you do not verbalize your needs for pain medication until it is well out of control. You are incontinent and wear Depend diapers. This in itself makes you believe you are less than human. I know from experience, Mom, I'm not pulling your chain.

You have lost more than 10 percent of your bodyweight since you were hospitalized a couple months ago. You only weigh 110 pounds. They have you on morphine patches as well as your breakthrough morphine, liquid, every hour as you request it.

*

Sept. 9, 1999. Your weight is 104 pounds and Dr. Taylor and Julie Bartolini, your social worker, thinks they have your pain under control.

On Oct. 1, 1999. Dr. Taylor took you off the morphine patches. He has ordered two, 110mg morphine tablets per day along with your liquid morphine. Your nurse, Mary Boyle, the social worker, and Dr. Taylor all seem to be very caring about your needs. During the next couple months, Mom, your body will continue to deteriorate and you will have massive episodes of confusion and hallucinations. These they attribute to your medications.

*

Beth and I, or sometimes just me if Beth can't go, come to visit you at least every other day, mostly daily. You don't seem to want us around, but what's new. I call Ron at least once a week to give him the latest updates on you. They live about 50 miles away and make the trip as often as they can.

The Care Center notifies me of your various bruising and skin tears as they develop due to your hallucinating and putting your arms or legs through the side rails on your bed.

*

Nov. 1, 1999. You have been up a couple times eating. This is a good thing. The hospice aide comes in at least twice a week to shower or bathe you and the hospice nurse comes in at least twice a week. The staff says you are always pleasant to them. They have increased your pain needs.

Dec. 26, 1999. The open wound on your right buttock has increased to .5cm from a .2. When you were entered in August, you told the staff that you look forward to Beth and I coming to see you, but you don't exhibit this to us when we do come.

*

Remember, I mentioned earlier you had befriended a Jan Moore who is the recreational supervisor and seems to be a really neat lady who I have seen quite a few times on my visits? Guess what, Mom, the day you decided to start giving her information to be put in letter form was Jan. 2, 2000, my birthday, coincidence or premeditated? I don't believe in coincidences. I am going to put the letter in here verbatim as to what Jan wrote because some of the contents were enlightening and chilling.

*

The following letter was written by Jan Moore.

I'm writing this letter for Louise Haw, to be given to her sons Ken and Ron.

I have been talking to Louise, trying to convince her to talk to them when they come to see her. It seems very important to her that this be given to them only after she is gone, telling me I will know when.

Louise started out by saying maybe the letters weren't a good idea today, but I told her to get started. She told me I was bossy and laughed. She has a way of clamming up, but very warm to me almost always.

When you boys were very little, she wanted to do the things she had always done. She didn't want to be tied down to only being a wife and mother, but wants both of you to know she always loved you, but didn't do a good job of letting you know how she felt.

She said the arguments between your dad and her were always about them going places together and not taking care of you two. Drinking was a big part of what was a daily argument. She felt he was to blame for how she felt about both of you. She wanted to go with him not stay home with you two.

I was surprised at a visitor she had in her room one day when I walked in. She introduced her to me. At the time, I thought she looked a great deal like you Ken. Same eyes and smile. A pretty lady, sometime between Christmas and New Year's).

On Jan. 3, 2000, Louise wants to go to Church Sunday and have Ken and Ron there to be with her to talk to them after about how she felt all those years. Ken will be there, but Sonja couldn't reach Ron by phone.

Sunday, Louise went to church, but Ken couldn't get there because, as we found out later, he had hurt his back. He tried to reach me to let me know, but I didn't get the message. Louise was truly heart broken because she asked me if that was God's way of punishing her, "If there was a God." Ken, your mom is so stubborn. She told me you are just like her. Hard to imagine that.

Ron and Ken, you have a sister Deborah. She has told me, a half sister in Chandler. She only told me because I asked her about her visitor. She comes to see her every other week. I really think I had seen her there before with Louise.

These are her words. "Sons, I was not good to you like a mother should have been. I need you to forgive me for being the best mom I could be, but it wasn't good enough. You were nice boys, but I wasn't always a nice mother. I always put your Daddy first."

She doesn't want to live with something from her past to cover up any longer in her mind.

Ron, Ken, your mother does love you both as she has stated before, but don't ever expect her to say it to you in person because love isn't something that comes easy to her because she feels like she has failed as a mother and she probably is right. Actions, not love.

I have stressed if she can only let you know how much you both need to hear it from her that she will feel better about the way she was all those years.

In the end of her life on this earth, I really believe she will try to let you see her deep feelings to you both.

Just always know it was her choice. Not yours! God, will forgive her because I know she has been sincere and she has asked Him to. Please try.

Jan Moore
Louise's friend

*

Mom, why, why, why didn't we talk about some of these things. You can discuss these with a relative stranger, but not with your own flesh and blood. Maybe this has been one of our problems all our lives. We couldn't or wouldn't communicate.

Jan did not give me the letter until after you passed Mom, but I know she wanted to because of my frustrations and a lot of unknowns. Mom, I'm going to rush through the next few months as there is really not much change.

*

April 19, 2000. When I came to visit, I had a note to see C.K., the on-site pastor. He stated he had seen Mom around 10:30 this morning and she was relatively content and is at peace with knowing that her condition is terminal. He stated that they, he and mom, prayed daily for her family. She says she is ready to die and has made peace with God.

I noticed today that your left leg is bent at an almost 90-degree angle and you can't move it or you won't try. I don't know which but I suspect you can't. Your weight is 84 pounds. You have had a significant weight loss in the last 30 days. On your quarterly report, the aides said you have become more anxious and express the wish to die. Your condition has worsened.

If and when you eat, it is only very small amounts and you are refusing the liquids they try to give you for sustenance. I talked to your hospice nurse about your leg and she said it could not be moved.

June 3, 2000. You pulled a large piece of skin off your upper right arm and began screaming that a rattlesnake had bitten you. You had this piece of skin on a tissue paper and when you showed me, I couldn't convince you that this was no snake and you had me crawl around looking for it. I patronized you 'till my knees were hurting and I think convinced you the snake was gone. You wound had already been dressed by 2 that morning. The staff had called me about 9:15 a.m., reference the wound.

June 4, 2000. The nurses are able to see bone and muscle in the wounds, holes, in your buttock. The second hole is 3cm by 3cm with the original one being larger. You are still joking with the staff.

July 17, 2000. You have become even more confused as you keep asking why you're living so long, very hallucinatory and worried facial expressions. You're sleeping most of the time and this is your request which will be honored. You have keratonic growths on both sides of your face from the cancer in your body. Dr. Taylor said he will cut them off.

July 18, 2000. You have stated you are losing your vision and have no interest in improving. You are in the end stages of your cancer and the thrust of care is only on pain management. You constantly tell the staff that you have lived too long, you want to die. You cannot move on your own and have to be manually lifted.

Sept. 21, 2000. Your weight was up to 87.2 pound and you have gained a few pounds. This could be a good thing.

Mom, Beth and I still continue to see you at least every other day. I don't think you even know who we are anymore. We both feel your pain and only hope the meds they are giving you keeps the pain under control. You have been bleeding quite profusely from the wounds in your buttock, but all they can do is change the dressing and keep you medicated. Your restlessness is causing you lots of skin tears and they keep these cleaned and dressed. You are highly agitated and confused. You have began to fight with the nurses when they try to attend to you.

Oct. 22, 2000. Beth and I went to see you. You are still not responsive about the same as the past couple months when we have visited. Not

221

really wanting us there. Why should this surprise me? You have always been more warm, open and friendly to total strangers entering the room than with your oldest son.

Oct. 23, 2000. I went from work to see you before I take off for the annual Lake Powell trip. You are about the same as the last time I saw you. You did not even acknowledge my presence. I had bad feelings about things. I told you that Ron and I would be gone for a week or so on our trip to Lake Powell and that you may be taking a trip also. I wanted you to know that I really cared, loved you as much as I could. You responded, "I think I love you too."

I knew what she meant as love was not something readily available in my family. I'm now really undecided on whether to go on the trip or cancel out. On leaving Mom's room, I stopped by the nurse's station to let them know I was having second thoughts about going on my trip. They advised me that I should go ahead as planned that sometimes loved ones will not pass on until they know the family members will not be around. After leaving the second floor, I went to talk with C.K. I told him of my concerns, reference the trip. He told me the same things as the nurses.

That evening, I still had a sense of uneasiness and paged Mary Boyle. I told her that I felt I had said my goodbyes to Mom and I knew in my heart that I would not see her again. Mary told me that this was probably true and she thought that was what Mom was waiting for. She said she would advise me to go ahead with my plans.

Oct. 23, 2000. You are now unresponsive to the nurses and everyone who comes in. You do not respond to anyone who calls your name. All they can do is reposition you and try to make you as comfortable as possible. The cellulite in your body is getting worse and the nurses tell me this is close to the end stage. Your skin has turned a grey-molted color. The nurses tell me that you are still somewhat responsive to them at least with eye contact.

Oct. 28, 2000. Ron and I were on our way to Lake Powell when I told him how close I was to backing out on the trip and that we would not see Mom again. This trip was miserable from the time we got to Lake Powell until we left two days early to come home. Wind, rain, snow and cold for four days.

Oct. 31, 2000. Your condition is grave. Your extremities are cold to touch, purplish and molted. Beth was called and advised of your condition. You have lapsed into a comatose state.

1   *Nov. 1, 2000.*
2   12:30 a.m. You remain unresponsive. They are unable to obtain a blood pressure reading.
3   1 a.m. No change in your condition.
4   2:15 a.m. Mottled feet, legs, arms, hands and neck.
5   2:20 a.m. Pronounced deceased. Beth was called. She gave the information earlier, reference the funeral home, arrangements and credit card number. Heritage Funeral Home was called.
6   2:55 a.m. Dr. Taylor, Hospice nurses and C.K. were called.
7   3:45 a.m. Body was released to Heritage.

*

At about 11 a.m., Nov. 1, 2000, we finally got off the lake and started home. At about 1:30 p.m., Ron was finally able to get out on his cell phone and had 10 waiting messages, all work related. At about 2:30 p.m., Ron was asleep and I was driving on Interstate-17 near Camp Verde when Ron's phone beeped, indicating a waiting message. He answered it. The message was from Beth. Mom had died at 2:20 a.m.

There were no tears, no regrets for not being there.

When we got to Sunset Point, I called Beth to see how she was doing and let her know we were only an hour or so from home. She had Timmy today and she had told him that Great Grandma Haw had gone to be with Sasha in heaven. Beth had already taken care of giving the funeral home the credit card number and the OK to proceed with the direct burial as we had requested.

*

Mom would have been 77 today (Nov. 3, 2000), but died two days short of her birthday. I would have been home from my trip late this evening except for the bad weather or premonition that brought the trip short.

Mom was buried this morning at 10 at the VA cemetery on top of Dad's casket. Her casket was bright, light blue, square top and made of wood which I know she would appreciate because of her love for wood. It was not of the quality she could have made herself, but it was the only wood casket available from Heritage.

The entire process, burial, lasted only about 15 or 20 minutes. The grave was dug and covered with a yellow-wood covering when Beth and I arrived at about 9:50 a.m. A van bearing Mom's casket arrived promptly at 10 a.m. The casket was lowered into the ground. After the van pulled out, a truck with the concrete cover to go over the casket pulled in and lowered the cover over the casket. After that truck pulled out, a dump truck, with dirt, backed in and filled the grave. An attendant from the cemetery smoothed the dirt and we left.

The entire process was quick, efficient and I felt Mom would have appreciated it. C.K., Beth and I had previously arranged for a memorial service. The service was set for Nov. 10 at 2 p.m.

Mom's obituary notice was published in The Arizona Republic on Nov. 8, 2000. It was a simple notice and gave the information reference the memorial service. When I read the notice, I thought, will I see my older sister, Deborah? Do I really have an older sister? Many circumstances led me to believe that I might. Will she see the notice? Would she have called on Mom and been told of the services? So many ifs, only God knows!

*

Christine called from Texas and told me that her, Paul and his wife would not be able to attend, but would send flowers. Robert Stanford and Dorothy Tison called and wanted to know where to send flowers. It really surprised me to hear from either of them, especially Dorothy as there's a lot of history, mostly bad between her and me.

Uncle Aubrey called on Nov. 9, 2000, and a few times before this, but on the 9th he was not feeling good. He still thought he should be here for Ron and I. I told him we were both doing well and I didn't want him making the drive if he didn't feel well.

David, Aunt Ola Mae and Judy had all called. David was thinking about making the drive of about five hours just to be with us. I talked him out of it and told him he would be here for Mom in spirit and he need not come at the last minute. I know if I had encouraged him in the least, he would have been here.

Aunt Ola Mae and Judy, on the other hand, seemed somewhat put out with me for having a direct burial without an open-casket ceremony where they would be able to see "Mom" one last time to say their goodbyes.

I told them they would not even have recognized her as she had dwindled down to 70 or so pounds and they had the past 14 to 15 months to have seen her, spoken to her and been able to say their goodbyes. I also explained to them that this was what I thought was the best way, having a direct burial and later a memorial. The stated they would not be over if they couldn't see her.

*

When Beth and I arrived at Good Shepherd at 1:30 p.m., Friday afternoon, Nov. 10, 2000, there were two bunches of flowers—one from the Stanfords and one from Christine and Paul and his family. Janelle brought another one with her. C.K. had everything under control and the service started at 2 p.m. C.K. told me he was having a hard time finding the song, "You Are My Sunshine." C.K. did a very nice job and related an experience he had with Mom a couple weeks back when she was in a semi-comatose state.

He had come into her room to say a prayer over her and when he finished, he was holding her hand. She opened her eyes briefly and asked him how he was doing. He stated she was a fighter and battled a lot longer than anyone thought she would.

Amber saved the day as she had found a copy of "You Are My Sunshine." As C.K. put it on and started to play it, people in the back of the room said that there appeared to be a ray of sunshine coming through the stained-glass windows behind C.K. When I heard this, it did not surprise me as I know Mom was again getting in the last word in her own way. A ray of sunshine to the tune of "You Are My Sunshine."

After the services, some 13 people came back to our place for sandwiches. Beth had done an excellent job of preparing this. It was appreciated and devoured by those who came. Deborah was a no show.

225

Attachment I

Places Where I Lived

Kansas
    Salina (birth place)
    Ellsworth

Texas
    Dallas, Dallas Police Department, 2.5 years

Arizona
    Casa Grande, this was to become our primary location
    Coolidge
    Tacna
    Wellton
    Superior
    Mesa
    Phoenix
    Flagstaff
    Springerville
    Holbrook
    The Gap
    Cameron
    Tuba City
    Shadow Mountain
    Page (Actually Wahweap Trailer Park)
    Fredonia
    Gila Bend
    Sunflower
    Payson

    Ash Fork
    Sierra Vista (DPS sergeant assignment with BAG)
    Tucson
    Glendale

California
    Visalia
    Stockton
    Ivanho
    Eureka
    Tulare
    Woodlake (Ron's birthplace)

Oregon
    Portland

U.S. Air Force assignments:
    Lackland Air Force Base—San Antonio, TX
    Davis-Monthan Air Force Base—Tucson, AZ
    Goose Air Force Base—Canada
    McGuire Air Force Base—Trenton, NJ

We also traveled to Washington state to pick apples with Mom's side of the family—the Browns.

I was told we spent some time in Idaho harvesting beans.

We moved to some of these cities numerous times, such as Casa Grande and Flagstaff, as well as many of the Arizona locations as we followed the crops.

Attachment II

Family

Father: Kenneth R. G. Haw
Deceased: Feb. 9, 1991

Mother: Anna Louise Haw
Deceased: Nov. 1, 2000

Brother: Ronnie Lee Haw (divorced)
Daughter: Stephanie

Daughter: Debora Lainhart (divorced)
Granddaughters: Valarie and Ashley

Daughter: Denise Warren, married to Jay Warren
Grandsons: Jason and Nathan
Granddaughter: Sara

Daughter: Jennifer Nguon, married to Dwatt Nguon
Grandsons: Timothy Bushee and Lance Nguon
Stepson: Travis Rogers, married to Janelle Rogers
Granddaughters: Miranda and Marissa

Attachment III

Surgeries

Right shoulder, rotator cuff, repaired

Hernia, right abdomen, repaired (escaped from hospital, big mistake)

Pneumothorax, lung collapsing, hospital stay, repaired

First back surgery, 1982, herniated disk, repaired

Brain aneurysm, 1997, hospital stay, repaired

Second back surgery, 2000, different herniated disk, repaired
Gall bladder, belly-button hernia, 2000, repaired

Third back surgery, January 2002, fused L4 and L5 and put in hardware as bracing. They took bone scrapings from my right hip for the fusion material.

Fourth back surgery, January 2003, removed the hardware from right side of spine. Fusion was OK, but the upper screw holding the plate had irritated a nerve. From the third surgery, I was in constant pain. I was supposed to be in the hospital for one or two days, but I was so combative when I came out of recovery, it was one day. I felt great for the first time in a year and wanted to go home. They conferred with the doctor and I went home.

Right knee arthroscopic surgery, March 2008.

Right knee replacement, May 2008

Prostate cancer surgery, June 2008. Prostate removed.

Skin cancer surgeries. Numerous over the years with three being confirmed as cancerous, the rest were benign.

Beth had pancreatic surgery in 2008 after spending at least 20 visits to emergency over a few years. Each visit resulted in a 5- to 7-day stay in the hospital. We had been told that no doctor would operate on the pancreas. We finally found one who would. Dr. Koep performed this surgery and removed the spleen and the tail end of the pancreas. Beth has been pain free since the surgery.

Beth had thyroid cancer surgery and radiation treatment in 1990.

Attachment IV

Awards

1975
Valor Award. Highest award recognized by the Arizona Department of Public Safety.

1976
Officer of the Year Award. Presented by the Phoenix Rotary Club

1978
Certificate of Appreciation from DPS Class 32 for being a class counselor.

1987
Three certificates of appreciation for seminars I presented to the American Legion statewide on gambling and liquor enforcement.

1988
Plaque for instructing at a DUI/homicide conference hosted by the Governor's Office of Highway Safety.

1988
Director's Unit Citation, with ribbon, for outstanding performance

1988
Commendation from the Department via the sheriff of Hot Springs, AR, for identifying and apprehending a murder suspect

1995

Certificate of Appreciation for Operation Safe Streets and anti-gang details conducted between March 23-April 8, 1995. This operation resulted in 394 arrests of gang members, the seizure of 62 weapons and 13 recovered stolen vehicles

1996

Plaque for supporting Mothers Against Gangs (MAG). Presented by Sylvia Lopez, founder and president of MAG.

1998

Second plaque for supporting Mothers Against Gangs (MAG). Presented by Sylvia Lopez, founder and president of MAG.

1998

Retirement plaque and certificate from the Arizona Department of Public Safety upon my retirement after 26 years of service with this state law enforcement agency. Beth also received an award for being with me and supporting me during my years of service.

*

The two certificates or degrees I most cherish and would not have obtained, but for Beth's support and encouragement are:

1975

Glendale Community College, associates of arts (AA) degree, graduated with distinction.

1977

Saint Mary's College of California, bachelor of arts (BA) in public management.

Attachment V

DPS Work Shops, Conferences, Training Classes

1975
Basic training, cadet officer

1978
Analytical investigation
Basic criminal investigation

1980
Medico-legal homicide investigation

1981
Organized crime investigation
How to conduct interviews and interrogations

1983
Advanced criminal investigation
Burglary investigation
Drug laws—basic and advanced

1985
Instructor workshop
Investigating Pit Bull Dog Fights

1986
Counter surveillance school

1987
Intelligence
Booby traps and explosive devices
Death notification

1988
Fundamentals of supervision
Search and seizure
Gambling scams, emphasis on card and shell games

1989
Performance management
Staff skills, basic and advanced

1992
Arizona Narcotics Officers Association training (ANOA)
Case management system

1994
Gang recognition. Two-week school reference Black, Hispanic Asian, Indian street gangs; extremist groups; motorcycle gangs; tactical speed cuffing and searching.

1995
FBI two-week school in Marana. Topics: Team movement/command and control; pistol marksmanship with live-fire training; vehicle assaults; assault process and planning; close-quarters battle; aircraft and breaching technique. This training resulted in numerous mock field problems. This course was very rigorous. We also had physical agility tests daily.

Warrant service and building entry tactics.

1996
Police bicycle training
Patrol officers "talking hands" training

1997
Advanced gang training

*

These training seminars were over and above our annual drivers training; FATS firearms course which are video simulated shoot-don't shoot scenarios; supervisor training (after I promoted to sergeant); medical/first aid; stress management among various other things.

You are probably thinking how I got any actual work done with all this training. You just worked it into your schedule.